Moral Imagination

Mark Johnson

Moral Imagination

Implications of
Cognitive Science
for Ethics

The University of Chicago Press
Chicago and London

THE UNIVERSITY OF CHICAGO PRESS, CHICAGO 60637
THE UNIVERSITY OF CHICAGO PRESS, LTD., LONDON
© 1993 by The University of Chicago
All rights reserved. Published 1993
Paperback edition 1997
Printed in the United States of America
02 01 00 99 98 97   3 4 5

ISBN: 0-226-40169-3 (paperback)

Library of Congress Cataloging-in-Publication Data

Johnson, Mark, 1949–
    Moral imagination : implications of cognitive science for ethics /
Mark Johnson.
        p.   cm.
    Includes bibliographical references and index.
    ISBN 0-226-40168-5
    1. Ethics.   2. Imagination—Moral and ethical aspects.   I. Title.
BJ1031.J64   1993
171'.2—dc20   92-29896
                                                         CIP

For George McClure, 1928–1992

CONTENTS

PREFACE

All people of broad, strong sense have an instinctive repugnance to the men of maxims; because such people early discern that the mysterious complexity of our life is not to be embraced by maxims, and that to lace ourselves up in formulas of that sort is to repress all the divine promptings and inspirations that spring from growing insight and sympathy. And the man of maxims is the popular representative of the minds that are guided in their moral judgment solely by general rules, thinking that these will lead them to justice by a ready-made patent method, without the trouble of exerting patience, discrimination, impartiality—without any care to assure themselves whether they have the insight that comes from a hardly-earned estimate of temptation, or from a life vivid and intense enough to have created a wide fellow-feeling with all that is human.

George Eliot, *The Mill on the Floss*

A great many people believe that the way out of our present moral confusions is to get clear about the ultimate moral principles or laws that ought to govern our lives and to learn how to apply them rationally to the concrete situations we encounter every day. Some people believe that these moral laws come from God, others regard them as derived by universal human reason, and still others see them as based on universal human feelings. However much these people may disagree about the source of moral principles, they all agree that living morally is principally a matter of *moral insight* into the ultimate moral rules, combined with *strength of will* to 'do the right thing' that is required by those rules.

Something crucial is missing in this widely held conception of morality. What is missing is any recognition of the fundamental role of imagination in our moral reasoning. We human beings are imaginative creatures, from our most mundane, automatic acts of perception all the way up to our most abstract conceptualization and reasoning. Consequently, our moral understanding depends in large measure on various structures of imagination, such as images, image schemas, metaphors, narratives, and so forth. Moral reasoning is thus basically an imaginative

activity, because it uses imaginatively structured concepts and requires imagination to discern what is morally relevant in situations, to understand empathetically how others experience things, and to envision the full range of
possibilities open to us in a particular case.

Moral principles without moral imagination become trivial, impossible to apply, and even a hindrance to morally constructive action. Eliot's "men of
maxims," when they are not on the battlefield, tend to do more harm than good,
for they are incapable of the subtle discriminations required to act sensitively and
responsibly toward others. Moral imagination without principles or some form of
grounding, on the other hand, is arbitrary, irresponsible, and harmful. Those who
believe that there are no moral constraints and that the only sanctions are the
'external' ones of fear of punishment and hope for reward, often do even more
harm than those who claim absolute principles. Both types of people are detrimental to morality, because they both ignore the pivotal role of imagination in our
moral understanding and reasoning.

In this book I am attempting to say what moral imagination is and why it is so
important for morality. I am aware that, at best, I have taken only a few exploratory steps into this vast, relatively uncharted territory in our moral landscape. My
initial exhilaration about the possibility of laying claim to this previously ignored
region of our moral understanding has been tempered by the considerable
difficulty I encountered in surveying even a small part of it. Perhaps the greatest
obstacle has been the lack of a conceptual framework that could adequately
describe these imaginative dimensions of our moral experience. In order to give
an adequate account, I have had to discard some of the most basic conceptual
dichotomies that underlie our traditional conceptions of morality, such as the
distinctions between intellect and feeling, reason and imagination, mind and
body.

My attempt to describe the nature and implications of moral imagination develops in three successive stages. The first is to identify the chief imaginative
structures that make up our common moral tradition. The second is to determine
the extent to which certain aspects of our culturally inherited view of morality
might be inconsistent with what we know about the imaginative character of human conceptualization and reasoning. The third is to sketch the outline of an alternative, constructive view of imaginative moral reasoning that would replace
the views I have criticized.

About the first project, that of analyzing the imaginative character of our tradi-

tional folk theories of morality, I am confident that I have given a fair and revealing account, as far as it goes. Decades of further work, of course, would be
required to give a comprehensive analysis, since virtually every one of our moral
concepts and the complex imaginative structures that relate them would require
detailed, exhaustive examination.

With regard to the second project, that of criticizing the cognitively inadequate
aspects of our received folk theories of morality, I have mixed feelings. On the
one hand, I have shown how several of the major kinds of imaginative structure
raise very serious questions about the adequacy of our moral tradition. On the
other hand, because my analysis is limited in scope, it is possible that some of my
claims about the ways in which empirical studies of the imaginative nature of
human thought challenge the view of concepts and reasoning that underlies our
traditional morality may turn out to be less devastating than I have suggested. But
whatever limitations my analyses and criticisms might have, I am convinced that
to take seriously the imaginative nature of morality requires an extensive revision
of our traditional conception of ethics.

About the third project, that of delineating a constructive alternative view of
morality as fundamentally imaginative, I have experienced a mixture of frustra-
tion and anxiety, tinged with occasional flashes of hopeful anticipation that I am
onto something morally significant. The great problem with this positive project
concerns the nature of moral theory itself. According to the traditional view of
morality that I am criticizing, a theory of morality claims to give us moral *guidance* by clarifying our moral principles and their proper applications. Having
criticized the entire framework on which this conception of morality rests, along
with many of the conceptual distinctions that underwrite the project of giving
strict moral guidance or governance, I am left with the problem of saying how my
alternative view is going to give us moral guidance for our lives. The kind of
'guidance' my view gives is not the kind that will tell us 'the right thing to do.'
Rather, it explains why it may be harmful to think that there *is* one right thing to
do. It gives the kind of guidance that comes from moral understanding, insight,
and empathy. It helps us develop the kind of knowledge and awareness that is
necessary if we hope to be morally sensitive.

For the most part, the grand project of working out an alternative conception of
morality as irreducibly imaginative in a way that helps us be better people still
remains to be done. In chapters 8–10 I have tried to say what the basics of this
alternative view would involve, but I am very far from understanding all of the

significant implications for ethics, politics, and social theory. One thing is clear—if we take moral imagination seriously, we are going to have to do some radical rethinking of our culturally inherited notion of morality. We are going to have to take as our principle task, not the formulation of moral laws, but the cultivation of moral imagination.

ACKNOWLEDGMENTS

For fifteen years George McClure has reminded me that it is never enough to have moral principles, unless you also have a sense of the tragic in life, the fragility of human well-being, and the importance of moral imagination in everything you do. He taught me that moral principles without compassion and goodwill can be empty or even harmful. George spent hundreds of hours talking with me about the embodied and imaginative nature of our concepts and the reasoning we do with them, and he helped me see how this wreaks havoc with certain aspects of our received conception of morality. This book is dedicated to his memory.

My intellectual and personal debt to George Lakoff is immense. Whatever adequacy my analyses of the concepts underlying our sense of morality might have is due in large measure to his profound understanding of the way human conceptual systems work and his spectacular ability to analyze language. I have been able to write only a small part of the project we envisioned concerning the importance of cognitive semantics for morality, politics, economics, psychology, social theory, and art. But I hope that what I have been able to accomplish is at least true to the spirit of our vision.

In a similar manner, I have turned again and again to Steven Winter for his remarkable insight into morality and law. In his repeated commentaries on successive drafts of my work, he helped me discover what I was trying to say and how I might find arguments and evidence with which to say it. Steve's work on the metaphoric and imaginative character of legal reasoning has been an exemplary model for me in my investigations of moral reasoning.

Bob McCauley provided extensive comments on the first draft, and his critical, yet supportive, discussions over several years forced me to get clear about some of the epistemological, ontological, and moral implications of my view of meaning. His insistence that I do justice to our Enlightenment moral heritage kept me in mind both of what is good about our tradition and what is problematic.

Tom Alexander has patiently and enthusiastically worked with me to articulate a viable conception of moral imagination, and he has helped me to see how it is possible to go beyond a morality of rules. I am indebted to him for what is, in many respects, my Deweyan conception of morality.

Eve Sweetser's suggestive comments led me to reorganize the structure of the book, and I cannot thank her enough for our ongoing conversations on a broad range of related issues, especially the narrative character of human experience and understanding. I have also learned a great deal from Mark Turner's comments on an early draft and from his work on the nature of human understanding and reasoning.

I wish to thank Owen Flanagan and an anonymous reviewer for their extremely helpful comments and suggestions, which led to the book in its present form.

Jane Espenson, Adele Goldberg, Alan Schwarz, and Sarah Taub, at the Institute for Cognitive Studies, University of California, Berkeley, helped me work out some of the metaphor analyses included in chapter 2.

An early draft of this book was prepared in 1989–90, while I was supported by an American Council of Learned Societies research fellowship, for which I am extremely grateful. I also benefited from an NEH Summer Research Fellowship during the summer of 1989.

I would like to acknowledge the important role that Alan Donagan played in the formation of my understanding of morality. He taught me most of what I know about moral theory. More important, he supplied me with a model of a life lived nobly and in a principled manner.

Finally, I am indebted to Sandra McMorris Johnson for showing me what love and compassion—the deepest sources of morality—can mean, and for laughing at me whenever I spouted stupid claims that stemmed more from abstract theory than from a deep understanding of the reality of human moral experience.

How Cognitive Science Changes Ethics

Moral Imagination

My central thesis is that human beings are fundamentally *imaginative* moral animals. This is a provocative and potentially disruptive thesis, for, if we take seriously the imaginative dimensions of human understanding and reasoning, we will discover that certain basic assumptions of our shared Western conception of morality are highly problematic. We will see that there are many things wrong with our received view of moral reasoning as consisting primarily in discerning the appropriate universal moral principle that tells us the single 'right thing to do' in a given situation.

Exploring the imaginative character of human reason can be both unsettling *and* liberating. It will tend to be unsettling insofar as it requires a thorough reevaluation of the conception of morality that we have inherited from our moral tradition. We will see that this traditional picture of morality as rule-following presupposes a view of concepts and reason that has been shown by empirical studies in the cognitive sciences to be false. Such problems with our traditional conception of ethics often result in the deep tensions many people encounter between their inherited view of their moral task, on the one hand, and the way they actually experience their moral dilemmas, on the other.

Fortunately, focusing on the imaginative nature of moral deliberation does not leave us merely in a state of moral anxiety and destabilization, for it can also provide a constructive alternative view of morality that is liberating. Profound moral self-examination of this sort can free us by giving us a psychologically and philosophically realistic understanding of morality. Recent empirical research in the cognitive sciences has revealed that both our concepts and our reasoning about them are grounded in the nature of our bodily experience and are structured by various kinds of imaginative processes. Consequently, since moral reasoning makes use of these same general cognitive capacities, it, too, is grounded in embodied structures of meaning and is imaginative through and through. This means that the quality of our moral understanding and deliberation depends crucially on the cultivation of our moral imagination.

Moral reasoning is a constructive imaginative activity that is based, not primarily on universal moral laws, but principally on metaphoric concepts at two basic levels: (1) Our most fundamental moral concepts (e.g., will, freedom, law, right, duty, well-being, action) are defined metaphorically, typically by multiple metaphoric mappings for a single concept. (2) The way we conceptualize a particular situation will depend on our use of systematic conceptual metaphors that make up the common understanding of members of our culture. In other words, the way we frame and categorize a given situation will determine how we reason about it, and how we frame it will depend on which metaphorical concepts we are using. Thus, the liberating aspect of our inquiry will turn out to be the way it gives us a depth of moral understanding that is based on our learning *that* moral reasoning is imaginative, *what* the imaginative structures of our moral knowledge are, and *whether* and *how* we can change them so that we may live better lives.

Because of the nature of our traditional conception of morality, most of us will regard the term 'moral imagination' as an oxymoron, the juxtaposition of two incompatible or contradictory concepts. In Western culture, we have inherited the mistaken view that morality is nothing more than a system of universal moral laws or rules that come from the essence of reason. According to this view, correct moral reasoning is a matter of applying these moral laws to the concrete situations we face in our daily lives.

We have been taught to regard imagination, by contrast, as a subjective, free-flowing, creative process not governed by any rules or constrained by any rationally defined concepts. We are thus led to see imagination as an enemy of morality, as though it would introduce into our allegedly rational moral deliberation various idiosyncratic, indeterminate, and emotion-laden flights of fancy. The presence of imagination in moral reasoning is thought to destroy the rational, universal character of morality by making moral laws or rules of any sort impossible. Presumably, if you were left solely to your imagination in deciding how to act, and I were left to mine, then there would be no rational basis for morality, no binding rules we could share, and nothing to ward off the most extreme forms of moral relativism.

The idea that imagination is subjective and nonrational is both false and dangerous. I will show how this rigid separation of reason from imagination, coupled with the mistaken idea that imagination is an unconstrained play of images, is shared by the two dominant views of morality that confront us today, namely, moral absolutism and moral relativism. These views are radical opposites, yet they are both based on the same erroneous assumptions about imagination and its relation to reason.

Moral Absolutism and Moral Relativism: Two Misguided Views

Moral absolutism asserts the existence of universally binding, absolute moral laws that can tell us which acts are right and which are wrong. It assumes that imagination is 'merely' subjective and that it has no place in a morality of laws.

The opposite position, moral relativism, argues either that there are no moral laws of any sort, or else that if there are moral laws, they could have force only relative to a particular cultural group and within a particular historical context. Hence, relativism claims that there are no *universally* valid moral laws and that all standards of evaluation are utterly contingent and culture-specific. If moral relativists embrace imagination, they do so only because they regard it as entirely unconstrained, as opposed to reason, and as undermining the possibility of moral universals.

Contrary to both of these views, we can show that imagination is neither subjective, unconstrained, nor irrational. The fact that our moral understanding is imaginative is not something to be feared or worried about. It does not undermine the possibility of a shared moral knowledge. The metaphors that make up our shared moral understanding—our 'folk theories' of morality—are held in common by all of us within a moral tradition, and they are part of what makes it possible for us to inhabit a shared world.

Neither does the pervasiveness of imaginative processes in moral evaluation preclude the idea of moral critique. Humans are fundamentally imaginative creatures whose understanding of experience is built up with the imaginative materials of cognition. Contrary to the received view, such metaphors and other imaginative structures are what make criticism possible in the first place, for they give us alternative viewpoints and concepts from which to evaluate the merits of a particular moral position. They make it possible for us to envision the probable consequences of a proposed course of action, such as how other people are likely to be affected, how it might change our relationships, and what new possibilities it might open up (or close off) concerning how we can grow.

Moreover, it is principally metaphoric reasoning that makes it possible for us to learn from our experience. Such reasoning is necessary if we are to draw out the implications of our previous experiences for a present situation. We must be able to project beyond clear cases that are morally unproblematic to those that are either nonprototypical or completely novel in our experience. There are no rules to tell us how to perform this crucial task, yet it is the essence of our moral deliberation. We will see that metaphoric reasoning makes this projection possible because nonprototypical cases are often metaphorical extensions from core cases within a radial category.

Moral absolutism and moral relativism, then, are *both* fundamentally mistaken and misleading. They are mistaken, as I will show, because they assume false views of reason and imagination. Consequently, they lead us to false expectations about what is or isn't possible in morality and about what moral understanding consists in.

Moral Law Folk Theory

To see why absolutism and relativism lead us astray it is helpful to see how, though they appear to be opposites, they both presuppose similar assumptions that underlie what I will call the Moral Law folk theory. By a 'Moral Law theory' I mean any view that regards moral reasoning as consisting entirely of the bringing of concrete cases under moral laws or rules that specify 'the right thing to do' in a given instance. The Moral Law theory and all of its assumptions turn out to be so pervasive in our cultural heritage that they form the shared folk theory of morality that underlies both religious ethics and our dominant nontheological rationalist ethics alike. Most of us are never even aware that such a folk theory underlies our sense of morality. We simply take it unreflectively as an unquestionable fact, and we mold our lives around it. It operates for us so automatically and unconsciously that it becomes extremely difficult even to conceive of an alternative moral framework.

Moral objectivism assumes the Moral Law theory straightforwardly. Objectivism claims that there are absolute moral laws, that they can be discovered by reason, and that they can be applied directly and objectively to real situations.

The two forms of moral relativism also accept assumptions of the Moral Law theory, but in different ways. One version claims that morality *is* a matter of following moral laws, but regards them as binding only relative to particular cultures or societies. The other version denies that there are any rationally defensible shared moral standards at all, and so it concludes that morality is irrational and subjective. But this argument implicitly accepts some of the major concepts and assumptions that lie behind the Moral Law theory, for example, that there can be objectivity, rationality, and criticism only if there are universal moral laws. It mistakenly assumes that Moral Law theory is the only way to secure the possibility of rational criticism. It then concludes that, since we cannot have absolute moral laws, morality must be nonrational and relativistic.

My principal critical thesis, then, is that the traditional Moral Law theory that most people live by is quite mistaken. It is mistaken in its unsophisticated form as a cultural folk theory, and these mistakes are carried over into all of the philosophical theories of ethics that are based on the Moral Law theory. I will suggest that it is morally irresponsible to think and act as though we possess a universal, disembodied reason that generates absolute rules, decision-making procedures, and universal or categorical laws by which we can tell right from wrong in any situation we encounter.

I do not mean to deny the existence or usefulness of very general moral principles. Such moral ideals exist within cultures and are an important part of moral knowledge. But the idea that our primary moral task must be to discover and apply absolute moral laws misses most of what really matters in morality. An exclusive focus on moral laws and rational principles is a threat to human well-being because it blinds us to the cultivation of moral imagination that is necessary if we are to be morally sensitive and fully responsible to other people. The narrow and simplistic conception of morality as the following of moral laws completely ignores the crucial imaginative dimensions of moral understanding that make it possible for us to discern what is important in any situation or relationship and to act wisely in light of our discernment. The Moral Law theory impoverishes our moral knowledge because, as we will see, it is premised on bad psychology, bad metaphysics, bad epistemology, and bad theories of language.

I will argue that the Moral Law theory is wrong primarily because it presupposes a false account of the nature of human concepts and reason. Its two offspring, absolutism and relativism, are both equally wrong because they each inherit this same erroneous theory of reason and imagination. The absolutist/relativist split is a false dichotomy. It forces us to choose between two opposite views, both of which are false. We are forced to say that either all moral rules are absolute because they have a basis in universal human reason, or else all values and principles are utterly relative to specific cultural contexts. But empirical studies in the cognitive sciences concerning conceptual structure, meaning, and reason show that neither of these views is correct and that they do not exhaust the options we have for explaining morality. There is ample evidence to show that, although our moral understanding cannot be absolute, there are constraints on the forms it can take.

A similar false dichotomy asks us to choose between the view that imagination is strictly rule-governed (and so not different from reason), or else that it is utterly unconstrained and nonrational (and therefore unfit to support a shared morality). As we explore the imaginative structure of our moral understanding, we will see that the reasoning we do on the basis of metaphorical concepts and other imaginative structures is not primarily a matter of deducing implications of universal moral principles. Yet this reasoning is constrained in a number of ways that keep moral deliberation from being utterly relativistic or subjective. Both of these false dichotomies thus turn out to rest on the same erroneous view of reason and its correlative view of imagination.

The Cognitive Science of Moral Understanding

The question of the nature of human reason and imagination is an empirical question. There are a number of empirical scientific disciplines—cognitive psychology, developmental psychology, linguistics, neuroscience, anthropology, computer science, and so forth—that study the nature of mind and reason. Combined with philosophy, these various disciplines, related both by the questions they share and by their converging lines of research, are known collectively as the cognitive sciences. Cognitive science today has gone far beyond the early narrow concerns and methods of traditional artificial intelligence, which presupposed the metaphor of MIND AS COMPUTER PROGRAM. The new generation of cognitive scientists are much broader in their interests and more empirically responsible in developing their models of concepts, mind, and reasoning. Second-generation cognitive science now embraces far-ranging studies of cognition, language, and understanding that are changing our view of how the mind works. A new view is emerging of concepts as grounded in structures of our bodily interactions and as irreducibly imaginative in character. Psychology, linguistics, and anthropology are beginning to give us ways of empirically evaluating generalizations concerning cognitive structure. They are also beginning to acknowledge the importance of bodily, social, and cultural dimensions of cognition.

I will argue that the cognitive sciences have extremely important consequences, both critical and constructive, for our understanding of morality. Critically, they teach us that what we are learning about conceptual systems, category structure, conceptual frames, and reasoning is radically at odds with our traditional Moral Law folk theory of morality. On the more constructive side, these empirical findings give us a conception of moral reason as imaginative, and they require us to foster a new kind of moral understanding that our received moral tradition cannot even recognize as existing.

In order to get a preliminary idea of how these new studies of cognition and language force us to change our received view of morality, it is useful to have a preliminary account of this pervasive folk theory of Moral Law. It is a 'folk theory' we share, as members of our culture, concerning what counts as a moral issue, how moral reasoning works, and what this means for how we ought to live our lives. In the next chapter I will give a detailed account of the assumptions and tenets of the Moral Law folk theory. For purposes of contrasting its assumptions with various empirical results in the cognitive sciences concerning concepts and reasoning, we need only the following brief summary:

THE MORAL LAW FOLK THEORY
Human beings have a dual nature, part bodily and part mental. It is our capacity to reason and to act upon rational principles that distinguishes us from brute animals. The free will, which humans possess but animals do not, is precisely this capacity to act on principles we give to ourselves to guide our actions. Therefore, our freedom is preserved only in acting on principles our reason gives to us. There is a deep tension between our bodily and mental aspects, because our bodily passions and desires are not inherently rational. That is why we need reason to tell us how we ought to act in situations where our actions may affect the well-being of ourselves and other people.

Reason guides the will by giving it moral laws—laws that specify which acts are morally prohibited, which are required, and which are permissible. Universal reason not only is the source of all moral laws but also tells us how to apply those principles to concrete situations. Moral reasoning is thus principally a matter of getting the correct description of a situation, determining which moral law pertains to it, and figuring out what action that moral law requires for the given situation.

This is the Moral Law folk theory in the general form that everyone will recognize, and that most of us accept as true, whether we believe in a religious basis for morality or espouse a nontheological morality based on reason. What is seldom recognized, except perhaps by moral theorists, is that, in order for this view to be plausible, certain other assumptions must also be true. For example, if a moral law is to apply directly to a situation, then our conceptualization of the situation must match exactly the concepts in terms of which the moral law is stated. This requires that three additional things be true: (1) There must be one and only one correct conceptualization for any situation. Otherwise, we could never figure out which moral rule is supposed to apply to the situation. (2) There must exist literal concepts with univocal meanings, in terms of which the moral laws are stated and which also apply to the situation being considered. (3) Situations must be conceptualizable by a list of features that uniquely describe them (which is to say that concepts must be defined by sets of necessary and sufficient conditions for their application).

There is much in this Moral Law folk theory that captures important aspects of our moral experience. But there is also much in the theory that is incompatible with what the cognitive sciences are revealing about the nature of concepts, reason, and understanding. Consequently, most of us who accept and try to live by the Moral Law theory, whether consciously or unconsciously, are likely to experience a certain inescapable tension and cognitive dissonance in our attempts to decide how we ought to act. The problem, as I will argue, is that we are trying to live according to a view that is inconsistent with how human beings actually make sense of things.

To give a brief introductory idea of how taking second-generation cognitive science seriously would change moral philosophy, we need only consider a few relevant findings about concepts and reason that call into question various assumptions lying behind the Moral Law folk theory. In later chapters I will go into these empirical results in more detail. For now, it is necessary only to suggest how what we have learned about human conceptualization and reasoning bears directly on the specific case of moral reasoning.

Theory of prototypes. The classical theory of categories and concepts that is still held by most people understands categories as picking out sets of properties possessed by objects that exist objectively in the world.[1] Every concept or category is supposedly defined by a set of necessary and sufficient features a thing must possess if it is to fall under that concept.

Psychologists, linguists, and anthropologists have discovered that most categories used by people are not actually definable by a list of features. Instead, people tend to define categories (e.g., *bird*) by identifying certain prototypical members of the category (e.g., robin), and they recognize other nonprototypical members (e.g., chicken, ostrich, penguin) that differ in various ways from the prototypical ones.[2] There is seldom any set of necessary and sufficient features possessed by all members of the category. In this way our ordinary concepts are not uniformly or homogeneously structured.

Our basic moral concepts (e.g., person, duty, right, law, will) have prototype structure, too. This is utterly inconsistent with the Moral Law theory, which requires the 'classical' theory of category structure, in which concepts defined by sets of necessary and sufficient conditions directly fit states of affairs that exist objectively in the world. If our moral concepts aren't like this, then it is not possible for moral laws to fit situations in the highly determinate way required by Moral Law theory.[3] Since our basic moral concepts do not have this essentialist structure, we cannot, therefore, simply determine the features of a situation, find the relevant concepts under which it falls, and apply the relevant moral law to get one definite imperative for our action.

On the positive side, the prototype structure of our fundamental concepts allows us to expand them to fit new cases, while still retaining a certain part of the conceptual structure as relatively stable and unchanged. This would be impossible on the classical view.

Moreover, moral precepts turn out to be formulated only with reference to prototypical ('clear') cases. Those precepts seem to work unproblematically only for prototypical cases. But most of our moral problems arise for nonprototypical cases, or for novel cases. In deciding how to treat those cases, it is necessary to know in what ways they differ from the prototype.

Frame semantics. Cognitive linguists have discovered that our terms and concepts get their meaning relative to larger frames or schemas that we develop to understand the kinds of situations we encounter.[4] For example, terms such as 'bat,' 'home run,' 'steal,' 'balk,' 'strike,' and so forth get their meanings by their role in a complex 'baseball' frame. These frames are not objectively *in* the situations they allow us to understand. Rather, they are idealized models and frameworks that grow out of our experience and that we bring to our understanding of situations. For any situation we encounter, there will be different possible framings by which we may understand it, each of which supports different ways of reasoning about that situation.

In morality, this means that there are multiple possible framings of any given situation, and hence different moral consequences depending on which way we frame the situation. If a fetus is understood as a 'person' in one frame and as a 'biological organism without personality' in another possible frame, then we are likely to understand the moral requirements of the situation in two very different ways. However, there are limits to the ways we can frame situations, and so there are limits to the range of possible moral evaluations of a particular case.

Metaphorical understanding. Contrary to traditional views of meaning, concepts, and reason, linguists and psychologists have shown that our conceptual system is, for the most part, structured by systematic metaphorical mappings.[5] In general, we understand more abstract and less well-structured domains (such as our concepts of reason, knowledge, belief) via mappings from more concrete and highly structured domains of experience (such as our bodily experience of vision, movement, eating, or manipulating objects). Language, and the conceptual system that underlies it, does not give us a literal core of terms capable of mapping directly onto experience. Instead, it is based on systems of related and interlocking metaphorical mappings that connect one experiential domain to another.

The existence of conceptual metaphor in our moral understanding is devastating for the Moral Law theory of morality. The traditional view requires moral principles and rules that can apply directly, by means of literal concepts, to situations whose features are objective. The classical view regards metaphor as an indeterminate, nonrational play of imagination. If our fundamental moral concepts turn out to be metaphorical, then it would be impossible to have determinate, univocal applications of the moral rules that contain such concepts.

On the contrary, the metaphoric character of our moral understanding is precisely what makes it possible for us to make appropriate moral judgments.[6] Metaphor enters our moral deliberation in three ways: (1) It gives rise to different ways of conceptualizing situations. (2) It provides different ways of understanding the nature of morality as such (including metaphorical definitions of the central concepts of morality, such as will, reason, purpose, right, good, duty, well-being, etc.). (3) Metaphor also constitutes a basis for analogizing and moving beyond the 'clear' or prototypical cases to new cases. It gives us constrained ways to pursue these metaphorical extensions. It thus allows us to learn from experience in a way that is necessary if we are to grow in our moral understanding.

Basic-level experience. Not all levels of experience and categorization are the same. Given the kinds of bodies we have, the way our brains work, the nature of our purposes, and how we interact socially, certain levels of experience will become more important for our functioning than other levels.[7] Concepts applying to those 'basic' levels of experience will achieve priority in the way we organize and structure our conceptual system. The classical theory of categories cannot make sense of this fact, since it regards all categories as equal with respect to the way they apply to experience.

Basic-level experiences of pain, pleasure, harm, and well-being, for example, may provide universal bases in experience for an account of universal human rights. It would, at least, place general constraints on the nature of any account of rights. It may thus give us a place to look for counterarguments to extreme forms of moral relativism. Giving up moral absolutes needn't throw us into the abyss of moral anarchy, where anything goes.

Narrative. There is abundant empirical evidence that narrative is a fundamental mode of understanding, by means of which we make sense of all forms of human action.[8] There are various types of narrative structure that play a role in how we understand actions, evaluate moral character, and project possible solutions to morally problematic situations. Narrative is not just an explanatory device, but is actually constitutive of the way we experience things. No moral theory can be adequate if it does not take into account the narrative character of our experience.[9]

A View of Morality as Imaginative

Empirical findings of this sort from the cognitive sciences require a radical re-thinking of morality.[10] They require us to give up most of the Moral Law view that has been the foundation of our morality since its origins in the Judeo-Christian moral universe. They demand a very different view of moral reasoning as imaginative through and through. And they place an obligation upon us to cultivate a new kind of moral understanding that is grounded in what we are learning about human reason and the way the mind words.

What is needed is a new, empirically responsible moral philosophy. It would be grounded on what the cognitive sciences are teaching us about concepts, understanding, and reasoning. Such a philosophy will provide a way to analyze both our commonsense (folk-theoretical) moral understanding and our philosophical moral theories that are based on our folk theories. We might call this part of moral philosophy the 'cognitive science of moral understanding.' It will show us which parts of our folk theories are mistaken and need revision. And since philosophical theories of morality are ultimately based on folk theories and their assumptions, there may be much in traditional moral theory that needs to be overhauled. An empirically adequate account of concepts, imagination, understanding, and reason will reveal which traditional ethical questions are based on false assumptions or false dichotomies. These pseudoquestions can be discarded, as irrelevant to human moral experience and reasoning.

Another liberating consequence is an account of why the Moral Law theory itself can never give us the laws it promises, and therefore why that entire project is unable to give us genuine moral understanding. Investigations of the imaginative structure of human understanding are not going to replace moral laws with some other form of moral guidance that 'tells us what to do.' Except for obvious, unproblematic cases, the Moral Law theory never did *that* either. So it is not as though we are losing something precious and are left with nothing to replace it. Instead, we recognize that the few moral principles we actually have should not be understood as prescriptions for action, but rather as summaries of the collective experience of a people. Such 'laws' are reminders of important considerations that we have found significant and helpful in our past efforts to live responsible, caring, considerate lives.

There cannot be any replacement form of moral guidance, because we were mistaken to think that we ever had strict rules in the first place. What is more likely, as I will argue, is that our attention to the imaginative dimensions of our understanding will give us a *new* set of questions to investigate that couldn't even be asked under the influence of our previous assumptions.

The new account of moral understanding that I envision will make us far more modest in our claims to moral knowledge. By showing us the imaginative nature of morality, it will make us aware of the variety of possible framings for any given situation and the variety of metaphorical concepts that define our most important moral concepts. The moral philosophy that emerges from this new understanding of mind and reason won't give us a system of rules for living, and that is as it should be, given what we have come to know about human cognition and reasoning. What it will give us, instead, is *genuine* moral understanding, which is the prerequisite for sensitive, critical, and constructive moral deliberation. It will help us in our task, not of finding moral laws, but of cultivating moral imagination.

Reason as Force: The Moral Law
Folk Theory

The Moral Law Folk Theory

In the next few chapters we will see that every aspect of morality is imaginative—our fundamental moral concepts, our understanding of situations, and our reasoning about those situations are all imaginatively structured and based on metaphor. Once you start looking at how those concepts are structured and at how we reason, you can no longer get along with anything like our traditional view of morality. According to the traditional picture, moral reasoning consists in figuring out the proper description of a situation and then finding the particular preexisting universal moral law that tells you what you ought to do in that situation. We will see that such a view has no way of accounting for the imaginative nature of our conceptual system and our reasoning. Consequently, we need to rethink our conception of moral reasoning.

In this chapter I want to characterize more fully our traditional model of morality, which is based on what I am calling the Moral Law folk theory. It consists of a cluster of related assumptions about human nature, how the mind works, what counts as a moral issue, and where moral laws come from. I want to show how the Moral Law folk theory is grounded in the Judeo-Christian moral tradition that lies behind almost all Western morality. I will then show how it underlies, not only our dominant religious ethics, but also various rationalistic views of morality that are not theologically based, that is, theories that see moral laws as coming out of human reason, rather than divine reason.

In setting out the Moral Law folk theory we will begin to notice that it is defined chiefly by metaphors. Once we analyze (in the next chapter) the sets of metaphors that make up its basic assumptions, its central claims turn out to be anything but the universal truths we mistakenly take them to be. They look more like just one possible structuring of our key concepts, and one of several possible ways of understanding our moral experience. Some of its claims are half-truths, at best. Others presuppose false metaphysical or epistemological dichotomies, and thereby generate pseudoproblems that are utterly unsolvable if taken on their own terms.

In order to get an idea of what is involved in the Moral Law folk theory and its assumptions, imagine yourself caught up in the following situation: You have been in a healthy and satisfying monogamous relationship with another person for several years. But then something begins to happen to you that you neither sought out nor anticipated. Over a period of weeks you find yourself more and more attracted to a new colleague at work. You certainly weren't looking for trouble, but there it is, staring you right in the face. And there is no doubt about it that this is *trouble* for you, because your growing sexual attraction toward the other poses a problem for your monogamous relationship.

Now, of course, *your* problem is how you're going to deal with these conflicting feelings and desires. "Well," you say to yourself, "I've got to get a hold on myself. Obviously, what I'm feeling is lust for him (her) because he (she) is so damned attractive in so many ways and is obviously also strongly attracted to me, which, no doubt, is one reason I probably find him (her) so appealing. But I've got to get control of myself. I don't want this to jeopardize the relationship I've had all these years. It means far too much to me to risk losing what we have built together. I know it's not right to be unfaithful to my partner. Nobody should be treated that way. So, yeah, I've gotta get a hold on myself and stop this before it gets out of hand."

The question I want to ask about this scenario is this: Just why in the world should you feel, as presumably most of us would, that such a situation *is* 'trouble'? After all, not everyone would perceive this to be a problem the way you do. Somebody from another (nonmonogamous) culture might very well not experience any moral tension in this situation. Nor would someone in our own culture who held different values about sexuality, or the nature of relationships, or what moral obligation consists in. The obvious point here is that *we* experience this situation as morally problematic because we implicitly accept our culture's values concerning meaningful human relationships and our very conception of what makes something a *moral* issue. We would feel that we had gotten ourselves in a mess here, because we are brought up within a loosely shared cultural framework that defines a common moral tradition. That common moral tradition involves shared presuppositions about the nature of morality, reason, motivation, and a host of related philosophical notions. What counts for us as a moral *problem* is thus defined relative to such a tradition.

There is nothing special about the particular example I've given here. It is structurally similar to a vast range of mundane moral difficulties of the sort we encounter daily, all of which are experienced and understood in terms of th same basic assumptions of our moral tradition. Those assumptions form a general folk model of morality (the Moral Law folk theory) that defines the way we understand our moral problems. This Moral Law folk theory is based on another folk theory we share concerning the mind and human nature—a folk theory defined chiefly by different metaphors for the various aspects of mind.

THE METAPHORICAL FOLK THEORY
OF FACULTY PSYCHOLOGY

— There is a mental realm.
— This mental realm contains a society of mind with at least four members (the faculties): Perception, passion, will, reason.
— Perception receives sense impressions from the body and passes them on to reason and/or passion. Therefore, perception can be metaphorically either a person or a machine.
— Passions become active through bodily experience, either directly (from perception) or indirectly (from memories or from inferences made by reason on the basis of earlier perceptions).
— Will is capable of *freely* making decisions to act. Therefore, it must be understood metaphorically as a person.
— Reason calculates; it analyzes sense data and passes the information on to will. It also formulates principles, either theoretical descriptions of the world or practical imperatives telling us how we ought to act. Therefore, it must be either a person or a machine.
— Passions exert force on will, are unpredictable, and are difficult to control. Therefore, they are either people, wild animals, or forces of nature (e.g., floods, fires, storms).[1]
— Will can exert force on the body, causing it to act.
— Reason can exert force on will and can thus guide action.
— Will is always able to resist the force of reason, and it may choose to do so or not. It can at least sometimes resist the force of passion. The stronger will is, the better it can resist the force of passion.
— Commonly, passion and reason exert opposite forces on will, placing them in a struggle for control over will.

This folk theory of Faculty Psychology is shared by virtually everyone in Western culture. It isn't something we think about very often. In fact, it operates mostly unconsciously for us to determine how we understand our mental operations. As we will see in the next chapter, it shows up everywhere in the ways we think and talk about human motivation, reasoning, moral problems, and the nature of our actions. For now, it is important to notice that it is a folk theory defined by basic metaphors. It understands our cognitive faculties metaphorically as either machines, animals, or people interacting with one another. It treats the relation of these faculties in terms of entities exerting *force* on other entities. Reason exerts force, passion exerts force, will exerts force, and perception sometimes exerts force. There is a never-ending power struggle going on among the faculties to determine which will rule. Actions are understood metaphorically as motions along paths. Freedom to act is understood as absence of impediments to motion. And the different metaphorical 'forces' in this mental domain jointly determine how we will 'move' along various action-paths.

We will examine many of these metaphors in more detail in chapter 2, showing how they structure our moral understanding, our moral reasoning, and the language we use to talk about morality. The existence of these metaphorical systems indicates that our understanding of action, motivation, and morality is somehow deeply and pervasively metaphorical in nature. Such metaphors *define* our conception of mind, and they therefore define part of our conception of morality. In particular, they support the dominant folk theory of morality in our culture.

THE MORAL LAW FOLK THEORY

— *Faculty Psychology.* The folk theory of Faculty Psychology is assumed.

— *Our dual nature.* Humans thus have a mental (or spiritual) dimension and a physical (bodily) dimension. We are driven by our bodily passions to pursue pleasure (i.e., satisfaction of our needs and desires) and to avoid pain and harm to ourselves. Therefore, since our passions and desires are not intrinsically rational, our bodily and rational parts will tend to exist in tension.

— *The problem of morality.* The problem of morality arises from the fact that people can help or harm other people, depending on how they act. Unlike animals (who can also help and harm), however, only people can be moral or immoral, because only people have *free* will. Humans alone can use their reason to formulate principles concerning how they ought to act. And they alone can then decide freely whether or not to obey those principles. This raises the fundamental question of whether reason can give general guidelines to will about how to act when issues of help or harm (i.e., issues of well-being) arise.

— *Moral laws.* The answer to this question is that there most definitely *are* general laws given by universal human reason concerning which acts we *must do* (prescriptions), which acts we *must not do* (prohibitions), and which acts we *may do,* if we so choose (permissible acts). Reason both generates these laws and tells us how they ought to be applied to particular cases. It does this by analyzing situations to see how they fall under concepts contained in moral laws.

— *Moral motivation.* Reason is what separates people from animals. Lacking reason, animals have passion alone to determine their actions. What makes people better than animals is that reason can guide their actions. What we most essentially are, then, is *rational* animals. Therefore, it is better in general to be guided by reason than to be guided merely by passion. When will chooses to go against reason and with passion, it is seen as being immoral, since it is better to be guided by reason whenever it conflicts with passion. When will lacks the power to resist passion, it is seen as being weak. Acting morally requires building a strong will that can resist passion. And we have a moral duty to do so, since it is better to be guided by reason than by passion alone.

According to the Moral Law folk theory, then, morality is a massive, ongoing power struggle between the forces of reason and the forces of passion. Moral behavior thus requires us to keep our moral reason pure (so that it will give us the right principles of action) and to keep will strong (so that we have the willpower to do what our reason tells us is right). We thus come to experience our moral lives as ongoing struggles to develop and preserve purity of reason and strength of will in the face of constant pressures that arise from our embodiment in the world.

This folk model is present in the hypothetical case described above. For example, in such a morally problematic situation, I would experience myself as suffering the strong pull of bodily based sexual desire, which, if given free reign, would lead (by natural causes) to a sexual relationship. I experience myself as having a problem because my desires toward my new colleague come into conflict with my feelings toward, and attachments to, my partner. My reason tells me that I shouldn't let myself be overwhelmed by sexual desire, that my relationship to my partner is far more meaningful, and that I have obligations to promote the well-being of someone to whom I have made certain sorts of commitments and with whom I have shared my life. I *feel* the conflicting pull of the two sides of my dual nature. I *experience* the need for a strong moral will to do what I reason would be the morally correct thing.

One could give an increasingly fine-textured description of the moral conflict involved in this case, but the key point is clear enough—namely, that our very experience of this situation as morally problematic is based on our (mostly unreflective) acceptance of the Moral Law folk theory, which carries with it a large number of deep philosophical assumptions about the nature of mind, reason, action, and value. Therefore, in order to understand the core of our Western conception of morality, we must explore more carefully the basic concepts upon which it is founded. What this will eventually show us is the following key points.

1. Our moral tradition is but one among various competing moral traditions, and it came to its present form through a series of historical transformations.

2. Because the key concepts that define the Moral Law folk theory are metaphorical, there is nothing absolute about our moral tradition.

3. The Moral Law folk theory tends to ignore or deny imaginative aspects of our ordinary moral deliberation that turn out to be crucial. It overlooks these important dimensions of cognition principally because it is grounded on views of conceptual structure, action, and reasoning that recent empirical research has shown to be inadequate and in need of substantial revision.

By sketching the chief features of our Western moral tradition, I hope to show how some of its fundamental concepts and assumptions have developed historically, how it incorporates the Moral Law folk theory, and how it ultimately leaves us with an inadequate conception of moral reasoning. Our moral tradition is essentially a morality of constraint and limitation. It is founded on metaphorical conceptions of reason as a force, moral laws as constraints, and moral action as movement that does not violate these constraints. I shall argue that, by virtue of its negative and restrictive character (as a *morality of force*), our moral tradition, with its attendant conception of moral theory, overlooks imaginative cognitive resources that are the very means by which we are able to make morally sensitive and humane judgments.

It is important to be quite clear about the status I am claiming for our Moral Law folk theory. Like any other folk theory, it consists of a system of interrelated assumptions that define our understanding of some aspect of our world. In the case of the Moral Law folk theory, these are primarily assumptions about the self, reason, concepts, action, meaning, freedom, duty, and so forth that constitute our shared conception of morality. This folk theory forms the mostly unreflective horizon out of which our explicit moral views emerge. Churches and synagogues preach this view of morality, many people consciously entertain this view as defining their ethical values, and moral philosophies try to analyze, refine, and systematize the fundamental concepts that make up the folk theory.

But a serious problem arises when we try to live by some version of the Moral Law folk theory. The problem is that virtually none of the defining assumptions of the theory are compatible with the way people *actually* conceptualize, reason, deliberate, and so forth. This reveals a deep tension and dissonance within our cultural understanding of morality, for we try to live according to a view that is inconsistent with how human beings actually make sense of things. I am trying to point out this deep tension, to diagnose the source of the dissonance, and to offer a more psychologically realistic view of moral understanding—a view we could live by and that would help us live better lives.

The Roots of Our Morality in the Judeo-Christian Tradition

Whether we like it or not, we are all, as Westerners, caught up in a complex narrative web whose roots lie deep within the Judeo-Christian moral tradition. And this remains true regardless of our theological commitments, because what we have inherited is not so much a theological ethics, but rather the Moral Law folk theory—a set of shared values plus certain assumptions about human nature, reason, and action that underlie and support those values. Even where a theologically grounded ethical system has been rejected, its replacements (such as Kantian rational ethics, utilitarianism, emotivism, Marxism, and existentialism) have preserved most of these shared assumptions in one form or another.

Therefore, to understand ourselves we must understand the origins of our morality in the Judeo-Christian tradition. That there is such a dominant moral tradition is quite clear, so much so that Alan Donagan has confidently identified it as "*the* theory of morality" in the Western world. According to Donagan, this theory is essentially "a theory of a system of laws or precepts, binding upon rational creatures as such, the content of which is ascertainable by human reason."[2] The core idea in our tradition is that human beings possess a universal reason which, when it functions correctly, gives us a system of moral principles and precepts that are supposed to tell us how to act. These moral precepts allegedly specify for us which actions are morally permissible, which are absolutely forbidden, and which are obligatory for us whenever we have an occasion to perform them.

Our Judeo-Christian moral tradition articulates one version of the Moral Law folk theory, the version in which all moral constraint originates in the power of divine reason. According to this religious picture, we feeble human creatures are born into a world created, sustained, and governed by a divine intelligence. We have a split nature, part animal (our bodily being) and part rational (our mental and spiritual being). In light of this dual nature, we occupy a very special and unique place within God's purposefully designed creation. By virtue of our bodily nature, we share certain characteristics with brute animals. But, by virtue of our rational nature, we transcend the bodily, the animal, and the physical, for we alone, among all created things, are 'made in the image of God.'[3] That is, we humans are '*rational* animals'—the only animals who possess the spark of divine reason. This means that we can use our finite but universal human reason to grasp at least some parts of divine reason. In other words, our reason can 'participate' or take part in divine reason.

And so we bridge the gap in the Great Chain of Being between pure animality and pure spirituality.[4] Our dual nature (as 'rational *animals*' and as '*rational* animals') places us morally within a unique niche. Among the animals, we alone have duties to obey God's will, because we alone are able to discern rationally what is required of us, both in our relations with others, who, like ourselves, are made in God's image, and also in our dealings with nonrational creation.[5] Consequently, we find ourselves with duties of two basic sorts: those toward nonrational nature (i.e., brute animals and the environment) and those toward rational nature (i.e., people). Regarding the former, we are given dominion over a morally neutral nature,[6] although we must be good stewards of this marvelous gift. This means that nature, in itself, is not morally significant and that we are given the moral right to use it for our advantage within the limits of reason. Notice that nature is regarded essentially as a *tool* and *resource,* and animals are either *tools* or, at best, *pets.*

Regarding rational nature, our duties stem from the fundamental requirement to treat every human creature (every rational will) with the proper respect due him or her as a person made in God's image.[7] The duties pertaining to rational creatures (people, angels, and God) are specified as a set of absolute laws that come from divine reason and that hold universally for all humans. These moral laws are supposed to tell us both how we should *not* treat people and what we have a moral obligation to do toward them. In the Hebraic tradition those laws are specified narrowly in the Decalogue (e.g., Exodus 20) and more expansively in the Torah, consisting of the entire Pentateuch (the written law) and the Talmud (rabbinical writings). Within the Christian tradition there is considerable debate about the nature and extent of moral law, and there emerges a special emphasis on the inward 'spirit' rather than the 'letter' of the law,[8] but the basic picture of human creatures subject to divine law is never questioned.[9]

Out of this Judeo-Christian tradition there thus emerges a very definite conception of human nature and morality.

THE JUDEO-CHRISTIAN MORAL LAW THEORY
Humans occupy a special place in the order of being. We alone bridge the metaphysical gap between physical or bodily nature, on the one hand, and rationality (as mental or spiritual), on the other. We alone are both *animal* and *rational*. This unique position confers upon us special rights and privileges (e.g., control over the earth, the right to be treated with respect proper to our rational nature), but it also brings with it special duties and obligations (e.g., to be good stewards, to treat every other human being as an image of God). There are absolute, universally binding moral laws given by divine reason which we must obey if we are to receive God's favor, succor, and protection. Determining how we ought to treat ourselves and others is essentially a matter of figuring out the relevant moral laws (given by universal reason) that specify minimum conditions for respecting rational creatures. In short, this Judeo-Christian picture of morality is merely a specific version of the Moral Law folk theory.

As Donagan has noted,[10] once divine commands were divided into those that express divine reason and those that do not, it became possible to envisage a purely rationalistic theory of morality. If moral law is equated with divine command per se (as it apparently was at the earliest stages of Judaism), then humans are dependent solely on revelation to determine how they ought to act. This minimizes the role of reason in morality, since strict adherence to divine command alone would be sufficient. Morality of this sort is basically a matter of 'doing what you are told' by a superior moral authority (typically, God). But as soon as morality comes to be understood as based on commands that are essentially rational (i.e., expressions of divine *reason*), morality becomes rational, since all of the relevant moral laws can be grasped by human reason. Traditional Western morality is 'rational,' just insofar as it involves the use of human reason to determine which actions are correct and to realize those actions concretely in the world. To paraphrase Plato,[11] we come to see that moral action is moral not just because God commands it, but rather because God commands it *for good reasons* (i.e., because it is the rationally correct thing to do). In other words, morality ceases to be the result of inscrutable and perhaps arbitrary commands and becomes, instead, an issuance of (divine) reason, available to us through a universal reason possessed by all normal adult humans.

It is this rational conception of morality upon which I want to focus. The analysis I will provide applies both to theologically and nontheologically based theories of morality, insofar as they assume that, with respect to our duties toward others, ourselves, and our world (and excluding requirements for our salvation), reason is sufficient to generate a system of rules that specifies morally correct action. The critique I will mount of this view also applies in large measure even to strictly religious moralities not founded on reason, since they typically share most of the fundamental assumptions of the Moral Law folk theory that I will be scrutinizing.

Kantian Rational Ethics: Judeo-Christian Morality Minus God

The Moral Law folk theory assumes that morality is a matter of *reason*. In that way it cuts across the distinction between a theological and a humanistic ethics, since they both accept the Moral Law view that reason can discern the appropriate moral laws for a given case. They are both what I call 'rationalistic ethics.' Whether the moral laws come from divine reason or from human reason alone, they can be rationally discovered and applied to concrete situations.

As a representative instance of rationalistic ethics in general, I want to look briefly at what is surely the most profound and subtle analysis of a purely rational morality ever developed in Western moral theory. Immanuel Kant gave the fullest formulation and defense of such a morality of reason. Holding Kant up as model for any rationalistic ethics, I would like to show how his view is merely a sophisticated articulation of the Moral Law folk theory. This is not surprising, since Kant saw himself as revealing the rational foundations of that part of our common moral tradition that is not based on any theological assumptions.

The first thing to notice is that Kant's analysis has an ineliminable 'conditional' or 'hypothetical' character of the following sort: Kant's project was to provide a rational foundation for the nontheological part of the Judeo-Christian moral tradition,[12] that is, the part that sees moral laws as coming out of a universal human reason, independent of divine reason. He did not wish to deny the existence of a moral God; however, he argued that morality is not, and cannot be, based on divine commands. Rather, morality must be grounded in Universal Reason. Kant *assumed* the basic correctness of this traditional morality—as he says, "Who would want to introduce a new principle of morality and, as it were, be its inventor, as if the world had hitherto been ignorant of what duty is or had been thoroughly wrong about it?"[13] A theory of morality must then unpack the principles presupposed by our commonly shared morality, reveal their philosophical underpinnings, and give a rational exposition of them. And, while such a rational reconstruction of our common moral tradition would not create *new* principles, it might reveal deep principles at the heart of our morality that would require us to revise some of our unreflectively held moral judgments, insofar as they prove to be inconsistent with those fundamental principles.

This conception of the nature of a theory of morality is manifested in the structure and sequence of Kant's writings on morality. The *Foundations of the Metaphysics of Morals* (1785) is "the search for and establishment of the supreme principle of morality."[14] This search starts with our "common rational knowledge of morals" (*F*, 393) and attempts to extract the philosophical presuppositions upon which it rests. Kant is not claiming, of course, that we are ordinarily conscious of these principles, or that we have ever analyzed their nature; rather, we are educated in a culture that is based upon these philosophical principles, and we operate relatively unreflectively and habitually within this framework.

This first analysis of our shared morality gives us a formulation of the supreme moral principle, but only in terms taken from "popular philosophy," which Kant describes as a "disgusting jumble of patched-up observations and half-reasoned principles" (*F*, 410). In the second section of the *Foundations*, therefore, we need to move from this inadequate popular philosophical understanding to a proper "metaphysics of morals," that is, to a "pure" moral philosophy based on reason alone and "meant to investigate the idea and principles of a possible pure will" (*F*, 390). A "pure" will would will solely in accordance with the dictates of *reason*, which supplies the principles for morally correct action. A complete metaphysics of morals would thus systematically elaborate the basic moral laws that would be followed by someone who always acted rationally (i.e., by a 'pure will'). Since no actual human being is a 'pure will,' these moral laws are, for us, moral imperatives telling us how we ought to act if we are to be moral (i.e., fully rational).

By the end of the second section of the *Foundations* Kant has completed a subtle and sophisticated analysis of traditional Western morality that is, however, *entirely hypothetical* in its basic structure. It is hypothetical because it claims only this: *if* our common rational knowledge of morals (as embodied in part of the Judeo-Christian tradition) is roughly correct, *then* the notions of duty, moral worth, will, and reason that are presupposed as grounding this tradition will place certain strict requirements on the nature of the supreme moral principle. Given such constraints (e.g., that moral law commands unconditionally), we can determine rationally what the supreme moral principle must be. However, this entire chain of reasoning is conditional upon two sorts of basic assumptions which are *not susceptible of any form of proof:* (1) that our common morality is, in its essentials, correct, and (2) that the conceptions of moral agency, duty, will, reason, and freedom that are presupposed by our common morality actually apply to human beings. We can reason about these key notions, but we cannot give proofs for them. Thus, it is still possible that the entire framework Kant has laboriously erected is built on shaky foundations.[15] It remains possible, for example, that the conceptions of reason and will presupposed by our common moral tradition are simply false, or that they have nothing to do with the way people really are.

Of course, Kant never *proves* that the will is autonomous or that pure practical reason has the character he ascribes to it (as necessary to support our shared conception of morality);[16] rather, he tries to show only that it is at least possible (i.e., not contradictory) that will is autonomous and reason practical in the required sense. The elaboration of his lengthy argument for this possibility occupies the third section of the *Foundations* and most of the *Critique of Practical Reason.*

Thus, Kant's conception of moral theory is very different than many have supposed, since it in no sense involves proofs, deductions within axiomatic systems, or claims to intuitions of first principles. It is an informal analytic argument that is highly conditional or hypothetical in structure, since it presupposes the basic correctness both of his northern European moral tradition and of a certain view of reason, will, freedom, and human nature implicit within that tradition. It presupposes all of the Moral Law folk theory, and therefore all of the folk theory of Faculty Psychology.

It is important to emphasize this 'if-then' conditional structure of Kant's rationalistic theory of morality, for it reminds us that there is no way to demonstrate, by proofs, the ultimate correctness of our analysis of any key concept within our theory. Kant understood that we are never in the epistemically certain position that would allow us to make such foundationalist claims as "*This* is the essence of practical reason, therefore X, Y, and Z are universally binding moral duties." But this tendency to absolutize is very strong, especially when we are dealing with issues of considerable moral and political importance. Later, I want to examine this powerful temptation to take certain concepts that happen to fit into *our* moral tradition—concepts that make up our Moral Law folk theory— and to treat them as though they were somehow absolute, universal notions. We are then led to regard the central concepts of our tradition as somehow built into the essence of universal reason itself. We forget that a rationalistic theory of this kind is but a rational reconstruction of *our* way of dealing with the kinds of social, political, and moral problems we have tended to encounter in our recent history.

We forget that we are dealing with a Moral Law folk theory that is, for the most part, defined by systems of metaphors. I will examine the nature and extent of these metaphorical systems in later chapters.

Kant's project is the epitome of a rationalist ethics. He replaces divine reason with a universal reason, but he preserves the absolute and transcendent character of reason. He argues that morality cannot be based on God's will as the source of divine moral law, for that would reduce human freedom to a sham freedom to obey an 'other.' Yet he argues that morality *can* be based on universal law which we rationally give to ourselves as an expression of what we most essentially are (namely, free *rational* creatures). On this view, we are free just insofar as we are autonomous, that is, just to the extent that we give moral laws *to ourselves* as an expression of our rationality and our freedom.

In this way, Kant tried to maintain moral absolutes and ultimate foundations without grounding them in the will of an 'other' (namely, God). But it is only by hypothesizing a transcendental Universal Reason that Kant can maintain the possibility of moral absolutism. In sum, Kantian rational ethics preserves (and reinterprets) the fundamental conceptions of the Judeo-Christian moral tradition as follows:

1. Divine reason is replaced by an equally transcendental Universal Reason.

2. Divine moral laws are translated into universal moral laws (of practical reason).

3. Being 'created in God's image' reduces to 'possesses Universal Reason and free will.'

4. Treating oneself and others as unique creatures 'made in God's image' translates into 'respecting rational nature, whether in ourselves or others.'

5. Freedom to choose whether or not to obey God's law is transformed into freedom realized as autonomy, that is, giving the law (rationally) *to oneself.*

6. The Judeo-Christian emphasis on purity of heart and 'inwardness' is translated into an emphasis on correct willing that overcomes an external influence (such as passion) and that is not based on contingent consequence, which may be out of one's control.

Since Kant attempted a reconstruction and defense of traditional Judeo-Christian morality, it is not surprising that he, too, adopts all of the metaphorical concepts that make up the Moral Law folk theory that provides the framework for that morality. Just as in the Moral Law folk theory, Kant construes reason as *force,* morality as *law,* and human nature as fundamentally bifurcated into a rational versus a bodily nature.[17] What we most essentially are, on this view, is a *rational* ego, lodged in a body that is the source of desires and inclinations that tend to pull against our freedom and reason. Acting morally becomes a matter of *restraining, channeling,* and *forcing* our physical natures to conform to the dictates of pure practical reason. Embodiment, therefore, comes to be construed as a pressing moral *problem,* on the assumption that, if we were disembodied rational egos with pure wills, we would then act morally by nature. In such a case reason would constitute no constraint for us, since there would be no body to need restraining.[18]

Kant's acceptance of a fundamentally bifurcated reality—a reality that aligns reason, freedom, concepts, and understanding in one metaphysical realm set over against a realm of causally determined physical objects wherein all our bodily manifestations (sensation, feeling, emotion, movement) occur—caused him problems with which he struggled, unsuccessfully, throughout his entire philosophical career. His problems with explaining the possibility of human freedom, without which traditional morality would be an illusion, are legendary.[19] I shall not discuss these problems raised by such metaphysical dichotomies in Kant's theory, though I will later return to the question of what a theory of morality that is not based upon such a metaphysical split might involve. My point for now is that, following the Judeo-Christian tradition, Kant preserves a dichotomized view of human nature and a conception of reason and will as in no way dependent on human embodiment.[20] We are left with a picture of ourselves as bodies driven mechanistically by various needs, desires, and inclinations, which yet must somehow be constrained by *forces* of reason and will meant to have an effect on our bodily action. We are left, again, with the folk theory of Faculty Psychology and the Moral Law folk theory woven together into the structure of our moral experience.

Contemporary Variations on Traditional Morality

Rational ethics in the Kantian mode, construed as a rational nontheological grounding of traditional Judeo-Christian values, has survived in the twentieth century in many widely varied forms in the work of such figures as Hare, Gewirth, Rawls, Nozick, and Donagan.[21] It would be tedious and obsessive to set out each of these views, identify their Kantian elements, and show how they presuppose the REASON AS FORCE metaphor of moral deliberation. Despite their real, and sometimes substantial, differences, however, these theories all share the Moral Law folk theory, insofar as they each view morality as a rationally derived system of rules that tell us how we ought to act. Hare thinks we can only identify the ultimate principle constraining the form of any possible set of moral rules. Gewirth, Rawls, and Nozick argue for universal constraints on the kind of principles we can have, and they then specify some of the kinds of moral rules that would meet such constraints. Donagan, like Kant, argues that it is possible to derive a fairly comprehensive system of moral rules applicable to typical kinds of cases. But these differences among the various theories pertain chiefly to the question of how specific the rules can be and to the question of the precise nature of the derivations of those rules. What these theories share is much more important, namely, the idea that a theory of morality ought to give moral *guidance* concerning what is right and wrong, that it should specify moral laws, that reason is a force, and that morality is a system of restrictions.

One distinctive twentieth-century twist on these themes is worth noting. Contemporary philosophy's obsession with language has led, as one might expect, to strong analogies between morality and the speaking of a language. One consequence of this linguistic emphasis has been the emergence of a metaphor of *moral grammar* as a way of articulating our traditional notion of practical reason as moral *force*. In *A Theory of Justice* John Rawls suggests that constructing a theory of justice (or, more generally, a theory of morality) is akin to constructing a grammar of a natural language.[22]

Rawls argues that in constructing a grammar we seek principles that would account for our intuitive sense of grammaticality, keeping in mind that the principles so formulated might later require criticisms of some of our intuitions about what is grammatical. In moral theory, by analogy, we would search for principles that would generate our considered moral intuitions (i.e., our reflectively considered judgments about what acts are right or wrong in specific kinds of situations), keeping in mind that our confidence in these principles might later lead us to question some of our moral intuitions.

A more extensive elaboration of the MORALITY AS GRAMMAR metaphor appears in the work of Alan Donagan, who is quintessentially Kantian in his conception of the nature of a moral theory, in his commitment to absolute rational foundations, and in his setting forth of a system of universal moral precepts. Recall that Donagan sees morality as a system of laws or precepts that are derivable by the use of human reason and that are universally binding upon all humans.[23] Hegel had argued that such a morality inevitably becomes abstracted from its grounding in the ethical life of an actual historical community. So abstracted, it loses its concrete content and "evaporates" into mere subjectivity. For Hegel, then, ethics ought not to consist merely in a theory of morality in Donagan's sense, but rather in a theory of the historically and culturally embedded and embodied morality of ethical life (*Sittlichkeit*).

It is in response to this criticism of morality (*Moralität*) that Donagan introduces the MORALITY AS GRAMMAR analogy. He grants Hegel's point that the moral life cannot consist merely of the conscious, reflective following of explicit moral principles. Rather, these laws and precepts are embodied in the practices, values, and dispositions of a particular, historically situated community. In this respect, these principles are quite like those of the grammar of a natural language. Each of us is born into a linguistic community and learns its particular language. We almost never reflect on the grammatical principles that structure our linguistic practices, and most of us would do a poor job of articulating any of those principles. Yet our language *is* grammatically constrained, even though individual speakers will frequently violate this or that particular grammatical rule.

Donagan thus concludes, correctly, that there are "conditions . . . imposed by the grammar of a particular language upon speech in that community" (13). The 'grammar' in the moral realm is also a set of restrictions and constraints, consisting of the laws and precepts that structure a moral tradition, which underlies the attitudes and dispositions of those whose lives are informed by that tradition. We are born into the concrete life of an ethical community that is partly defined by its sharing of such a tradition. Most of our decisions and actions are the result of unreflective dispositions and attitudes that we share with others in our community, and that manifest our shared morality (i.e., our 'moral grammar'). That such a moral grammar exists is supposedly attested to by the possibility of our conscious reflection on, and debate over, moral principles and their proper application to particular cases.

Donagan thus analogizes morality to grammar according to the following mapping from the domain of language onto the domain of moral practice:

Language Domain	*Moral Domain*
Speaking a natural language ⟶	Acting within a moral community
Linguistic tradition ⟶	Moral tradition
Grammatical principles ⟶	Moral principles
Constraints on linguistic form ⟶	Restrictions on form and nature of principles governing action

Speaking correctly (i.e.,   ————————→ Acting in a morally cor-
grammatically)   rect manner
Speaking well ————————————→ Acting well

This last mapping is crucial for Donagan's reply to the Hegelian criticism that morality (in Donagan's sense) is too abstract and too divorced from the ethical life of a community to encompass the full richness of the moral life. We must distinguish, Donagan argues, 'acting well' from 'acting morally': "The grammar of a language is ascertained from the usage of those who speak and write that language well. Its authority is that of the speech and writing which exemplifies it. But speaking or writing well is more than doing so grammatically: being grammatical is a necessary condition of it, but not a sufficient one. And so it is with the relation of morality to acting well: nobody can act well unless he acts morally; but, for the most part, to act well it is not enough to act morally" (11).

True to the Judeo-Christian moral tradition as developed in rationalistic ethics, and thus true to the Moral Law folk theory, Donagan construes morality as a set of rationally derived limiting or constraining principles. It is a "morality largely confined to *restrictions* on how one may pursue legitimate ends" (11; emphasis mine). Donagan follows Kant's view that "common morality is disclosed in what a man will not do: it consists in the *limitations* he observes in his pursuit of happiness" (12; emphasis mine).

This view of morality is well expressed by Robert Nozick as a set of absolute "side constraints" or "limiting conditions" on our actions specifying what we must never do toward others,[24] though Donagan would add that there are also obligations to pursue certain ends, and not just to refrain from proscribed acts. In other words, it is a morality of the *force* of reason to constrain and limit one's action in accordance with universal restrictions.

What's So Compelling about the Traditional Rationalist Theory?

The heart of the Western moral tradition, in its theological and nontheological versions alike, is moral *law*. And the core conception of such law is concisely expressed by Aquinas as "a rule and measure of act, whereby man is induced to act or is restrained from acting. . . . Now the rule and measure of human acts is the *reason*."[25] Law *induces* or *restrains,* by virtue of the *force* of reason. We are moral insofar as we bring our will*power* under the constraint of such universal law, and thereby exert *force* and *control* over our bodily actions.

We thus get the following picture of the fundamental structure of Western morality: According to the Judeo-Christian tradition, divine commands can be distinguished by whether or not they express divine reason. Only those that express divine reason are regarded as issuing in divine law. Human reason (that spark which is God's image in us) is capable of grasping or participating in divine reason, so that all humans have access to the fundamental principles or moral laws that are binding on all rational creatures. The central focus of this picture is reason's capacity to be practical, that is, to give principles that are meant to guide our acts of will. Once reason becomes the locus of moral reflection, then theological grounds for law become superfluous, at least with respect to humans' duties to one another and to nonrational creation. Reason becomes autonomous, or self-governing, and we are left with a purely rationalistic ethics based on the Moral Law folk theory.

The deep human appeal of this Moral Law folk theory lies in our desire for moral order and control. It takes very little reflection to become aware of the fragility that characterizes every aspect of our lives: our self-identity, our health, our personal relationships, our work, and our public projects can all be shattered by events over which we have no control. The most contingent events can drastically rearrange our lives, visiting upon us suffering and moral confusion. The aggression, potential violence, and evil we encounter daily, both in ourselves and in others, is a constant reminder of the moral chaos lurking on the horizon or just beneath the surface. Notwithstanding Nietzsche's attack on our common morality as slavish and weak, we need be neither cowards nor blind fools to want moral guidance and governance in our lives. Some acts of violence just do seem to us to be unequivocally inhumane and impermissible for morally sensitive beings. Our conviction about these standards leads us naturally to the more ambitious ideal of morality as an entire *system* of laws that would jointly articulate our fundamental moral obligations. The vision of universally binding moral rules for our conduct thus emerges in the most natural way from our encounter with the contingency of human existence.

I grant that there are moral rules, and that some of these might come quite close to being human universals of conduct, although they will necessarily be so general as to be useful only as guidelines concerning how we ought to act in particular situations. As accretions of the moral wisdom of a tradition or culture, moral rules can serve as summaries of the experience of a people. But it does not follow at all from this that acting morally is reducible to acting in strict accordance with a system of rationally derived rules. I am going to argue that the Moral Law view of morality misses the imaginative activity that is crucial to humane moral deliberation. What rules there are get whatever meaning they have only from our interpretation of them, and all interpretation is irreducibly imaginative in character. Moreover, I will argue that morality can never be merely a matter of obeying restrictive rules, because acting morally requires acts of imaginative exploration of possibilities open to us in morally problematic situations.

Furthermore, I will show how the REASON AS FORCE metaphor that defines our Enlightenment conception of morality depends on assumptions about conceptual structure, meaning, action, and personal identity that are radically incompatible with empirical results from recent cognitive science. This empirical research on human cognition, in turn, introduces an ecologically adequate account of human conceptual structure and rationality as being irreducibly imaginative. And it turns out that this view of reason as imaginative is precisely what is required for beings like ourselves who encounter changing environments and situations and who must adapt to, act within, and transform those situations in a creative fashion.

Before setting out my constructive view of imaginative moral deliberation, it is important to get clearer about why we so badly need such a new view. What is the motivation for my claim that the very capacity—moral imagination—that has been marginalized and devalued in our moral tradition must become the central focus of any theory of morality that is both consistent with what we know about human cognition and morally useful to us? Having identified the restrictive, negative, rule-governed character of our Moral Law folk theory, I want to determine why and how it is that we come to regard the assumptions of our moral tradition as metaphysical, epistemological, psychological, and moral absolutes, when, in fact, they capture very little of our experience as human beings and cause us to overlook some of the most important features of morally problematic situations. I do not wish to deny the importance of constraint and limitation for human community and personal growth; however, I will argue that the exclusive focus on this dimension within traditional morality has led us to overlook a conception of morality as a means of exploring possibilities for human flourishing—a conception that is primarily expansive and constructive.

Metaphoric Morality

Poor Mr. Casaubon had imagined that his long studious bachelorhood had stored up for him a compound interest of enjoyment, and that large drafts on his affections would not fail to be honored; for we all of us, grave or light, get our thoughts entangled in metaphors, and act fatally on the strength of them.

George Eliot, *Middlemarch*

The Pinto Case

On August 10, 1978, three young Indiana women were driving to volleyball practice in a 1973 Ford Pinto when their car was rear-ended by a 1972 Chevy van. The Pinto was crushed, the gas tank ruptured, and the car burst into flames. Two of the occupants died instantly, and the third died two hours later in the emergency room.

The Ford Motor Company was charged with negligence with regard to its design of the Pinto gas tank. Ford internal memos revealed that executives had debated the advisability of installing a $6.65 part designed to help protect the gas tank in the event of direct impact. A cost-benefit analysis was performed which balanced the expense of installing the part (which would raise the cost of the car) against costs assigned to possible injury, death, and lawsuits that might result from future collisions. Ford decided not to install the protective part. The court ruled that the internal memos were not admissible as relevant evidence in the case.

The jury found Ford Motor Company not guilty.[1] Whether or not Ford exercised reasonable care is a difficult issue—there were conflicting accounts of the incident that supported two opposing judgments. One witness said that the Pinto driver had stopped for gas and failed to replace the gas cap just prior to the accident. Another said that the Pinto was standing still when it was rear-ended, in which case it would be unreasonable to expect the gas tank to survive the impact. Another witness described the Pinto as moving slowly, in which case the impact would have been less severe, and the gas tank should have remained intact. So the facts of the case were not clear. But what was perfectly clear was that certain Ford executives had engaged in a form of moral mathematics in which monetary values were assigned to human lives, as a basis for comparison with the increased cost of a Pinto fitted with the reinforcing bar.

Many of us find such reasoning shocking. Ford executives took the metaphor of a moral mathematics quite seriously, to the point of accepting simple cost-benefit analyses that put a price on human beings and inanimate objects alike, without distinction. It is perhaps in retrospect too easy to blame these people for moral callousness and for failing to appreciate the implications of the MORAL ARITHMETIC and LEGAL ARITHMETIC metaphors they employed as the basis for their decision.

Whatever else this sad case teaches us, it shows us at the very least that we do often reason, typically without being aware of it, on the basis of fundamental metaphors that underlie our ethical decisions. This raises the crucial question of whether it is possible, or even desirable, to try to eliminate metaphors from our moral deliberations. I am going to argue that metaphor is pervasive in our moral deliberation, that it cannot reasonably be excluded from our reasoning, and that it is, in fact, the chief means by which we are able to imagine possibilities for re-solving moral conflicts, to criticize our values and institutions, and to transform ourselves and our situations. In short, metaphor lies at the heart of our imagina-tive moral rationality, without which we would be doomed to habitual acts.

The So-Called Problem of Metaphor

My central claim in this book is that human moral understanding is fundamen-tally imaginative. Metaphor is one of the principal mechanisms of imaginative cognition. Therefore, we should expect our common moral understanding to be deeply metaphorical, too. *It is,* and in this chapter I propose to show that meta-phor is essential to our moral understanding at two basic levels: (1) Our most important moral concepts (e.g., will, action, purpose, rights, duties, laws) are defined by systems of metaphors. (2) We understand morally problematic situa-tions via conventional metaphorical mappings. Consequently, our everyday moral reasoning is based on metaphor at these two levels. In later chapters I will investigate another form of metaphorical projection, one in which we extend be-yond prototypical cases within a category to nonprototypical and novel cases that do not share every feature with the prototypical ones. I will also show that even our most formalized moral theories adopt some of the same metaphors that define our folk theories of morality. I hope thereby to identify metaphors as indispens-able to every part of our moral understanding, reasoning, and theorizing, so that it becomes inconceivable to think of morality—in our ordinary understanding and our philosophical theories alike—as anything but metaphoric and imaginative.

Why should anyone think it such a horrible thing that most of our moral reasoning is shot through with metaphors? The general answer is that our traditional conception of morality has no place for reasoning based on metaphors. We have seen that our Moral Law folk theory requires moral rules that can apply directly to situations by means of literal concepts that define the objective features of those situations. Metaphors, on the other hand, are viewed as being semantically indeterminate and unstable. The received view holds that, if our fundamental moral concepts were metaphorical, then it would presumably be impossible to apply the moral principles containing such concepts to concrete situations in any definite or determinate way. The traditional view thus requires literal concepts with univocal meanings, and it eschews the use of metaphor.

The prejudices that underlie this literalist conception of morality are deeply rooted in our culture.[2] There are typically two standard sorts of reasons why people think it necessary to exclude metaphor from morality. The first is based on the assumption that metaphors are strictly poetic and rhetorical figures of speech that express emotions, moods, and attitudes. As such, they are alleged to have no rational structure or conceptual content. This strategy is simply a turn on the old logical positivist splitting of language functions into two opposing kinds, the 'cognitive' (descriptive, truth-conditional) and the 'emotive' (expressive, non-truth-conditional). From this perspective, metaphors in morality are seen as emotional expressions of approval or disapproval for certain acts or states of character. As such, they could have no role in our conceptualizing of situations or our reasoning about them.

The second objection to metaphors in moral reasoning is that they are too cognitively indeterminate. They are seen as generating an indefinite imaginative play of meanings that never gives any specific concept. Metaphors are taken as ambiguous, multivalent, and radically context-dependent. Applied to morality, this would mean that moral reasoning is irreducibly indeterminate—that there can be no one correct answer or right action for a given situation.

What frightens people who hold either of these views of metaphor is that both of them lead directly to moral relativism. Moral 'reasoning' is seen either as emotive persuasion or as an imaginative playing with indefinitely many equally valid (or equally invalid—one cannot tell which) assessments of a given act. In neither case are there rational standards for criticism. So, it is thought that if moral reasoning turns out to be irreducibly metaphorical, this confirms the Moral Law advocate's worst fears about subjectivism and relativism.

Fortunately, both of these views of metaphor are quite mistaken, as we will see. Once we understand the nature of metaphor as a process of cognition constrained by our biological, social, linguistic, political, and economic interactions, the specter of an extreme relativism fades into the shadows. It will turn out, however, that we must learn to live with (what we have always lived with, whether we knew it or not) the fact that, for any given situation, there may be more than one morally appropriate course of action. This is a highly constrained form of relativism that gives us a basis for criticizing many possible views, judgments, and actions as being unwise, morally deficient options. This pluralistic view allows us to appreciate metaphor as the locus of our imaginative exploration of possibilities for action, and as the basis for our self-critical reflections on our values, ideals, and institutions. Metaphoric reasoning becomes the chief means for our ability to transform our situation and ourselves in limited and criticizable ways.

The Metaphoric Character of Our Commonsense Morality

Once you start to look for the metaphors that define our Moral Law folk theory, you soon discover that metaphor is everywhere in morality. As far as I have been able to determine, our most basic moral concepts are structured by metaphor, and typically by multiple metaphors that are not always consistent with one another. I propose to examine a large representative sample of such fundamental moral concepts in order to see how they are defined by metaphor, how they are systematically related to each other by metaphor, and how they form hierarchical levels of metaphoric systems. I intend to demonstrate the irreducibly metaphoric character of our ordinary moral understanding, to identify several of the most important systematic metaphors that underlie the Moral Law folk theory, and to explore the implications of this for our understanding of moral reasoning.

I will focus specifically on two major sources of evidence for my central claim that moral experience is metaphoric through and through: (1) linguistic evidence concerning the way we ordinarily talk about morality—our conventional language of ethical discourse is based on systems of metaphor that define our fundamental moral concepts—and (2) patterns of inference in our moral reasoning that are based on metaphorical concepts.

The following sections consist of fairly detailed analyses of some of the more significant metaphorical concepts that make up key parts of the Moral Law folk

theory. Such analyses require spelling out the semantic structure of each metaphor and showing how our moral reasoning and our moral discourse are based on
these metaphors. It is sometimes easy to get lost in the details of how the particular metaphors work, but this deep level of analysis is necessary if we are to reveal
the metaphoric character of our morality. In working through these accounts it is
useful to keep in mind that the central point of all of this is to show how the
various metaphors build upon one another to form vast, interconnected systems
of metaphorically structured concepts that make up the bulk of our moral understanding.

There appear to be three primary clusters of metaphors that define our shared
conception of morality: (1) those that are concerned chiefly with the *action* performed and that involve metaphorical structurings of our notions of action, purpose, law, duties, rights, and so forth; (2) those by which we decide *what we owe
others* and *what others owe us* as a result of our helping and harming each other;
and (3) those by which we evaluate *moral character*. Let us examine each of
these three clusters of metaphors in turn.

METAPHORS FOR ACTIONS, PURPOSES, AND RIGHTS

The idea that even our conception of something as basic as action is irreducibly
metaphoric can be unsettling, especially for anyone who accepts the Moral Law
folk theory. And what is even more unsettling is that we have recently discovered
that our concept 'action' is defined typically by at least *two different* metaphorical
systems. George Lakoff and several of his students have recently been undertak-
ing a massive systematic analysis of the fundamental conventional metaphors of
the conceptual system that underlies the semantics and syntax of English.[3] One
of their most significant findings to date is the existence of a vast metaphorical
system that defines our notion of an event, including our concepts of action, purpose, cause, state, change, and means. Since actions, purposes, and causes are
all understood relative to this EVENT STRUCTURE metaphor, it is necessary to lay
out its structure in considerable detail.[4]

The EVENT STRUCTURE *Metaphorical System*

The EVENT STRUCTURE metaphor is actually two different metaphorical mappings
—one by which we understand events metaphorically as motions along paths toward locations, and the other as actions that give us possession of some object.
Let us consider each in turn.

The LOCATION *Version of the* EVENT STRUCTURE *Metaphor*

According to the LOCATION version of the EVENT STRUCTURE metaphor, we understand an *event* as a *motion along a path* toward some destination. The metaphoric system consists of an extensive mapping of structure from the source domain (i.e., motion in space along a path) onto the target domain (i.e., events). The arrow represents the mapping by which an element in one domain (source) is correlated with and mapped onto an element in the other (target) domain.

Spatial Motion Domain	*Event Domain*
Locations ⟶	States
Movements (into or out ⟶ of bounded regions)	Changes in states
Physical forces ⟶	Causes
Self-propelled movements ⟶	Actions
Destinations ⟶	Purposes
Paths to destinations ⟶	Means
Impediments to motion ⟶	Difficulties
Travel schedule ⟶	Expected progress
(Large) moving objects ⟶	External events
Journeys ⟶	Long-term, purposeful activities

This version of the EVENT STRUCTURE metaphor is so basic to our conceptual system that we are virtually never aware of the way it automatically structures our understanding of events of every kind. Consider, for example, only the part of it that pertains to actions. We conceive of ourselves as directed toward various ends or goals, and as motivated by various interests and purposes. Understood metaphorically ACTIONS ARE MOTIONS ALONG PATHS from one location (= state) to another state-location. This deep metaphorical concept underlies a massive system of linguistic expressions that we use to talk about events of various kinds (as in "Her surgery is *going along quickly,*" "The construction of their home is really *moving* now," "We're *getting nowhere* in solving this quadratic equation—we're just *plodding along*"). STATES ARE LOCATIONS along such metaphorical action-paths, and they are understood metaphorically as bounded regions ("He's *in* love," "While we are *in* flight, please remain seated," "Stay *out of* trouble"). CHANGES ARE MOVEMENTS from one state-location to another. We speak of being *in* or *out* of a state, of *going into* or *out of* it, of *entering* or *leaving* it, and of getting *to* a state or emerging *from* it. PURPOSES ARE DESTINATIONS toward which we move.[5] We understand them as metaphorical places we try to reach as we move along action-paths ("They finally *reached the end* of their job search," "I *started out* to get a math degree, but I *got sidetracked along the way,*" "Have we finished the job? I thought we'd never *get there*").

DIFFICULTIES ARE IMPEDIMENTS TO MOTION; that is, the difficulties we may encounter in our purposeful actions are metaphorically understood as people, things, or objects that either block or divert us from our action-paths. Among the more prominent types of impediments to physical motion that we experience are blockages, features of the terrain, burdens, counterforces, and lack of an energy source. Each of these impediments has its metaphorical counterpart in the target domain. Thus we have a large range of expressions concerning difficulties in action based on these five forms of impediments.

1. *Blockages:*
    He never *got over* his divorce.
    He's trying to *get around* the regulations.
    She *went through* the trial.
    We've *run into* a brick wall.
    She's *backed into* a corner.
2. *Features of the terrain:*
    He's *between a rock and a hard place.*
    It's been *uphill* all the way.
    Don't get *bogged down in* the details.
    We *hacked our way through* a jungle of regulations.
3. *Burdens:*
    She's *carrying too much of a load* to ever finish.
    He's *weighed down* by a lot of assignments.
    Don't try to *shoulder* all of the responsibility yourself.
    Get off my back!
4. *Counterforce:*
    Quit trying to *push me around.*
    She's *leading him around by the nose.*
    He's been *holding her back.*
    Don't come in here and think you can *throw your weight around.*
5. *Lack of energy source:*
    I'm *out of gas.*
    We're *running out of steam.*

This is but a small part of the structure of the LOCATION metaphor that underlies our conception of events, actions, causes, purposes, and means.[6] Moreover, this metaphor is not merely about isolated events and actions. A series of 'smaller' actions can be part of a long-term purposeful activity of the sort we perform as part of our larger life plans and goals. According to the LOCATION metaphor, those component actions are each small motions along paths, and they can be chained together to form larger paths, which constitute our more comprehensive purposive actions. This gives us the metaphor LONG-TERM PURPOSEFUL ACTIVITIES ARE JOURNEYS along life-paths. Many of our actions—both physical actions toward spatial locations, and mental actions directed toward abstract goals—are metaphorically construed as journeys toward destinations. We might understand ourselves, for example, as having *started out to* help the homeless find shelter, but *along the way* we *got sidetracked* by other less noble concerns. We are *led astray* and may even *lose our way* for awhile. Finally, we *gain sight of where we were going* and may be able to *arrive at our original goal*.

In our culture, living a life is conceived of as a massive purposeful activity made up of a huge number of intermediate actions directed toward various purposes. We are expected to have goals in life and to formulate life plans that make it possible for us to attain those goals. Since life is a long-term purposeful activity, it, too, is a journey. It has goals (= destinations), actions (= self-propelled motions), a course (= the path made up of the smaller action-paths chained together), difficulties (= impediments), progress (= keeping on course toward your destination), and so forth. In short, A PURPOSEFUL LIFE IS A JOURNEY is perhaps the dominant metaphor by which we structure our experience, understanding, and language concerning our ongoing life projects.

The OBJECT *Version of the* EVENT STRUCTURE *Metaphor*

Event structure is dually metaphorical. Besides the LOCATION metaphorical system there is a parallel system in which achieving a purpose through one's action is understood metaphorically as acquiring an object. The basic mapping is as follows:

Object Domain	*Event Domain*
Possessable objects ⟶	Properties
Acquisition/loss of object ⟶	Change of state
Control over acquisition ⟶ or loss of object	Causation
Desired possession ⟶	Purpose
Getting desired object ⟶	Achieving a purpose
Impediments to acquisition ⟶ or loss of object	Difficulties

According to the OBJECT mapping, a property or state is a possession (as in "She *has* a pleasant *disposition,*" "He *lost* his *virginity,*" "She *gave away* her *tranquility*"). Changing from one state to another is thus acquiring (or losing) an object ("She *got* ill yesterday," "The candidate *lost* his composure," "He *acquired* a bad habit"). Causation is control over the acquisition or loss of the object ("He *gave* me the jitters," "She *took* my confidence *away*"). The achieving of a purpose is acquiring the desired object or losing an undesirable object ("I finally *found* happiness," "She *got rid of* her insecurity").

There is a close structural parallel between the LOCATION and OBJECT systems for events. In both cases, achieving a purpose involves relative motion between the agent and some purpose or goal. In the LOCATION version the agent moves along an action-path toward a destination, while in the OBJECT version either the agent moves toward the desired object (as purpose) to possess it, or else the object comes (or is brought) to the agent. As we will see below, this parallelism shows up in our dual metaphorical conception of rights.

The SOCIAL ACCOUNTING *Metaphor: Rights and Duties*

So far, I have been arguing that our most basic concepts pertaining to action (e.g., cause, event, purpose, act, means, difficulties) are structured metaphorically. But what does this have to do with morality? The answer is that every moral concept that is in any way connected to action turns out to be metaphorical. This includes our conceptions of will, rights, duties, obligations, moral debt, and moral credit. Let us begin with our correlative notions of rights and duties. They are both defined relative to an extensive systematic mapping that I will call the SOCIAL ACCOUNTING metaphor. The EVENT STRUCTURE metaphor and the SOCIAL ACCOUNTING metaphor are connected via what I will call the CAUSATION IS A COMMERCIAL TRANSACTION metaphor.

Let us consider our conception of causation more closely. Recall that, in the OBJECT version of the EVENT STRUCTURE metaphor, causation is control over the acquisition or loss of a possessable object (= property or state). An effect is understood metaphorically as an object that one receives. Thus, a transitive action is the transfer of an object from an agent to a patient (i.e., the CAUSAL TRANSFER metaphor). The mapping from source domain (transfer of objects) to target domain (causation) is the following:

The CAUSAL TRANSFER Metaphor

Object Domain	*Causation*
Object ──────────────────⟶	Effect

Source of object ————————————→ Cause
Recipient ————————————————→ Affected party
Size of object ————————————→ Magnitude of effect
Attribute of object ————————→ Nature of effect
Additional object(s) ————————→ Repeated effect(s)

According to the CAUSAL TRANSFER mapping, an agent or cause *gives* an effect to the affected party. Thus, we say, "The noise *gave me* a *headache*," "He *got* his red hair *from* his mother," and "I *couldn't take* her abusive behavior anymore." The magnitude of the effect correlates with the size of the object transferred (as in "The noise gave me a *big* headache," "Reagan left us with *huge* social and economic problems"). Repeated effects are additional objects given ("He *handed* me *one* defeat *after another*").

If the object given or received is understood as a *commercial* object, then we get a specific version of the CASUAL TRANSFER metaphor known as CAUSATION IS A COMMERCIAL TRANSACTION (or, for short, the CAUSAL COMMERCE metaphor), which plays a central role in our moral understanding. CAUSAL TRANSFER is turned into a commercial transaction by the addition of two important metaphors, as follows:

The CAUSATION IS A COMMERCIAL TRANSACTION *Metaphor*

This metaphor consists of three metaphors:

1. CAUSAL TRANSFER.
2. WELL-BEING IS WEALTH: Well-being is understood metaphorically as the possession of many valuable commodities. Money can stand as a surrogate for such commodities. Thus, we say, "Music has *enriched* my life," "It is a *poor man* who has no love of himself," and "The cynics of the world lead *impoverished* lives."
3. EXCHANGE FOR VALUE: An object, actual or metaphorical, is worth what someone is willing to give in exchange for it, either in terms of other commodities or money.

CAUSATION IS A COMMERCIAL TRANSACTION creates a realm of exchange, debt, credit, and balance within our physical and social interactions. Any event that increases your well-being is understood metaphorically as one that gives you money (as in "He *profited* from his experience," "She was *enriched* by the relationship"). Suffering a decrease in your well-being is understood as losing money

("He *paid for* his mistake with his life," "Her improprieties *cost* her her job"). Causing beneficial effects is giving someone money ("She *bought* herself some time with her delaying tactics," "They *paid me* with gratitude for all my efforts"). Causing detrimental effects is taking money ("Reckless skiing *cost* her a leg," "The wind *robbed* him of the 200-meter record").

This pervasive monetary conceptualization of causation gives rise to a vast commercial interpretation of our most basic social and moral interactions. In our social and moral worlds people's actions affect the well-being of themselves and others. These effects on a person's well-being are understood as increasing or decreasing their wealth. The result is a conception of SOCIAL ACCOUNTING in which one's actions earn credits or create debts to others, according to the following mapping:

The SOCIAL ACCOUNTING Metaphor

Financial Domain	*Social Domain*
Wealth	→ Well-being
Getting money	→ Achieving a purpose
Earning money	→ Achieving a purpose by honest toil
Payment	→ Actions that increase well-being
Debts	→ Duties
Letters of credit	→ Rights
Debtor	→ Person with duty
Creditor	→ Person with IOU
Inexhaustible credit	→ Inalienable rights
Contract	→ Exchange of rights

Rights and duties are metaphorically defined! That is a striking conclusion that is incompatible with the Moral Law folk theory, which requires literal concepts for its foundation. According to the OBJECT version of the EVENT STRUCTURE metaphor, having a right is having a letter of credit (an IOU) that gives you access to a desired object (which is an action you can perform or a state you can be in). Where you have a right to such a desirable object, other people have a duty not to block your access to that object. They have a *debt* to you, which you have a *right* to collect on. They *owe* you whatever you have a right (i.e., a metaphorical IOU) to.

The OBJECT version is only one part of the EVENT STRUCTURE metaphor, and so we should expect to find a correlative conception of rights and duties generated by the other part, the LOCATION version. And we do. Recall that, according to the LOCATION mapping, action is motion along a path, and a purpose is a destination.

This entails that RIGHTS ARE RIGHTS-OF-WAY, that is, paths we ought to be able to traverse without obstacle or hindrance to our motion toward our destination (= purpose). In other words, there are some purposes we ought to be able to achieve without being blocked or interfered with by other people. Their duty (i.e., what they owe us) is not to place impediments in our way on those specified paths of action.

Notice the parallel structure of rights in both the LOCATION and OBJECT metaphors. In the LOCATION version, a right as right-of-way gives the traveller access to the destination (his purpose). In the OBJECT version, the person is given access to either a valuable commodity or to money, as a surrogate (= the purpose). So, in both cases, the right is what gives the person access to her desired end, and there is relative motion between person and end. That is why, according to both metaphorical conceptualizations, we have a right *to* something.

In both the LOCATION and OBJECT versions, it is people who have rights and toward whom we have duties. But since our notion of personality is metaphorically defined and extendable, we can understand ourselves as having duties, for example, toward anything to which we can attribute personality. Consequently, our tradition recognizes duties to particular persons, to God (as having personality), and to society (via the SOCIETY IS A PERSON metaphor[7]). The existence of such metaphorical extensions of personality has made it possible for recent animal rights advocates and environmentalists to argue that rights might be extended beyond the human realm to include animals and even nature as an organic system.

The EVENT STRUCTURE metaphor also makes sense of some other aspects of our moral understanding. The basic conception of action as metaphorical motion along a path receives a very strict interpretation within most moral traditions. According to the Moral Law folk theory, for example, moral principles would be rules telling us which action-paths we *may* take, which ones we *must* take, and which we *must never* take. Certain action-paths to various sanctioned ends or purposes (as destinations) are marked out as moral directions. Such actions will be those that tend to realize either individual or communal states of well-being. These paths are typically *straight and narrow,* leaving little leeway for which motions (= actions) will bring us to the required destinations (= ends).

DEVIATION IS IMMORAL ACTION. It is immoral because it fails to get you where you ought to go, that is, to the state you ought to be in or realize, and it fails to get you there directly. This sense of 'going where you ought to go' translates as pursuing certain ends, the ultimate of which is the comprehensive end of becoming a morally worthy agent, however we might define moral worth. So, moral deviation can involve losing our directedness toward any of a number of prescribed particular ends or else toward the end of moral purity itself (as a state of being of the agent). The greater the deviation from the path, the more immoral the action is, for it takes you farther from the 'proper' destination, or it hinders your progress toward that moral end.

In traditional Judeo-Christian morality, deviation keeps you from realizing your essential nature as autonomous moral agent. Though I do not understand all of the relevant psychological motivations, I suspect that this accounts in part for the extreme abhorrence many people have to any form of deviance from established norms. Some people, for instance, regard sexual deviance as a threat to the entire moral order by calling into question fixed norms that presuppose a very particular view of an essential human nature. It is as though failure to be on our way toward realizing our moral nature denies everything that makes us capable of moral agency.[8] What seems to be presupposed is an ideal of what a person most essentially is, or may become, if they realize their full nature. Getting off the path toward that self-realization is seen as sabotaging the whole purpose and point of morality. Thus, immoral behavior on this view consists chiefly in *going astray, losing the way,* and willfully taking *forbidden paths.*

The Procedure for Assessing Moral Worth

The SOCIAL ACCOUNTING metaphor sets up a framework within which we have rights and duties. It *defines* what it is to have rights and duties, in terms of letters of credit and debts owed. It does not, however, explain fully how we assess *what we owe* or *what is owed us* as a result of actions on our part that help or harm other people. It does not tell us *when* we have a right or a duty as a result of some action performed by ourselves or others. It does not tell us what it means to have moral credit or moral debt. To explain these dimensions of our moral experience, we need to examine a version of the SOCIAL ACCOUNTING metaphor that I will call the MORAL ACCOUNTING metaphor, which defines procedures for determining what we 'owe' others and what they 'owe' us under various conditions.

Roughly, within the MORAL ACCOUNTING metaphor, well-being is understood as wealth, so that doing something that increases the well-being of another is a moral act understood via metaphor as giving her a commodity that increases her wealth. Just as in standard financial dealings, a balance of transactions is required—in the economic domain we exchange goods and services, and we understand fair transactions as those in which the values of the goods exchanged

balance out—analogously, in the moral domain we understand our actions metaphorically as commodities exchanged, and we expect their (metaphorical) values
to balance out in the end. If I perform good acts, I build up a form of moral credit.
If I harm you, then you deserve a certain restitution or payback that balances out
the harm done.

This MORAL ACCOUNTING metaphor thus involves the following mapping between the domains of economic exchange and moral interactions:

The MORAL INTERACTIONS ARE COMMODITY TRANSACTIONS Metaphor[9]
(i.e., the MORAL ACCOUNTING Metaphor)

Commodity Transaction	*Moral Interaction*
Objects, Commodities ⟶	Deeds (actions), states
Utility or value of objects ⟶	Moral worth of actions
Wealth ⟶	Well-being
Accumulation of goods ⟶	Increase in well-being
Profitable = causing ⟶ increase in wealth	Moral = causing increase in well-being
Unprofitable = causing ⟶ decrease in wealth	Immoral = causing decrease in well-being
Money (as surrogate ⟶ for goods)	Well-being
Giving/taking money ⟶ or commodities	Performing moral/immoral deeds
Account of transactions ⟶	Moral account
Balance of account ⟶	Moral balance of deeds
Debt ⟶	Moral debt = owing something good to another
Credit ⟶	Moral credit = others owe you something good
Fair exchange/payment ⟶	Justice

The particulars of this systematic mapping show up everywhere in the way we
conceive of and talk about our moral experience. Below are some of the common
expressions that arise from the specific mappings within the general metaphor
MORAL INTERACTIONS ARE COMMODITY TRANSACTIONS.[10]

1. *Deeds/states are objects in transactions:*
   I'm *getting* help from Bif.
   In return for our kindness, she *gave* us nothing but trouble.
   Can somebody *give/lend* me a hand? (hand either as metonymy or as
   metaphor for help).

2. *Well-being is wealth:*
    I've had a *rich* life.
    She has *enriched* my life immeasurably.
    As a result of her illness, her life is *impoverished*.
3. *Moral account is record of transactions:*
    Don't judge him so harshly—*take into account* all of the good things
    he's done.
    I'm holding you *accountable* for this mess.
    His despicable lying *counts against* him in my book.
    When you compare his fine character with what he is accused of
    doing, it just *doesn't add up*.
4. *Moral balance is balance of transactions:*
    One good turn *deserves* another.
    Surely, all his recent sacrifices *balance out* the bad things he did years
    ago.
    His crimes *exceed* his good deeds.
    His noble deeds far *outweigh* his sins.
5. *Doing moral deeds is accumulating credit:*
    We all *owe you so much* for all you've done tonight.
    She certainly *deserves credit* for her exemplary behavior.
    It is *to your credit* that you kept the race clean.
    I've got to *give you credit* for your sacrifices.
6. *Benefiting from moral deeds is accumulating debt:*
    I *owe* you my life!
    He is *indebted* to her for her help.
    I couldn't possibly *repay* your kindness.
    Much obliged.
7. *Doing immoral deeds is accumulating debt:*
    I *owe* you a great deal for the hurt I've caused you.
    He *owes a debt* to society for his crimes.
    You must *pay* for your mistakes.

    The MORAL INTERACTIONS ARE COMMODITY TRANSACTIONS metaphor (or the
MORAL ACCOUNTING metaphor, for short) thus reveals itself in the way we experi-
ence, reason about, and talk about morality throughout most of Western culture.
It gives us the concrete structure and details of our sense of obligation and our
sense of what we deserve for our moral acts (i.e., 'what we *have coming to us*').
In other words, it establishes the framework in which we *owe* something to others

(including SOCIETY AS PERSON) and they *owe* something to us. Sarah Taub[11] has identified a number of metaphorical schemas that specify the precise kinds of 'debt' and 'credit' relations we use to evaluate people's morally significant actions. These schemas are *metaphorical* because they refer to an exchange of 'moral' goods rather than material commodities or their surrogate, money.

In the following schemas the phrase *something good* is a shorthand expression that should be understood as follows: Giving someone *something good* is giving him a valuable commodity (or its monetary equivalent), which, by the MORAL ACCOUNTING metaphor, amounts to increasing his well-being. Giving someone *something bad* is a more complex notion—it amounts to harming her in some way, or decreasing her well-being. Decreasing her well-being is understood as taking a valuable commodity (or monetary equivalent) from her. What is needed to work out the precise details of this metaphorical conception is an arithmetical notion of negative values. If giving someone *something good* is giving him a commodity of positive value, then giving him *something bad* is giving him a commodity with a negative value. The negative value amounts to taking something of *positive* value away from the other person, and so reducing her well-being. For the sake of clarity and simplicity, I am using the terms *something good* and *something bad* to elaborate the schemas, because those terms capture the intuitive idea behind the schemas in a way that is lost when all the details of negative and positive values are included.

Schema 1: RECIPROCATION: *'One good turn deserves another'*
EVENT: A gives *something good* to B.
JUDGMENT: B owes *something good* to A.
EXPECTATION: B should give *something good* to A.
MORAL INFERENCES: B has an obligation to give *something good* to A. A has a
    right to receive *something good* from B.
MONETARY INFERENCE: B pays A for getting *something good* by giving *something good* (of equal price).

EXAMPLES: I *owe you* a favor for that good deed.
          You saved my life! How could I ever *repay* you?
          You've been so kind; I'm deeply *indebted* to you.
          Your generous acts have *earned* you my respect.
          I *owe* you more than you'll ever know, for what you've done for
          me.
          She *bought* his respect with her constant good will.

Schema 2: RETRIBUTION: *'You'll get yours'*

EVENT: A gives *something bad* to B.

JUDGMENT: B owes *something bad* to A.

EXPECTATION: B should give *something bad* to A.

MORAL INFERENCES: B has the right to give *something bad* to A. A has an obligation to receive *something bad* from B.

MONETARY INFERENCE: B pays A back for getting *something bad* by giving A *something bad*.

EXAMPLES: I'll *pay you back* for what you did to me.
                I *owe you one* for that insult.
                You'll *get what you deserve* for that!
                Just wait till you *get what's coming to you!*

Schema 3: RESTITUTION: *'I'll make up for it'*

EVENT: A gives *something bad* to B.

JUDGMENT: A owes *something good* to B (i.e., to balance out the bad).

EXPECTATION: A should give *something good* to B.

MORAL INFERENCES: A has an obligation to give *something good* to B. B has the right to receive *something good* from A.

MONETARY INFERENCE: A pays B by giving *something good*.

EXAMPLES: You *owe me* an apology for your rudeness.
                I *demand* an apology!
                I'll do my best to *make it up* to you for any harm I've done.
                How can I *pay* you for the damage I caused in the relationship?
                The one mistake *cost* me years of suffering.

Schema 4: REVENGE: *'An eye for an eye'* (*'getting even'*)

EVENT: A gives *something bad* to B.

JUDGMENT: A owes *something good* to B.

COMPLICATION: A will not give *something good* to B.

EXPECTATION: B should take *something good* from A.

MORAL INFERENCES: A has an obligation to give *something good* to B. B has a right to receive *something good* from A.

MONETARY INFERENCE: B exacts payment from A.

EXAMPLES: I'll *make you pay* for what you did!
                I'll *take it out of your hide.*
                He'll *get even with* you for this.
                She *owes you one* for that (what she owes is *something bad*).

Schema 5: ALTRUISM/CHARITY: *'What a saint!'* [12]
EVENT: A gives *something good* to B.
JUDGMENT: B owes *something good* to A.
COMPLICATION: B cannot give *something good* to A in return. A does not expect B to do so.
EXPECTATION: A accumulates a certain moral credit in general but expects no concrete good in return.
MORAL INFERENCE: A has gone beyond what is normally required and expected of us.

EXAMPLES: She's a saint—she never expects anything for what she does.
I can't understand how he can be so selfless—all that giving without anything in return!

This last schema is interesting just where it diverges from the pattern of the other four. What is so striking is that, contrary to our normal expectations, an act is done without expectation of reciprocation. Taub notes that in such cases we ought not to say that 'B owes *something good* to A.' However, I have retained this judgment as part of the schema insofar as it reminds us of the general context within which acts of charity are performed, namely, a context of expectations that good acts create obligations and debts. Still, even if B (the recipient of *something good*) isn't expected to reciprocate, there is at least the assumption that moral credit will accumulate and be recognized by society as a whole (assuming the SOCIETY IS A PERSON metaphor). This raises the interesting question of whether there can be truly selfless acts not motivated by any hope for moral credit. I cannot answer this question, but it seems clear that our dominant folk theory of MORAL ACCOUNTING assumes that we act with the expectation of accumulating credit. Thus, Taub correctly observes that this CHARITY schema "is not widely practiced, as it violates our ideas of how giving GOOD and giving BAD should cancel each other out." [13]

To sum up, these metaphorical schemas, understood within the broad framework of the MORAL ACCOUNTING metaphor, constitute our primary conception of the way in which people can accumulate moral credit and moral debt. Such schemas do not, in themselves, define 'good' and 'bad.' Instead, they give the primary structures for forms of reasoning about what we owe others (including society as a whole) and what we are owed by others for our actions. The key point is that such forms of moral reasoning exist only by virtue of the metaphor systems we have been analyzing. Here we have a primary case of *moral reasoning based on metaphor.*

METAPHORS FOR MORAL CHARACTER

The Western philosophical tradition has been dominated by a view of human personhood as essentially bifurcated, split into two incompatible warring elements. This duality of the self runs through every part of our folk theory of Faculty Psychology, and it is characterized by a familiar set of recurring dichotomies in our descriptions of persons: subject/object, mind/body, mental/physical, cognition/emotion, reason/passion, and so forth. The split self appears with a vengeance in the view of moral character presupposed by the Moral Law folk theory, in which morality is construed as a battle between the 'higher' and 'lower' parts of ourselves. The metaphoric systems by which we articulate this tension fall into three general clusters.

1. *Power/control.* As we saw in the Moral Law folk theory, moral character is conceived as being principally a matter of control—the rational, moral self (or faculty) must bring the bodily, sensuous self under control. Since our physical, desiring self is strong and nonrational and manifests insatiable longing, it takes a strong, powerful moral will to control it. An incessant struggle ensues between these warring faculties, and one's character is revealed in the outcome of this conflict. Moral virtue requires a strong will that hears the call of reason and can bring the passions under control.

EXAMPLES:
   The spirit is willing, but the flesh is *weak.*
   She showed incredible *willpower* in breaking her addiction.
   You've got to *control* your passions.
   Get a hold of/on yourself!
   I guess I'm nothing but a *slave to my passions.*
   Manson was *overcome* with rage.
   Lust *drove/forced/compelled* him to do it.
   Sarah has a *strong* moral character.
   I *gave in to* my anger.
   Dan suffers from *weakness of will.*
   Such *virtue!* (from Latin, meaning strength, power).

2. *Uprightness.* In *Metaphors We Live By* Lakoff and I observed the ubiquity and importance of verticality metaphors. Being UP is typically associated with

control, health, consciousness, good, and happiness, while being DOWN corresponds to the opposite characteristics. We speculated that this particular alignment is the result of the nature of our bodily experience: being *up* correlates with power and control *over* some thing or person, when we are healthy we are *up* and about, and when we *wake up* we are conscious and *get up*.

Since, as we have just seen, our folk theory regards being moral as exercising *control* (= being up, on top), we find that a VERTICALITY (or UP-DOWN) schema, with its bipolar structure, correlates with high and low, good and bad, and thus provides an ideal structure for mapping our notion of a split self. The good, moral self is 'high,' while the bad, immoral self is 'low.'

EXAMPLES:

> Paul is so *high-minded*.
> Bubba is really of *low moral character*.
> That was a *dirty, low-down* thing to do.
> Hyde *sunk to the depths* of moral depravity.
> Mr. Poindexter, how *low* can a man go?
> Being around her is morally *uplifting*.
> Even Gandhi was not *above* unkind deeds.
> He *fell* into disgrace because of his actions.

3. *Purity/pollution*. The 'moral,' rational self is high, while the 'lower' self is associated with the body and bodily functions. This up/down, high/low orientation comes to be correlated with purity versus impurity. The body, with its passions and desires, ties us to that which is dirty, polluted, and impure. The mind, as the seat of reason and will, tries to maintain its purity by rising above and trying to control the body.

EXAMPLES:

> She kept herself *pure* throughout it all.
> His motives/intentions were *pure*.
> Sandi seems to have no moral *blemishes*.
> ". . . without *spot* of sin."
> "O Lord, create a *pure* heart within me."
> Nixon authorized *dirty* tricks.
> Scarlett was *washed clean* from sin.
> We must keep that *filth* out of our schools.
> That *trash* will ruin our children's character.
> Pornography *pollutes* the mind and soul.

He lives in a cocaine *sewer*.

That *stinks!* (said of an immoral action).

Metaphor in Framing and Reasoning about Moral Situations

Metaphors of the sort we have been examining above provide the basic structure of our common moral understanding. They are not merely optional, convenient words for expressing some allegedly nonfigurative moral knowledge. They are, instead, constitutive of our sense of morality. The idea that we might do without them, or some alternative set of metaphors, is ludicrous.

The clusters of metaphors listed above, along with some of their familiar linguistic manifestations, form only *part* of the vast system of metaphors that underlie our Western moral consciousness, in general, and the Moral Law folk theory, in particular. A comprehensive study would need to include metaphors that define our understanding of personal relationships, family, institutions, cults, and organizations. This would require an analysis of the metaphorical structuring of our notions of binding, ties, commitment, loyalty, honor, and so forth. We would also need to examine the metaphorical character of systems of related concepts concerning our emotional attachments, for instance, love, empathy, desire, passion, respect, charity,[14] and happiness.[15]

Our common moral understanding *is* metaphoric! Metaphors of the sort we have identified (e.g., SOCIAL ACCOUNTING, RIGHTS ARE RIGHTS-OF-WAY, MORAL INTERACTIONS ARE COMMODITY TRANSACTIONS) are the content of our understanding of morality. They are constitutive of our modes of reasoning, evaluation, and moral exploration. They are truly 'metaphors we live by.' What I hope to have shown with my very partial and preliminary analysis is that our fundamental moral concepts are defined by systems of metaphor, and often by more than one system for a given concept.

Most of the metaphorical systems we have examined so far are ones that structure our conception of morality itself, such as our notions of action, purpose, rights, and duties. But metaphor is operative, too, at a second, more concrete level of our understanding of morally problematic situations. The way we frame a given situation will determine what we ought to do about it, and our semantic frames typically involve metaphorical concepts. Consequently, our reasoning about these situations will be based on metaphors.

To get a clearer idea of how it is that we actually *live* and *reason* by means of deep metaphoric systems of meaning, I want to examine one real-life instance of moral reasoning that is so ordinary that we would typically not even notice either its *moral* or its *metaphoric* character. The case I examine involves reasoning of a sort that is often unconscious or only marginally conscious and that is based on metaphors that we use more or less unreflectively. Yet it is just this kind of metaphoric understanding and reasoning that makes up the fabric of our ordinary moral experience.

I want to consider one man's metaphorical understanding of his marriage, and the way he reasons on the basis of the metaphors. My analysis is based on data selected from a series of extensive interviews with husbands and wives conducted by Naomi Quinn.[16] Quinn is concerned with the way people organize and understand their marriages, and with how they act on the basis of these understandings.[17] What she discovered was a small number of systematic metaphorical mappings that underlie people's experience and conception of their marriage. Some of the more prominent metaphors for marriage were MARRIAGE IS A MANUFACTURED OBJECT, MARRIAGE IS AN ONGOING JOURNEY, MARRIAGE IS A DURABLE BOND BETWEEN TWO PEOPLE, and MARRIAGE IS AN INVESTMENT.[18] These are metaphors insofar as they involve understanding and experiencing a domain of a certain kind (e.g., the social, moral, legal, or religious institution of *marriage*) by means of structures and relations mapped from a domain of a different kind (e.g., a manufactured *physical object,* a *physical bonding process,* or a *physical journey*).

These metaphors are *systematic,* consisting of organized mappings of objects, events, states, causes, and relations from one domain onto another domain. Consequently, our very experience and understanding of marriage is metaphorical, and the language we use to talk about marriage is just one manifestation of the underlying metaphors. For instance, the MARRIAGE IS AN ONGOING JOURNEY metaphor, which is a specific case of the LONG-TERM PURPOSEFUL ACTIVITIES ARE JOURNEYS metaphor, is the conceptual structure behind ordinary conventional expressions, such as "We've *just started out* in our marriage." "They've *come a long way* in their sense of marital responsibilities." "She thinks it's been all *uphill* with her husband these last few months." "They're just *spinning their wheels* and *going nowhere fast.*" "I'm afraid their marriage is a *dead end.*" "Who knows, maybe they'll get *back on track* after all." The language we use concerning marriage is so heavily conventionalized that much of it does not seem obviously metaphorical. But we could not understand this language without presupposing the metaphorical systems (e.g., MARRIAGE IS AN ONGOING JOURNEY) from which that language is generated. Such systematic metaphors reach deep down into our *experience* and *understanding* of marriage, and so they involve consequences for *action* in our daily lives. These consequences might include goals for the marriage, expectations for oneself and one's spouse, criteria for evaluating the health or success of the marriage, and the range of (morally) permissible responses and actions sanctioned or suggested by the underlying metaphorical mapping.

My example of mundane moral reasoning is drawn from Quinn's interviews with 'Alex,' who is reflecting on the development and nature of his thirteen-year marriage. In retrospect, Alex sees that he first operated under the assumption that MARRIAGE IS A RESOURCE/INVESTMENT for satisfying his basic needs and wants. At first,

> I thought it was all going to be wonderful. You know it was—the problem of sex was going to be solved. You know I was an adolescent or barely out of adolescence, you know—this was a wonderful idea . . . there really are some things that I knew about and that I wanted. A companion and friend. Probably the most . . . that seemed important then—to have someone there all the time that you could rely on. And talk to all the time about things. Somebody to help and somebody to help you, you know, that seemed like a real good idea. That seemed like something that we got out of the marriage. Somebody always there.[19]

Alex entered his marriage with the MARRIAGE IS A RESOURCE metaphor dominating his thought and action. He saw marriage chiefly as a way for two individuals to satisfy needs and desires ("something that we got out of the marriage"), so that helping one's spouse (being a resource for her) was part of the bargain. In fact, this conception placed an obligation on the partners to do the right thing, to be "somebody to help you" and "someone there all the time that you could rely on."

Marriage is framed here as a form of COMMODITY EXCHANGE. Of course, Alex is not aware of the metaphorical character of the view he describes, yet it is nonetheless the basis of his explanation of what happened.

Early in his marriage, after joining the navy, Alex works his way toward a new understanding of his relationship, in which he and his wife form an ORGANIC UNITY:

> I got the first promotion with the idea that the second one might be coming. I think that's how it was and that was quite successful because Shirley got pregnant right away. And she, you know, when I got back from Guantanamo she told me and we told the news to everybody and it was a really big deal. And I think that the apartment and the baby and all

of that stuff really began to come down on us, you know, and we started believing that we were truly a couple. And we were truly a family and really married. (32)

Alex's shift in attitude and commitment involves the emergence of what I would call the MARRIAGE IS AN ORGANIC UNITY metaphor (which Quinn calls MARRIAGE IS BEING A COUPLE). MARRIAGE IS A RESOURCE is not given up, but it recedes into the background and is understood now in the context of the ORGANIC UNITY metaphor.

The ORGANIC UNITY metaphor entails a number of beliefs, attitudes, expectations, goals, and behaviors that a person would understand as possibilities contained in the metaphor. These possibilities are established by the mapping that constitutes the metaphor and that gives rise to a number of epistemic entailments (i.e., 'epistemic' in the sense of what one knows or concludes from the details of the mapping). The mapping consists of the entities, events, states, structures, causes, and relations that are projected from the source domain (biological organisms) to the target domain (marriage).

The MARRIAGE IS AN ORGANIC UNITY Metaphor

Biological Domain	*Marriage Domain*
Living physical entities (A and B)	→ Persons (spouses)
Unity of whole organism (composed of two entities)	→ Spiritual, legal, or psychological union of spouses
Emergent properties of organism	→ Creative possibilities emerging from relation of spouses
Interactive process between parts A and B of organism	→ Interactions (emotional, social) between persons
Causal effect of A on B or B on A	→ Emotional, psychological, physical effect of one spouse on the other

On the basis of this mapping across domains, there are a large number of possible epistemic entailments. For example, in an organic unity of previously independent parts, emergent properties of the organism seem to arise; consequently, in a metaphorical organic unity of spouses, we would expect that creative possibilities would emerge from their interaction that were not possible for them as independent units. Among the epistemic entailments of the MARRIAGE IS AN ORGANIC UNITY metaphor are the following:

Epistemic Entailments of the MARRIAGE IS AN ORGANIC UNITY Metaphor

— Spouses no longer exist as separate entities but are interdependent.
— As interdependent, each spouse must accept certain constraints on his or her freedom (which did not exist for him or her as independent units).
— The union creates possibilities for interaction and growth that were not available to the separate individuals.
— Shared experience is requisite for the maintenance of the relationship.
— Each spouse can expect certain exclusive relations with the other spouse.
— Physical closeness provides enhanced opportunities for shared experience and growth.
— There exist justified expectations of mutual aid, support, comfort, and constancy.

Such entailments must be regarded as only *potential*—they present connections to *possible* goals, values, obligations, expectations, commitments, and so forth that may come into play in one's moral deliberation. This multivalence of the metaphorical system means that what the metaphor requires of a given person will always depend on his specific circumstances. Independent of the context and the concrete situation of the person acting under the metaphor, we cannot say precisely what the metaphor will entail.

Furthermore, the multivalence of the metaphor will typically be rich enough to support pairs of entailments that, if not contradictory, are at least in tension. For instance, someone attracted by the emergent possibilities for creativity and development realized by the organic union of two people might at the same time lament the loss of independence, and the constraint on certain freedoms, entailed by this organic union. There may well be an inescapable tension set up by the ORGANIC UNITY metaphor of a sort that is characteristic of much of our moral deliberation. On the other hand, the loss of independence in some domains may turn out to be enabling in other ways (e.g., by what it brings in intimacy and support), and thus it may actually enhance freedom and independence in other areas of life. Conversely, so-called 'emotional independence' can sometimes give *less* freedom and may create isolation, which can hinder or even paralyze a person's moral growth.

In order to see how these entailments work, that is, which ones are taken up relative to a specific context and how they are organized, I want to consider three entailments that played a central role in Alex's moral reasoning. He does not consciously articulate these metaphors, nor does he emphasize the moral dimension of his marriage. Yet these deep systematic metaphors are morally significant with regard to Alex's sense of how both he and his wife ought to act, what they ought to be able to expect from each other, how they might justify their actions, what kind of character each has, and what values they feel an obligation to realize. For example, because Alex understands his marriage via the MARRIAGE IS AN ORGANIC UNITY metaphor, he is able to recognize at least three major implications for the nature of their relationship and their conduct: (1) the demand for a special exclusive relationship between husband and wife (what we might call 'duties of monogamy'), (2) the requirement of physical closeness or proximity (= 'duties of preserving unity'), and (3) the obligation to share experience (= 'duties of mutual growth'). Let us see how each of these entailments issues from the ORGANIC UNITY metaphor.

1. *Duties of monogamy.* Under the influence of the MARRIAGE IS AN ORGANIC UNITY metaphor, Alex looks back on his relationship with his wife, Shirley, before they were married. He was already beginning to embrace the ORGANIC UNITY metaphor: "I think I decided it was time for Shirley to stop fooling around with other guys. And that [getting married] was the one way I thought I could convince her to do that. Other than that she was going to party for the rest of her life" (33). For Alex, exclusivity—not the concept, but the attitude, the behavior, the obligation—is one of the entailments of the ORGANIC UNITY metaphor within the context of his experience. The metaphor grounds his sense that Shirley should stop fooling around. This line of reasoning is even more obvious once he is married and comes to feel justified in insisting that Shirley break away from her parents.

> I think it was significant because you know I made a very strong decision then and, you know, we—Shirley went along and I think that was one of the first times that I had said, "I'm going to separate you from your parents." In a very decisive manner and "This is what we're going to do." And you know, "You're going to follow me here, you're going to go with me here as your husband." Maybe it was, you know—looking back on that I—maybe that seems—sounds a little chauvinistic but I think it was a declaration that we have a marriage and it's just two of us in this marriage not four. (33)

Alex had a choice—either he could let things go on as usual, or else he could insist that Shirley break from her parents. He feels justified in demanding a certain kind of allegiance from Shirley by virtue of moral obligations entailed by the

MARRIAGE IS AN ORGANIC UNITY metaphor ("You're going to follow me here, you're going to go with me here as your husband"). Moreover, any justification Alex would have for placing the demand on his wife to break certain emotional ties with her parents also places moral constraints on Alex's own commitments and actions. For it is because he experiences their marriage as a unity of a special sort that he is able to perceive Shirley's relation to her parents as a threat to that exclusive marital relationship, and thus to assert the primacy of their marital union ("it's just two of us in this marriage not four"). The MARRIAGE IS AN ORGANIC UNITY metaphor functions for Alex unconsciously as a moral ideal and thus generates moral obligations (e.g., exclusivity), regardless of potential unpleasant consequences or restrictions on his freedom. Alex is not merely engaging in prudential considerations (though he is *also* at the same time doing that, too), but determining what rights and duties obtain in this concrete situation.

2. *Duties of preserving unity.* A second set of entailments of the MARRIAGE IS AN ORGANIC UNITY metaphor involves physical closeness as a basis for shared experience. Alex argues that to be forced into physical separation by external circumstances is an evil that can be endured, "but to be given a chance—to be told that you may stay together that everything has been cleared, . . . and then to say, 'I'm not going to go.' That would have been hard to overcome" (33). Alex is not merely suggesting that it is prudent to maintain physical closeness to one's spouse; rather, he regards it as a moral obligation stemming from his commitment to the moral ideal of emotional, psychological, or spiritual unity established by the ORGANIC UNITY metaphor.

3. *Duties of mutual growth.* MARRIAGE IS AN ORGANIC UNITY requires shared experience: "When I do go to someplace very good to eat or I get to go to a show, I really feel badly about her not being there because we don't have that shared experience anymore. And those shows and good meals and things like that that we've done as a shared thing are really important to us and have been—are good moments for us in our marriage" (34).

Two extremely important points stand out about this particular entailment. First, the moral obligations issuing from the MARRIAGE IS AN ORGANIC UNITY metaphor are *felt* inclinations, desires, and motivations. They involve entertaining in imagination the presence of one's absent spouse, the way this absence makes shared experience impossible, and the memory of earlier shared moments. *There is no separation of intellectual precepts from feeling and imagination.* Alex is motivated, just as all morally sensitive people are, not by the alleged purity of rules and abstractions, but rather by feeling and imagination that draw him to desire something as good. About this, Hume was quite right, stressing as he did that an emotional dimension is crucial in our moral deliberations.[20] He was wrong, unfortunately, to separate this emotional aspect from what he mistakenly took to be a pure cognitive or intellectual component. In fact, these two dimensions are blended in a way that makes it impossible to extract one from the other. One reason metaphor is so basic for our moral understanding is that it combines these very dimensions of our embodied moral awareness—projection of possibilities, relation of feelings, imaginative reflection—that make it possible for us to have any degree of moral sensitivity in the first place.

Second, the metaphoric character of Alex's understanding of his marriage cannot be dismissed as 'mere' prudential reasoning (as opposed to alleged 'moral' reasoning). There is no rigid distinction to be made between what some philosophers narrowly define as 'moral' considerations (e.g., "I have a *duty* to enhance possibilities for mutual growth with my spouse") and what they disparagingly call 'prudential' concerns (e.g., marriage is far more satisfying for both partners when they strive to promote mutual growth—i.e., it will tend to make them *happier*). We do not experience a combination of independent dimensions (the 'moral' and the 'prudential') that just happen, contingently, to occur together. On the contrary, these dimensions are woven into the fabric of our moral experience. Our experience is morally saturated, although some experiences are obviously more ethically significant and noteworthy by virtue of their greater impact on our communal welfare, our character, and our empathy for others. These more significant experiences we are likely to think of as 'moral,' but we must not forget that every experience is situated within a background context that is pervaded with moral import.

Moreover, the idea that what is moral is somehow utterly separate from and unrelated to our quest for well-being makes morality into an inexplicable fact that has no explanatory connection to what we know about ourselves. To divorce morality from prudence makes it virtually impossible to understand why we have the moral values we do and why we regard them as so significant. It makes morality seem as though it comes out of nowhere from on high, with only the most external relations to the kinds of beings we are, the motivations we entertain, and the purposes that give direction to our lives. It denies our ecological situatedness, as purposive beings who coevolve along with their material, biological, and social environments. In short, the idea that morality has nothing to do with our purposive search for well-being and happiness would make morality utterly inexplicable, at best, and a cruel joke, at worst.[21]

Alex certainly does believe that failure to promote mutual growth makes for a less satisfying and fulfilling marriage. And he thinks that he has a moral obligation to promote such growth. But these are not for him, nor are they for any of us, two distinct imperatives. They are simply experienced by him, felt by him, as a need and a strong motive that both inspires and constrains his actions, attitudes, and affections.

We have so far looked primarily at 'reasoning' that depends on mostly unconscious, tacit, and unreflective metaphorical understanding of a marital relationship. Most of our ordinary, everyday moral deliberation is very much like this, for it operates at a level that is barely reflective and that is only marginally self-conscious most of the time. We are almost never aware of our deepest assumptions, of the metaphors structuring our understanding of situations, and of the way our values are organized and redefined in concrete situations.

Yet there are moments of self-conscious reflection, moments when some of what was hitherto hidden, automatic, and sedimented shows a part of itself to our critical gaze. Alex, for instance, entertains possible alternative entailments of his metaphorically understood experience, in an effort to figure out where different entailments might lead. In one passage he deliberates about the moral consequences of his wife's possibly entering into therapy.

> There is [*sic*] certain kinds of analysis, encounter groups and all sorts of things are done now that do focus on the individual. Yes, and I think that is challenging to marriages. What it really comes down to, the big question is, should the couples that break up, as a result of having these things, should they have been married at all? Maybe those marriages weren't any good anyway. But you then begin to wonder—take this a step further—you wonder if any marriage would make it given the— given egotism. If you put the self ahead of the marriage, if any marriages would last. What I'm saying is that I myself don't know whether analysis destroys the type of relationship, or whether it just points out the problems with that type of relationship. (35)

Does analysis undermine the ORGANIC UNITY of the relationship by privileging a spouse's individual self-interest above the growth of the marriage? Or does analysis only point out the already existing weakness of the marriage? Alex cannot yet decide, so he is playing with these possible entailments in the context of the MARRIAGE IS AN ORGANIC UNITY metaphor. He is trying out each possible explanation to see how it 'feels,' how it makes sense of his experience. And as he performs this test he is glimpsing possible structurings of his marriage. How he acts toward his wife's analysis and whether or not he will enter analysis depends on his feelings about, reflections on, and past experiences with such matters. The issue of analysis is not morally neutral within the context of the MARRIAGE IS AN ORGANIC UNITY metaphor. It is only because of his moral commitment to the marriage, in the context of his metaphorical understanding of what it requires, that he can even define analysis as a *problem*.

Morality Is Metaphoric: A Summary

My claim in this chapter is that our commonsense moral understanding is deeply and pervasively metaphoric on two levels: (1) Our fundamental concepts (e.g., action, cause, purpose, will, rights, duties, law) are metaphorically defined, typically by more than one metaphorical structuring of each concept. (2) The conceptual frames in terms of which we understand concrete situations often involve systems of conventional metaphor (as, for example, in the case of marriage metaphors). Here, too, there are almost always competing metaphoric descriptions of situations. Neither at the level of our most important moral concepts, nor at the level of our framing of situations, can we eliminate metaphor. We can replace one metaphorical system with another, but we cannot get out of *some* set of metaphorical concepts. Consequently, most of the reasoning we do about ethical issues, most of the decisions we make, and most of our judgments about other people are based on metaphors.

It is terribly important to keep in mind that I am *not* asserting that all of our concepts are metaphorical. Nor am I asserting that all thinking is metaphorical. The claim that everything in cognition is metaphorical is simply false, and it has been shown to be false by a large number of empirical studies of concepts, meaning, reasoning, and language.[22] My particular theoretical orientation (known as cognitive semantics[23]) stresses the grounding of our conceptual systems in structures of bodily experience. Our concepts of many of these structures are not metaphoric, as we will see later.[24] But cognitive semantics also highlights the irreducibly imaginative character of human cognition, including the central role of metaphor in much of our conceptualization and reasoning. We have discovered that many of our nonmetaphoric concepts are implicated in, and extended by, conceptual metaphors. Consequently, it is impossible to perform any extended conceptual analysis without recourse to the crucial role of metaphor.

My claim, therefore, is that because so much of our common moral understanding is structured by systems of metaphor, no account of morality can be adequate that fails to examine the extent to which our conceptualization, reasoning, and language about morality involve metaphor (and other imaginative devices). I hope to have shown that enough of our moral concepts are metaphorically defined so that no adequate moral theory could ignore those metaphors and the way we think and live by them.

My strategy so far as been to identify and analyze so many of the systematic metaphors that make up our moral knowledge, that it becomes inconceivable to think of moral reasoning without reference to metaphor. The metaphoric structuring of our ordinary moral understanding is simply a fact. We must not deny it. We need not fear it. We need not wish that things were otherwise. What we should do, instead, is to *understand* this fact and the implications it has for morality. It should become a central part of the knowledge we bring to bear in our moral reasoning.

The Metaphoric Basis of Moral Theory

'Pure' Moral Theory

I have been arguing two points, that our culturally shared folk theories of morality (e.g., the Moral Law folk theory) are irreducibly metaphoric, and that our mundane moral deliberation typically depends on deep, usually unconscious metaphorical understanding. Those who see that the central role of metaphor in moral knowledge calls into question our traditional conception of morality might try to explain away these analyses as follows: "You have shown," they might argue, "only that the day-to-day reasoning of ordinary people rests on unconscious systematic metaphors most of the time. But it is the job of moral philosophy to tell us how we *ought* to reason and act, not how we actually *do* reason or act in a particular situation. A philosophically sophisticated moral theory will eschew such figurative devices as metaphor, for it will see reflectively beyond our actual reasoning to the pure literal concepts needed for an adequate specification of the ultimate rules of morality." The job of moral theory, they will insist, is to get behind our metaphorical understanding to the foundational literal concepts.

For such a moral theory to be possible, there must be an allegedly 'pure' moral rationality that is believed to be nonfigurative or, in some cases, even nonimaginative. Once we have recognized the metaphorical character of our folk understanding of morality and all of our most basic moral concepts, does it really make any sense to think that we might then construct an adequate philosophical theory that is free of metaphor? This is beyond belief. The systematic metaphors we have examined so far cannot be construed merely as convenient forms of expression that exist only in our ordinary folk understanding, but that might be replaced by nonfigurative concepts in a suitably refined philosophical theory. The two different metaphorical structurings of our concepts of 'duties' and 'rights,' for instance, actually define those concepts for us. The overwhelming empirical evidence just does not support the dream of a nonfigurative morality.

A literalist strategy cannot work, for it is based on the illusion of a 'pure' reason—a reason whose essence has nothing to do with our experience or with any empirical concepts.[1] There are two things wrong with such a view. First, it claims that fundamental moral concepts and moral laws come from a transcendental, nonempirical reason. Second, it takes the essence of reason to be logical structure, which has no place for metaphor. Reason defined in this way could have very little relevance to our actual human understanding and reasoning, which are grounded in bodily experience and are imaginative through and through. In short, 'pure' reason has almost nothing to do with human reason.

Views of reason as pure, transcendent, and nonimaginative ignore the fact that moral theories are expressions of the moral traditions they emerge from and reconstruct. Philosophical theories are, for the most part, attempts to develop internally consistent systematic accounts of various folk theories that exist within a culture. Philosophers analyze, refine, criticize, reconstruct, justify, and sometimes extend folk theories. As a result, they tend to adopt the same metaphorical concepts, forms of discourse, modes of argument, and so forth that are established within the folk theories they articulate. This is what makes it possible for philosophically sophisticated theories to sometimes seem intuitively correct to ordinary people. Unless philosophical accounts draw on and relate back to our folk theoretical understanding, they will not make any sense at all of our experience.

Alasdair MacIntyre has recognized this point in his argument that moral philosophies are rooted in, and take their life from, developing moral traditions: "Moral philosophies, however they may aspire to achieve more than this, always do articulate the morality of some particular social and cultural standpoint: Aristotle is the spokesman for one class of fourth century Athenians, Kant . . . provides a rational voice for the emerging social forces of liberal individualism. . . . Moral philosophies are, before they are anything else, the explicit articulations of the claims of particular moralities to rational allegiance. And this is why the history of morality and the history of moral philosophy are a single history."[2]

MacIntyre's claim that all moral theories articulate moral traditions does not entail that moral theories cannot also *criticize* those traditions from which they arise. In *After Virtue* and *Whose Justice? Which Rationality?* MacIntyre has mounted a sustained argument for the possibility of progress in moral theory. I will later argue the somewhat weaker claim that we can learn from our collective experience. My point for now is the modest one that we should expect to find in each moral philosophy the basic metaphors that structure the moral tradition (with its folk theories) from which that philosophy emerged, and which it seeks to articulate.

Kant's Metaphoric Morality

The only way to prove conclusively such a thesis about the metaphorical character of moral theory would be to survey every theory we know of. That would be an overwhelming, if not impossible, task, serving no significant purpose. What I propose, instead, is simply to examine briefly the one moral theory in our Western tradition that would seem to be the best candidate for a 'pure' moral philosophy—Kant's famous rationalist ethics. Kant saw himself as showing that our fundamental moral concepts and laws can be derived from pure practical reason alone. Moral theorists for the last two centuries have held up Kant's moral philosophy as a model of morality based on reason.

If any moral theory could ever have a chance of claiming to be free of metaphor and other forms of imaginative cognition, it would be Kant's. With respect both to its general form and its fundamental concepts, Kant's theory is *supposed* to show how morality stems solely from pure practical reason, without any dependence on imagination. Let us, therefore, examine Kantian rationalist ethics to see whether this is actually the case.

That it is *not* the case has been recognized by Hilary Putnam, who suggests that, contrary to Kant's explicit claims about pure moral theory, the Kantian project does not issue from a transcendent reason. Putnam sees Kant's theory as based primarily on a 'moral image' or set of moral images, rather than on strict rules, pure literal concepts, and logical judgments.

> Kant is doing what he would have called 'philosophical anthropology', or providing what one might call a *moral image of the world*. He is not simply providing arguments for the third formulation of the Categorical Imperative, arguments for the proper ordering of the formal and material principles of morality, and so on; he is also, and most importantly, providing a moral image of the world which *inspires* these, and without which they don't make sense. A moral image, in the sense in which I am using the term, is not a declaration that this or that is a virtue, or that this or that is what one ought to do; it is rather a picture of how our virtues and ideals hang together with one another and of what they have to do with the position we are in. It may be as vague as the notions of 'sisterhood and brotherhood'; indeed, millions of human beings have found in those metaphors moral images that could organize their moral lives.[3]

According to Putnam, the moral image we have inherited from Kant is complex and multifaceted, but its core is a notion of autonomy, that is, an image of a community of free and equal beings who are able to think and act for themselves in a manner that respects the right of other people to do the same.[4]

Contrary to Kant's purist view of his own project, Putnam is right in claiming that Kant's theory elaborates a moral image and is an imaginative articulation of a particular moral tradition. In order to see why Putnam is right, however, we need to look much more closely at the actual metaphorical structure of Kantianism, which I am taking as a paradigm of rationalist ethics. We have seen already that folk theories of morality involve systematic metaphors at two basic levels, (1) in the nature of the fundamental concepts of the theory (e.g., the concept of a person, action, end, reason, duty, right, etc.), and (2) in the conceptualizing of particular situations. We should expect to find the same two levels in philosophers' theories of morality. We do.

Before I launch into my analysis of the metaphorical character of Kant's moral theory, I want to anticipate one obvious objection that modern-day Kantians are likely to level at my account. They will accuse me of caricaturing Kant as the paradigmatic moral absolutist. They will cite a growing number of recent articles and books in which Kant's moral theory is presented as being far more subtle, far less formalistic, and far more psychologically realistic than traditional interpretations suppose.[5] Let me state at the outset that I regard Kant as one of the most profound and subtle thinkers to have influenced the Western moral tradition. I am extremely favorable to all of these attempts to rebut standard superficial criticisms of Kant and to explore the rich depths of his understanding of morality. Consequently, I regard as important recent attempts to delve into Kant's insights into the nature of motivation,[6] moral feeling,[7] virtue,[8] and integrity.[9] I am also very much taken by Richard Eldridge's attempt to show us, through literature, how Kantian morality can be contextualized and situated within our world.[10]

In short, I grant the considerable merits of these new interpretations, which set out an admirable field of inquiry into a more realistic Kantianism. But I do not see how this body of work challenges in any significant way the analysis of the metaphoric character of Kant's conception of morality that I am about to give. I will set out my textual evidence shortly. If it should turn out that there are passages in Kant's writings on morality that reveal that he is less absolutistic than I present him as being, then this would require some revision of my analysis. Still, I believe that I have given a fair, textually defensible interpretation that at least captures a mainstream view of Kantian morality that has survived for two centuries, and that epitomizes rationalistic ethics. With these qualifications in mind, we can now look into some of the metaphorical concepts operative in Kant's account of morality.

Kant saw himself as supplying a *rational* foundation for the key ideas of the Judeo-Christian moral tradition that has dominated morality in the West. His was a "moral philosophy articulating a moral tradition," *his* and *our* moral tradition. So, it should not be surprising to find in his theory the key metaphors we have already identified as constituting the Moral Law folk theory that dominates our tradition. And this is exactly what we do find, namely, instances of the same metaphors we analyzed earlier as defining our folk theories.

Kant's most central moral concepts, in terms of which he articulates the fundamental principle of morality, are metaphorical, and irreducibly so. Consider his argument for, and formulation of, the ultimate moral principle, the categorical imperative.[11] Recall (from chapter 1) that Kant's project is to provide a rational foundation for the nontheological part of the Judeo-Christian moral tradition. In the *Foundations of the Metaphysics of Morals* Kant analyzes our "common rational knowledge of morals" (*F*, 393) as it is embodied in our shared moral tradition. He claims to have identified the "supreme principle of morality" (*F*, 392) upon which all our moral knowledge is based.

We saw earlier that Kant's method has a hypothetical character. He argues that, *if* our common moral tradition is roughly correct, *then* the notions of duty, moral worth, will, and so forth that are presupposed by our tradition will require a very specific form for the supreme moral principle. Kant cannot prove the truth of his moral tradition. He can only analyze it to see what it assumes and what it entails. Putnam is right, therefore, when he says that Kant is not concerned with proofs of any sort.[12] Instead, based upon his rational analysis of the central concepts of our moral tradition, Kant tries to construct a consistent view of how those fundamental moral concepts are systematically related and how they jointly constrain the formula for the supreme moral principle.

Kant's pure moral philosophy (what he calls a "metaphysics of morals") is "meant to investigate the idea and principles of a possible pure will" (*F*, 390). A pure will would be one that always acted from duty, and thus in a morally correct manner. So, Kant's central question concerns the nature of the moral principles that such a pure will would act on, insofar as it acts morally. These principles would be 'pure' principles of morality. But what does Kant mean by a 'pure' principle? A form of knowledge is pure, according to Kant, when it is not mixed up with any empirical elements.[13] A pure principle of morality would have to be one that comes out of pure practical reason alone and is in no way based on any-thing tied to our bodily being, for example, sensations, feelings, emotions, im-ages.

Notice that Kant takes over wholesale the folk theory of Faculty Psychology and of Moral Law. Humans have a dual nature—a 'pure' rational side and an 'impure' bodily side. These two aspects, reason and passion, understood meta-phorically as persons, are in a struggle to gain control over will. Our deepest essence is our rationality, not our bodily, passionate being. Kant regards the body as a source of alien (what he calls "heteronomous") influences, chief of which are feelings of any sort. To act morally, then, we must not let the will be determined by sensations, feelings, or emotions, but only by *pure* reason. A 'pure moral law' is one that comes out of reason alone and is not based on any empirical experi-ence, empirical concepts, or imaginative mechanisms. Kant argues that an action gets its moral worth solely from the rational principle that determines it, "without any regard to the objects of the faculty of desire" (*F, 400*), and thus independent of our wants, inclinations, or feelings.

The crux of Kant's view is that *reason alone* must be able to determine our acts of will. Reason must be able to exert a constraining force on will. Reason's laws give the *form* of that constraint; that is, they specify what kinds of actions are morally required and what kinds are prohibited. Because we do not always act in a fully rational manner, reason's laws present themselves as restrictions on our willing. In Kant's terms, "the determination of such a will according to objective laws is constraint" (*F, 413*). This is exactly the same notion of REASON AS FORCE that we saw in the Moral Law folk theory.

To sum up, Kant claims that our notion of a good (pure) will is a will that acts from duty. Acting from duty involves acting from pure principles that come from the essence of practical reason (what Kant calls "a priori" principles), rather than being derived from experience ("a posteriori" principles). Such principles are laws that tell us how we ought to act, and they thus constrain our willing. Kant's view is that "the principles are completely a priori, free from everything empiri-cal, and found exclusively in pure rational concepts" (*F, 410*). He claims that it is clear from an analysis of our moral knowledge "that all moral concepts have their seat and origin entirely a priori in reason" (*F, 411*).

Imagination in the Application of Moral Law

Kant's assumption of the purity of all moral concepts, as containing nothing based on empirical experience, creates for him a monumental problem. How could any pure principles that are based only on a priori concepts ever apply to a particular experience? Any principle governing a specific action would seem to have empirical content, since it would contain concepts that apply to empirical situations in the world. So the problem is, how could a 'pure' moral principle (i.e., one without empirical content) ever be applied to experience?

Kant understands the problem of applying the supreme moral principle as a question of figuring out how to use it to determine whether a particular maxim of an action is morally acceptable. A maxim is merely a description of the principle upon which a person actually acts.[14] Maxims, as Kant frequently states them, typically have the following form: For the sake of X (the end), I will do Y (the action), in circumstance C (the situation). Thus, every maxim has a 'purposive' component (specifying the end in view), a 'performative' component (specifying the act done), and a 'circumstantial' component (specifying the type of situation in which the act occurs).[15] Assuming that a maxim of this form could be given for any action, Kant claims that deciding the moral acceptability of a maxim requires us to determine whether our actual (subjective) principle or maxim could also serve as a universally valid *objective* principle for all rational creatures. "The objective principle (i.e., that which would serve all rational beings also subjectively as a practical principle if reason had full power over the faculty of desire) is the practical law" (*F,* 401n).

The objective principle, the practical law, the law valid for all rational creatures, cannot be based on anything private or peculiar to me. It cannot be a mere hypothetical imperative that has the form "If I will end E, I ought to perform acts A, B, C, and so forth, which are the necessary means to that end." A merely hypothetical imperative is always contingent on my setting some particular end I wish to achieve. Such imperatives are hypothetical, because if I cease to will the contingent end, then I am no longer bound by the imperative to act in a certain way.

Kant also argues that the objective principle (the moral law) cannot depend in any way on my bodily feelings, inclinations, desires, or emotions, all of which Kant regards as subjective, contingent, and sources of heteronomous influences. In Kant's terms, the moral law must abstract from all material content (i.e., any particular end that is given by my contingent desires) and from any part of my bodily being. Only by keeping 'pure' in this way can the moral law command unconditionally and universally (i.e., categorically).

However, once we abstract from any particular *content* of a moral principle, then we are left with only the *form* of law as such, which is the form of *univer-*

sality, since all moral laws are universally and unconditionally binding (*F,* 420–21). Focusing only on the form of universality thus gives us the "only one categorical imperative," which is "Act only according to that maxim by which you can at the same time will that it should become a universal law" (*F,* 421).[16]

I want to point out, in passing, how Kant's entire analysis depends on a rigid distinction between 'form' and 'matter' and between 'pure' and 'empirical.' Numerous philosophers have challenged the radical form/matter dichotomy, arguing that 'form' makes no sense in itself, independent of something that has that form.[17] I would only add to this objection the further argument that 'form' and 'matter' are interrelated, metaphorically defined notions. Our basic understanding of form is grounded in our bodily perceptual and motor experience of shape and internal configuration of perceivable objects. The use of 'form' with regard to nonperceptual, abstract entities or domains (e.g., the form of an argument, logical form, mathematical relations, formal laws, etc.) is via metaphorical extension from our bodily sense of form. Similarly, 'matter' and 'content' are metaphorical concepts when applied to nonphysical or abstract domains.

Returning to Kant's problem of how pure moral laws can apply to experience, it is likely, at first glance, to strike us as laughable that deciding the morality of an action requires figuring out whether its maxim can serve as a universal law, for we haven't the slightest idea what that could mean. How can a particular maxim that specifies subjective ends to be achieved by our bodily actions in the natural, causally deterministic world, be evaluated by a purely formal principle? The problem is that such a formal principle is utterly unlike our empirical maxim, in that it abstracts from all material content, does not depend on subjective ends, and supposedly legislates for the realm of rational creatures (the realm of freedom, as opposed to causal necessity). Kant is well aware of this enormous problem when he says, "Since all instances of possible actions are only empirical and can belong only to experience and nature, it seems absurd to wish to find a case in the world of sense, and thus standing under the law of nature, which admits the application of a law of freedom to it, and to which we could apply the supersensuous ideal of the morally good, so that the latter could be exhibited *in concreto.*"[18]

Here we are at the crux of Kant's entire moral theory. Unless Kant can show how a pure formal principle can apply to experience, his entire project of a purely rational morality is undermined. Kant poses this critical problem as one of how it is possible to make a certain kind of practical moral judgment. Judgment is "the faculty of thinking the particular as contained under the universal,"[19] or the "faculty of subsuming under rules."[20] In the case of morality the 'rules' are laws for the realm of freedom—moral laws; and the 'particular' is some action in the natural world, governed by natural law. We seem to be confronted with an unbridgeable gap between freedom (the moral realm) and nature (the causally determined realm). Kant describes this ontological gap by saying that there can be no "direct presentation" (*CJ,* sec. 59; no instantiation in experience) of laws of freedom, since he assumed that the physical world was absolutely determined by causal necessity. In other words, the notion of freedom seems to have no place in a Newtonian universe, in which everything operates according to causal necessity. So it would seem that there is no way to apply pure moral rules (laws of freedom) to real-life cases! And this would make our traditional morality, which assumes that we can guide our actions by rational principles, a cruel illusion.

Kant's solution is that, although there can be no direct presentation (or "schematism") of moral laws in the natural world, yet there can be an *indirect* or *symbolical* presentation sufficient for our practical needs.

> A schema is a universal procedure of the imagination in presenting a priori to the sense a pure concept of the understanding which is determined by the law; and a schema must correspond to natural laws to which objects of sensuous intuition as such are subject. But to the law of freedom (which is a causality not sensuously conditioned), and consequently to the concept of the absolutely good, no intuition and hence no schema can be supplied for the purpose of applying it *in concreto*. Thus the moral law has no other cognitive faculty to mediate its application to objects of nature than the understanding (not the imagination); and the understanding can supply to an idea of reason not a schema of sensibility but a law. This law, as one which can be exhibited *in concreto* in objects of the senses, is a natural law. But this natural law can, for the purpose of judgment, be used only in its formal aspect, and it may, therefore, be called the *type* of the moral law.[21]

To put this extremely obscure account more straightforwardly: No pure moral rule can be applied directly to experience, because such a law of freedom cannot apply to our deterministic natural world. But the supreme moral law (the categorical imperative) involves only the *form* of all laws, that is, universality. Therefore, the universality of all moral law can actually be represented *figuratively* as the form of natural law (i.e., universality). Paul Dietrichson explains this by saying that abstract moral law can be applied to a maxim of action by means of "a merely *figurative substitute* for a schematization of the moral law, i.e., a *typification*."[22] Kant's "typic" of the moral law is the idea of treating a moral law *as if* it were a law of nature. By typifying the moral law, then, we can use the idea of a system of beings under natural laws as a device for deciding the morality of a particular maxim.

To assess a given maxim we ask whether, if our maxim (our principle of action) were to become a universal law of nature, we could still pursue the end we wished to achieve by following that principle.[23] The figurative test is to ask whether there could exist a system of nature whose 'natural' laws were actually those principles we are claiming to be moral laws. If there is something internally inconsistent or contradictory about such a figuratively envisioned natural world, then the proposed moral principle must be rejected.

Finding a type or symbol for moral law is thus a *metaphorical* procedure by which laws in one domain (the realm of freedom) are taken as acting like laws from another domain (the realm of nature) with respect to their form (universality). In short, the underlying metaphor that lets us apply the categorical imperative to concrete cases is MORAL LAWS ARE NATURAL LAWS.

Furthermore, Kant argues that the supreme principle of morality, so typified, really is the kind of principle people actually use to evaluate actions: "The rule of judgment under laws of pure practical reason is: Ask yourself whether, if the action which you propose should take place by a law of nature of which you yourself were a part, you could regard it as possible through your will. Everyone does, in fact, decide by this rule whether actions are morally good or bad. Thus people ask: If one belonged to such an order . . . , would he assent of his own will to being a member of such an order of things."[24]

But notice the startling conclusion we have arrived at: *that which is supposed to be the purest rational ethics possible turns out to involve rules that can only be applied to concrete cases on the basis of underlying metaphorical mappings!* Morality rests on metaphors. By Kant's own description, moral reasoning involves a figurative envisioning of a nonexisting world as a means for judging a proposed action. There is not literally a world in which all actions now freely undertaken (in our world) would be causally necessitated (in the envisioned world). But we are required to use such a figurative conception to evaluate the adequacy of a proposed maxim. The metaphorical mapping involves taking what we know of (the form of) natural law and projecting it onto the realm of freedom so as to transform free action into naturally necessitated events.

Based on this metaphoric transformation, we must then determine whether the envisioned world would involve some sort of internal contradiction. Typically, where there is a contradiction, it arises between what I have called the 'purposive' and the 'performative' components of the proposed maxim. That is, we see that acting on the suitably universalized maxim would make it impossible to achieve the very end or goal for which the action is allegedly done.[25]

Kant denies that typification involves imagination, for he wants to keep moral judgment a matter of pure practical reason. But what could be more thoroughly imaginative than this form of figurative envisioning that is based on a metaphoric mapping? As I have argued elsewhere,[26] this is clearly an imaginative metaphoric procedure of judgment, the nature of which Kant describes in his treatments of metaphor (*CJ,* sec. 59) and reflective judgment (*CJ,* "First Introduction," sec. V), both of which are imaginative processes.

Moreover, each of the other formulations of the categorical imperative that Kant gives are also elaborations of basic metaphors. As a general overview, we can summarize the metaphors that underlie the four most commonly identified formulas of the categorical imperative as follows:

1. "Act as though the maxim of your action were by your will to become a universal law of nature" (*F,* 421). *Metaphor:* MORAL LAWS ARE NATURAL LAWS. This is the formula we have just analyzed above. In Kant's system moral laws are not literally natural laws, but the typic sanctions the metaphorical understanding of the moral realm in terms of a natural system governed by universal laws of nature.

2. "Act so that you treat humanity, whether in your own person or that of another, always as an end and never as a means only" (*F,* 429). *Metaphor:* HUMAN NATURE IS AN END IN ITSELF. We typically understand ends as what Alan Donagan calls "producible ends,"[27] ends that can be brought about by some action. Such ends come to exist only as a result of actions by us that are directed to realizing those ends. But an 'end-in-itself' is, strictly speaking, not something we produce by our actions. So, in what sense can an end-in-itself be the *result* of our action, since it is not actually brought about by it? An 'end-in-itself' must be a metaphorical extension of our ordinary conception of an end as something brought about by us. Instead of being something we produce or realize through our actions, an end-in-itself is a rational creature who we *respect* by our action. In other words, we must take care to insure that our acts do not violate the integrity of other people as moral beings.

3. "Act only so that the will through its maxims could regard itself at the

same time as universally lawgiving" (*F*, 434). *Metaphor:* AGENTS ARE SELF-LEGISLATING BEINGS. We commonly understand legislation as enacted by another (or some group) to whom we are subject. A law is given to us, or perhaps we legislate for another. In both cases the person to whom the law is given, the person standing 'under' the law, is constrained by it to act in certain ways. But what sense can it make to see ourselves as not only subject to law, but subject to a law that we (autonomously) *give to ourselves?* Giving ourselves a law (*auto* [self]–*nomos* [law]) is a metaphorical extension of our ordinary notion of legislation. It requires a conception of a split self, in which one part gives a law to itself (regarded as another part). One part binds or constrains the other part, though these are both parts of the same person.

4. A rational being must act so as to "regard himself always as legislative in a realm [kingdom] of ends possible through the freedom of the will" (*F*, 434). *Metaphor:* MORAL AGENTS ARE MEMBERS OF A REALM (OR KINGDOM) OF ENDS. A 'kingdom of ends' is a systematic relation of ends-in-themselves (rational agents) and producible ends (the ends they bring about through their actions). In such a kingdom there is a harmonious balance of all of these ends, so as to minimize conflict and maximize freedom (as autonomy). Such a kingdom of ends does not actually exist, but we must imagine what such a kingdom would be like, as a guiding ideal in evaluating our actions. We must strive for this metaphorical 'kingdom' or systematic union of ends existing in harmony. This formula is perhaps not strictly a metaphor, but rather an imaginative ideal based on the metaphor of ENDS-IN-THEMSELVES.

Once we conceive of the various formulas of the categorical imperative as involving underlying metaphorical concepts, we can make sense of Kant's claim that each formula provides its own unique way of realizing morality: "The three aforementioned ways of presenting the principle of morality are fundamentally only so many formulas of the very same law, and each of them unites the other in itself. There is, nevertheless, a difference in them, but the difference is more subjectively than objectively practical, for it is intended to bring an idea of reason closer to intuition (by means of a certain analogy) and thus nearer to feeling" (*F*, 436). Each of the underlying metaphors, which Kant calls 'analogies,' that underlie the different formulas has its own special use, suggests its own perspective on the moral law, and calls up its own peculiar cluster of experiences, concepts, feelings, associations, images, and so forth, that guide us in seeing how the law applies in particular cases.

Summary: The Imaginative Basis of Kantian Rationalist Ethics

Even if we were to grant Kant's general rationalist framework (which we have reason to question), it would still be the case that his theory is metaphoric and imaginative in several ways.

1. The fundamental concepts of Kant's moral theory are, for the most part, concepts he took from the moral tradition he was articulating and defending. And just as these concepts were metaphorically defined in the Moral Law folk theory that predominates in that tradition, they are also defined by those same metaphors in his more rigorous and sophisticated philosophical theory. A comprehensive survey of the metaphorical concepts Kant adopts from the Moral Law folk theory would be a long and complex technical exercise that would lead me away from the constructive project of this book. Therefore, I have relied for my argument on only a few representative examples of such metaphorical concepts.

2. Even Kant's precise formulations of the supreme principle of morality, the categorical imperative, are based on metaphors. As we saw, it is the *metaphors* that make it possible for us to get even the vaguest understanding of what Kant's formulas mean.

3. The very possibility that the formulas of the categorical imperative could be used to assess the morality of proposed maxims of action depends on metaphor. The typification of the categorical imperative, which is necessary if it is not to be an empty formal principle, is a *figurative* procedure that requires an imaginative envisioning of situations that do not actually exist in our present world.

Moreover, imagination plays a crucial role in at least the following two additional ways in Kant's moral theory, or in *any* Moral Law theory, which I will take up in the next chapter:

4. Just to recognize that some rule might be relevant to our present case requires that we organize various details and select some as more significant than others. We do this by a process of imaginative reflection.

5. We must also imaginatively weigh similarities and differences between the situation at hand and various prototypical and noncontroversial cases where a certain rule proved applicable. This skill of weighing requires an educated imagination and cannot be usefully formalized or put in an algorithmic form. Often, deciding how to extend beyond 'clear' or prototypical cases to nonprototypical cases involves metaphorical projections.

What I am arguing is thus that Putnam is right when he suggests that, contrary to Kant's own belief that his view follows from the essence of a pure practical reason, what Kant *in fact* does is to provide us with compelling moral images that capture the deepest insights of our Western moral tradition, such images and metaphors as those of universal moral law, persons as ends-in-themselves, and autonomy as self-legislation. Moreover, the entire procedure for using the categorical imperative to assess the morality of particular maxims is a figurative, metaphorical process.

Once we recognize the imaginative character of moral reasoning, we see the need to detranscendentalize Kant's moral theory, rejecting his notion of a pure, transcendent, disembodied rationality. This leads us to regard his theory as an attempt to provide a rational, consistent, systematic analysis of the fundamental values, commitments, and implications of our moral tradition. The value and usefulness of such a nonabsolutistic theory would not be limited only to a knowledge of our moral tradition, its assumptions, and its limitations. Such a theory could also give us means for criticizing both our own tradition and other alternative traditions, as well. This would not provide a method for beating rival views into submission ('by a priori argument' grounded on 'pure' reason). Instead, as I shall argue, it gives us deep moral understanding and self-knowledge, and it gives us a basis for critical reflection, both about our own values and concepts and about the morally problematic situations we encounter in our daily lives.

Conclusion: Morality Is Metaphoric

To sum up the results of this and the previous chapter—morality is metaphoric through and through. Our folk models of morality are based on systematic metaphors. Our mundane, mostly automatic and unreflective moral understanding and reasoning are inextricably tied up with metaphors. And even our most abstract, 'pure' rationalistic theories of morality are shot through with metaphor. It would be obsessive and tedious to analyze all of our major moral theories for their metaphoric character. But I have tried to suggest that such a project would indeed be possible, since our most fundamental notions of action, purpose, rights, duties, personhood, and so forth are irreducibly metaphoric, so that any moral theory in our tradition will necessarily appropriate some set of basic metaphors for such concepts. This follows from the pervasively metaphoric character of human cognition, and not from any idiosyncratic conditions peculiar to morality. In short, I am suggesting that Kant, who above all others presumed to offer a 'pure' moral philosophy, is quite representative of moral theory generally, insofar as his basic concepts are metaphorically structured.

It is time to recognize that, whatever else we say about moral reasoning, we must acknowledge and seek to understand its deeply imaginative character. We must get clear both about the limitations this places on our moral perspective and also about the insight it gives us. In particular, our imaginative rationality is the chief means we have for dealing critically, creatively, and sensitively with the novel situations that arise for us each day. Failure to appreciate the imaginative character of our moral reasoning condemns us to misunderstand our situation in either of two equally mistaken ways: (1) by relying on illusory ideals of moral absolutes, pure reason, and algorithmic procedures, or (2) by falling into the opposite error of irrationalism, extreme relativism, or subjectivism.

There are two possible ways to take the argument, as I have developed it so far. The first, more modest, interpretation argues that traditional moral theory must be supplemented by a theory of imaginative rationality. On this reading, moral theory keeps its classic definition as supplying a set of rationally derived moral laws under which particular cases are to be subsumed. In this context, my argument would be construed as showing that the laws and principles don't have the alleged purity they were thought to have, that they are based on metaphorical concepts, and that their application requires various forms of imagination.[28]

The second, stronger, interpretation would regard my analysis as pointing out the need for a new conception of moral theory itself, one in which laws and formal decision procedures do not play the central role.

At this stage of my argument, I hope to have made what I regard as a very strong case for at least the first interpretation, having shown why we must bring imaginative rationality into moral theory as traditionally conceived. And I have suggested some of the ways in which this would change our conception of moral reasoning. I would consider it an important step to have made a contribution toward realizing this first project.

However, I believe that the imaginative nature of our conceptual system and reason supports the even stronger thesis, which calls for a revised view of morality and moral theory. This book as a whole is an attempt to make the case for the stronger reading, and thus to propose a different conception of moral theory. Such a theory would not be based primarily on discovering and applying moral laws, but rather on developing knowledge of the imaginative constitution of our moral understanding and what this means for moral reasoning.

Beyond Rules

The previous two chapters focused on the metaphoric nature of our moral understanding as a prime example of the imaginative character of moral reasoning. The pervasiveness and indispensability of metaphor, both in our fundamental moral concepts and our conceptual framing of situations, presents a major challenge to the literalist assumptions of our Moral Law folk theory. I now want to describe another type of imaginative structure that plays a central role in moral deliberation, namely, the prototype structure of concepts. The existence of prototype structure presents a second challenge to certain assumptions that lie behind the Moral Law folk theory. The implications of prototype phenomena are not merely negative and critical, however; they also give us insight into how it is possible for us to make informed moral judgments about difficult cases that are not clear or prototypical.

The recent discovery of cognitive prototypes has radically changed our understanding of conceptual structure.[1] The classical theory of category structure is based on the idea that categories or concepts are defined by lists of features an entity must possess if it is to count as a member of that category. Category membership is regarded as an all-or-nothing matter—an entity is either *in* the category or *outside* it—even though it is recognized that there might be a few difficult borderline cases. Moreover, the classical view has no conception of 'internal' structure of a category. Since every member must possess all of the features on the list that defines the category, there is nothing in the structure of the category that could differentiate one member from another. They are all equally in the category.

What Eleanor Rosch and her colleagues discovered in the early 1970s was that there is typically a great deal of internal structure to a category.[2] Not every member is equally central to our understanding of a given category. For a particular category (e.g., bird) some members (e.g., robins) turn out to be cognitively more central in our understanding of the category. These cognitive prototypes are important in defining our categories, but they do not exhaust the structure of the category, nor do they give us a list of necessary and sufficient conditions for category membership. In the category 'bird,' for example, other members will be less central or prototypical, such as chickens, ostriches, emus, penguins, and so forth. In most cases there will not be a single defining set of features possessed by every member of the category. Different members will be related by what Wittgenstein called "family resemblances," rather than by their sharing of a set of essential properties.[3]

In this chapter I want to explore briefly the way in which our new understanding of category structure is at odds with the Moral Law folk theory (in both its absolutist and relativist versions), and thus requires a different view of the nature of moral reasoning. In order to emphasize what is wrong with the view of moral reasoning as chiefly a matter of applying fixed moral laws to situations, I will focus primarily on the version of the Moral Law folk theory that I have called moral absolutism.

Moral absolutism is obsessed with the problem of grounding and securing moral objectivity, in an attempt to overcome skeptical fears that morality is nothing more than a cultural construct erected to reinforce the contingent values and interests of a particular moral tradition. It seeks this absolute grounding by searching for a definitive set of determinate moral rules that come out of a Universal Reason, are universally binding on all rational beings, and are unchanging across cultures and throughout history. It is not surprising, therefore, that an absolutist would think it possible to 'get it right' once and for all about the fundamental moral rules.

Something terribly important is missing from this vision of absolute moral rules. What is left out is any sense of the development, growth, and historical transformation of our experience and our moral knowledge. Absolute moral rules are supposed to be objective precisely because they are not affected by the contingencies and vicissitudes of our historical experience. As we shall see, such rules are thought to issue from the essential structure of a practical reason that allegedly remains fixed for all time. Our understanding of the central concepts may change, but the concepts themselves must never change in their essence. Our *understanding* of the moral laws may vary, or even regress, whereas the laws themselves must remain eternally fixed and valid in their pristine state.

This picture of moral concepts, laws, and reasoning has very little to do with actual human deliberation. I will argue that this picture is mostly at odds with what we are learning about human conceptual structure, judgment, and reasoning. However, some of the assumptions of the absolutist viewpoint must be at least partially right, or it would never have won and maintained the allegiance it has enjoyed throughout history and across cultures.

What absolutism gets right is the existence of a shared, stable part of our basic moral concepts. There are large numbers of clear, unproblematic cases where there is little or no question what we should do. These form a kind of stable core of morality that we assume unreflectively and even unconsciously most of the time. For such clear cases it will make perfectly good sense to say that they fall neatly under fixed moral laws. But the absolutist's mistake is to generalize incorrectly in claiming that *all* moral reasoning works this way.

It is true that intelligent moral deliberation is a *reflective* activity and that, as such, it typically operates under the general influence of imaginative ideals and principles. We should not, however, think of these principles as absolute moral laws. I will elaborate a different view of moral principles, not as restrictive moral laws, but rather as summaries of our collective moral experience that present important concerns we ought to figure into our moral deliberations. I view moral deliberation as expansive, imaginative inquiry into possibilities for enhancing the quality of our communally shared experience. Principles, in a sense to be explained below, are crucial for this kind of intelligent moral inquiry and self-criticism. I will urge that moral deliberation is better described as imaginative exploration and transformation of experience, instead of the pigeonholing of cases under a set of fixed rules.

If absolutism is right about the existence of a shared, stable part of morality, what it misses is relativism's insight that there is a part of morality that is unshared and unstable. What we have learned about the imaginative structure of concepts can explain why this is the case. It thus undercuts absolutism. But, at the same time, it also undercuts extreme forms of relativism by showing that morality is not radically unstable and indeterminate, either.

What is at stake in this discussion is thus of the utmost importance. It is the question of what moral reasoning consists in. This ought to matter to us because our view of the nature of morality commits us to a view of how we ought to live and what ought to matter most in our lives.

Moral Absolutism's View of Concepts and Laws

There are different forms of moral absolutism, but what I regard as a prototypical version involves the following cluster of closely related claims about moral deliberation.

1. *Universal moral laws.* There exists a set of moral laws, universally binding on all human beings, that specify which actions are morally impermissible, which are permissible, and which are obligatory for us.

2. *Universal Reason.* Each moral agent possesses a universal capacity for reason which, when it functions correctly, is able to grasp these moral laws and to apply them to concrete situations.

3. *Absolute character of moral values.* Moral values and laws are absolute. They are in no way dependent on cultural differences or historical contingencies. They are universally binding on all rational beings regardless of time or place. They are not subject to modification or replacement for any reason, or in any context.

4. *Moral concepts are univocal and literal.* If our fundamental moral laws are to be absolute and definitive of morally correct willing and action, then the concepts contained in these laws must be highly determinate and well-defined. They must have a single definite meaning, so that their application to concrete situations is simply a matter of determining whether the necessary and sufficient conditions defining the concept actually obtain in experience (i.e., actually apply to the concrete situation).

5. *Classical category structure of concepts.* In order for moral judgment to be the bringing of cases under fixed concepts and laws, the concepts must have classical category structure; that is, they must be defined by sets of necessary and sufficient conditions, and there must be no internal structure to these concepts beyond the set of defining features.

6. *Nonimaginative character of moral reasoning.* The absolutist's demand for univocity (through literal concepts) leaves no room for structures of imagination, such as metaphor, metonymy, or images of any sort, all of which are regarded as subjective, idiosyncratic, and highly indeterminate. Structures of this sort would supposedly render moral deliberation irrational and utterly indeterminate, at least according to the absolutist characterization of imagination as an unconstrained play of fancy.

7. *Hierarchical ranking of values and principles.* In any instance where two or more moral principles might seem to conflict, there must exist some rational procedure for rank ordering the values or principles involved. Universal Reason must, on this view, allow us to avoid any irreducible moral conflict of duties. It must be entirely coherent and internally consistent, and there must be one uniform standard of evaluation. Only in this way can we hope to have a single correct judgment for each case.

8. *Absolutistic logic.* For the absolutist, moral reasoning must be ultimately a matter of deductive logic, the subsuming of concrete cases under absolute moral precepts. Formal logic of this sort has no place for metaphors or any other kinds of imaginative structure. Only in this way, and assuming also the classical view of concept structure and the universality of reason, can the absolutist anticipate the existence of '*the* right thing to do' in a given situation. Absolutists may recognize other, less formalizable modes of reasoning, but they will all be regarded as less satisfactory to the degree that they diverge from the pure deductive model.

9. *Radical freedom.* Absolutism requires the possibility of radical freedom, that is, that moral agents must be capable of acting on the basis of moral *decisions* based on moral principles they give to themselves, independent of any 'external,' 'nonrational' causes, such as their contingent emotions, desires, habits, or obsessions. For the absolutist, moral responsibility requires that the agent always have the capacity to say yes or no to any contemplated act.

10. The *right thing to do.* If every aspect of the absolutist program were to fall into place, then there would be one and only one 'right thing to do' in any given case. We could then organize our lives around our attempt to maximize the number of times we deliberate correctly about given situations and act according to what moral law requires of us. Moral excellence would consist in the purity of mind and strength of will to determine exactly what ought to be done, and to do it.

The cluster of assumptions given above applies not only to moral absolutism, but even to certain forms of relativism that are versions of the Moral Law folk theory.[4] For, if you simply qualify most of the ten assumptions listed above for absolutism, so that they are relativized to a particular cultural or historical context, then you get a prototypical case of one version of moral relativism. For example, if you relativize 1 above by adding that the moral laws are binding on all humans *within some domain* and that the moral laws specify right and wrong *under given conditions,* then you have a version of relativism.

What makes it possible to move from absolutism to this particular form of relativism is that they are *both* based on the assumptions of the Moral Law folk theory. They both see morality as applying ethical laws to specific situations.

Consequently, the argument I am going to give concerning the imaginative prototype structure of concepts applies both to moral absolutism and to any form of moral relativism that is still tied to the basic assumptions of the Moral Law folk theory. I will focus my argument on the absolutist orientation, because it is easier to see how the prototype structure of concepts and their relation to idealized cognitive models is at odds with Moral Law theory in its absolutist formulation.

Donagan's Moral Absolutism

Moral absolutism is a normative ethics that sees morality as a set of universal rules of conduct. The last two decades have witnessed a remarkable recovery of normative ethics, that is, of philosophical attempts to establish fundamental moral principles. The disease that knocked normative ethics off its feet for some forty years prior to this recovery was a particularly virulent strain of logical positivism. Its chief symptoms were, and still remain, the cognitive/emotive and theory/practice distinctions, an antimetaphysical bias, and an obsessive concern with the 'grammar' of various types of rigidly separated discourses.

Ethics was reduced to an impoverished form of metaethics that consisted in the analysis of the nature of moral discourse as such, without any place for a constructive system of morals. Logical empiricist views of language, meaning, and knowledge reduced moral discourse to the status of emotive expressions, on the grounds that talk about morals could not meet the cognitive standards of descriptive scientific statements. Moral theory, reduced to this extremely narrow version of metaethics, turned out to be so unenlightening, so divorced from serious moral concerns and experience, and, frankly, so boring that it nearly succeeded in killing off moral theory altogether.

The revival of normative ethics was due in large measure to John Rawls's *A Theory of Justice,* which did not argue against the dominant metaethical views. Instead, it simply produced a remarkable theoretical work of normative ethics that incorporated nonessentialist and nonfoundationalist views of meaning and knowledge.

Emboldened by Rawls's unabashed construction of a normative theory, a number of philosophers returned to more traditional normative projects centered on the articulation of fundamental moral rules. To repeat my earlier description, a 'rule' approach is precisely defined by Alan Donagan as "a theory of a system of laws or precepts, binding upon rational creatures as such, the content of which is ascertainable by human reason."[5] For my purposes, we can lump together Hare, Rawls, Nozick, Gert, Gewirth, Donagan, and Brandt as rule (or Moral Law) theorists, and we may ignore the significant differences that distinguish their views. Each differs widely in his conception of the nature, number, and specificity of the rules.[6] However, in spite of these real and not unimportant differences, they all share the rule-theoretical view that, at one level or another, morally permissible kinds of actions are somehow picked out and evaluated by one or more rules, principles, or laws. They also share the claim that reason alone is competent to decide how these rules are to be applied in specific cases.

At this point, it is crucial to note that philosophers tend to use the term 'rule' in a very special way that can be confusing to linguists and other people not formally trained in philosophy. It is useful to contrast the linguist's and the philosopher's prototypical notions of rules. To a linguist or a cognitive scientist, a 'rule' is

1. unconscious, and typically unaccessible to consciousness;
2. a description of a regularity in actual normal behavior; and
3. automatic and effortless.

To a philosopher, a typical 'rule' is

1. conscious, or at least accessible to consciousness;
2. 'regulative'; that is, it is an imperative specifying which action ought to be performed in a given situation; and
3. reasoned and effortful.

A prototypical example of a rule for a linguist might be a phonological rule. In our pronunciations of words there are all sorts of regularities that make it possible for us to communicate. There are 'rules' at work concerning how we pronounce a word. But they operate unconsciously, and if we tried to consciously entertain them, this would make it impossible for us to speak. In our ordinary speech we follow these rules automatically and effortlessly most of the time.

At least since Kant, philosophers have recognized the existence of rules of this sort, which are unconscious and automatic. According to this notion of rules that is used by linguists and most cognitive scientists, there are many rules operative in the way we act. But this is not the prototypical notion of a rule that is used in moral theory. When philosophers speak of following moral laws or precepts, they mean following rules that can be consciously entertained and that are regulative for our action. The criticisms I am making of Moral Law theories are criticisms of 'rules' understood in the way that is typical for moral philosophers.

Keeping in mind what moral theorists tend to mean by 'rule,' I am going to focus my analysis on Donagan's work, because it seems to me to be the most representative, well-argued, and sophisticated version of rule (Moral Law) theory. Following Kant, Donagan assumes that there is a core Western moral tradition, that it is in large measure correct in its pronouncements, and that a moral theory ought to give some form of rational reconstruction of the foundations of that tradition.

Since my central concern is with the nature of laws and rules as such, and not with any particular precept within some system of morals, I shall accept Donagan's contention that in the Judeo-Christian moral tradition the fundamental principle for the assessment of actions is respect for persons. Donagan states the principle as follows: "It is impermissible not to respect every human being, oneself or any other, as a rational creature."[7] This is supposed to be the supreme principle of the first-order system, the system of moral laws or precepts that govern moral action. Our problem, as Donagan sees it, is to determine *which* and *how* specific kinds of actions fall under this principle. In other words, how do we know which actions are consistent with the principle of respect for persons? If we could figure out what the concept of respecting a person involves, then we could articulate a system of more specific precepts that tell us how to act in various kinds of situations.

These specific precepts, according to Donagan, will always fit one of three possible schematic forms.[8]

1. It is always permissible to do an action of the kind K (permissions).
2. It is never permissible to do an action of the kind K (prohibitions).
3. It is never morally permissible not to do an action of the kind K, if an occasion occurs on which one can be done (strict obligations).

In short, any given action is one that either we (1) may do, if we so choose, (2) may never do, or (3) must do, when we can. A complete system of morality is eventually supposed to give an extensive list of precepts (fitting the above schemas) covering all of the basic kinds of actions we encounter in our moral experience.

The chief problem for Donagan's theory, or for any Moral Law theory, is how to determine which kinds of actions fit which of the three possible schemas. We need, therefore, a set of additional premises telling us, for each possible kind of action, whether and in what way it does or does not respect human beings as rational creatures. These 'specificatory premises' are supposed to specify the fundamental principle of respect for persons down to the level of the variety of actions we encounter in our lives. Paralleling the three schemas for moral precepts, there are three forms of specificatory premises.

   i. No action of the kind K, as such, fails to respect any human being as
      a rational creature.
  ii. All actions of the kind K fail to respect some human being as a ra-
      tional creature.
 iii. If an occasion occurs on which an action of the kind K can be done,
      not to do it will fail to respect some human being as a rational crea-
      ture.

This makes up the first-order system, which consists of the supreme principle,
the specificatory premises, and an allegedly exhaustive set of lower-level, or
derived, precepts governing the morality of actions. The system is not axiomatic,
but rather involves the bringing of various kinds of actions under the one central
concept of 'respecting a human being as rational.'

Now, the obvious difficulties arise, as they do for all Moral Law theories, when
we ask how it is possible to judge which kinds of actions fall under the central
concept. Such acts of judgment cannot be guided themselves by more rules or
algorithmic procedures, for this would lock us into an infinite regress of rules for
applying rules. Thus, if morality is a system of rules, then at some point we must
somehow be able to determine that we are properly applying those precepts to
specific *kinds* of situations. Donagan's account of this procedure of application is
as follows:

> The structure consisting of fundamental principle, derived precepts,
> and specificatory premises is strictly deductive; for every derived pre-
> cept is strictly deduced, by way of some specificatory premise, either
> from the fundamental principle or from some precept already derived.
> But that structure is not the whole of the system. *For virtually all the
> philosophical difficulties that are encountered in deriving that structure
> have to do with establishing the specificatory premises; and that is done
> by unformalized analytical reasoning* in which some concept either in
> the fundamental principle or in a derived precept is applied to some new
> species of case. (71–72; emphasis added)

What Rule Theories of Morality Miss

Here we have the crucial problem for any Moral Law theory, namely, the problem
of explaining what is involved in this 'unformalized' reasoning, without which
the moral laws could not be applied to specific kinds of actions in specific real-life
cases. Donagan's answer is quite clear: As members of a shared tradition, we
each have a partial grasp of the fundamental concept of 'respecting a human

being' as a rational creature. Moreover, most of us also recognize certain kinds of actions as clearly (noncontroversially) falling under this concept in a certain definite manner. For example, no one would seriously claim that wanton, unprovoked slaughter of innocent people is compatible with respect for them as rational creatures. So Donagan recognizes, correctly, a stable core to certain moral concepts, and he sees that debate is hardly ever likely to arise for such clear core cases.

But what about the difficult cases that fill our everyday lives—the cases that are problematic precisely to the extent that they do not fit automatically under some moral concept? What we must do, says Donagan, is to figure out whether our present problematic case is enough like some previous case that we have already decided or that is clear-cut, so that we can extend our evaluation in the former case to cover our present difficult case. We must weigh likenesses and differences between these cases, and such a reflective activity "cannot be usefully formalized" (69). Donagan sees this procedure as analogous to that of legal reasoning, in which a concept that is a candidate for application to new cases "has a content which in part is comprehended by members of the law-abiding community and in part remains to be determined by reflecting on cases to which it and related concepts have been applied" (69).

The situation Donagan describes here might be interpreted as revealing the way in which our moral concepts are actually transformed over time as they are stretched to encompass ever new and unforeseen kinds of cases. But a moral absolutist must utterly reject such an explanation, for fear that it would undermine the absolute foundations of the system of morals. The fear is that an ineliminable indeterminacy would be inserted into the system if its central concepts were not fixed. Such indeterminacy would mean that we could never know for sure whether we were *correctly* applying a concept, or whether we were merely twisting and molding it to serve our interests and desires.

Consequently, Donagan insists that the fundamental concept of morality (i.e., respect for persons) "is in large measure understood in itself" (71). According to Donagan's absolutism, although our *understanding* of the concept of respecting rational nature may vary over time, or from culture to culture, that concept *in itself* must not change. For if it did change, then each application of it would potentially be a new normative act that might depend on our values, interests, and ends. Again, we would simply be molding the concept to fit our subjective purposes.

So, Donagan needs to argue for a fixed core for each of our fundamental moral concepts. He needs to argue that our application of these concepts in non-prototypical, problematic cases does not involve changing these concepts in any way. This explains why Donagan goes to some lengths to argue against R. M. Hare's view that additional normative judgments may, in fact, occur as new cases arise.

The Hart-Fuller Debate: A Study in Prototype Structure

In what follows, I am going to argue that what we have learned about the prototype structure of concepts explains both what Donagan (and all Moral Law theories) gets right and what he gets wrong. Prototype theory explains why there *is* a stable core to most of our moral concepts, but it also explains why there will always be an unstable part of such concepts. Moreover, it explains how we are able to make intelligent judgments about nonprototypical cases that do not fall within the core. I will be arguing, therefore, that, while Donagan is right to identify the stable core for which we have clear rules, he misses the rich imaginative structure of the nonprototypical part of our concepts, which is precisely where most of our moral problems arise. It is primarily in the nonprototypical cases where the Moral Law theory is completely inadequate.

Hare's argument is based on H. L. A. Hart's much-debated case of a statute prohibiting the use of wheeled vehicles in a park.[9] Hart puts the key issue as follows:

> A legal rule forbids you to take a vehicle into the public park. Plainly this forbids an automobile, but what about bicycles, roller skates, toy automobiles? What about airplanes? Are these, as we say, to be called 'vehicles' for the purpose of the rule or not? If we are to communicate with each other at all, . . . then the general words we use . . . must have some standard instance in which no doubts are felt about its application. There must be a core of settled meaning, but there will be, as well, a penumbra of debatable cases in which words are neither obviously applicable nor obviously ruled out. These cases will each have some features in common with the standard case; they will lack others or be accompanied by features not present in the standard cases. . . .
> . . . If a penumbra of uncertainty must surround all legal rules, then their application to specific cases in the penumbral area cannot be a matter of logical deduction, and so deductive reasoning, which for generations has been cherished as the very perfection of human reasoning, cannot serve as a model for what judges, or indeed anyone, should do.[10]

Donagan and Hare disagree about what goes on in such a case where deductive reasoning no longer serves. Hare argues that, in deciding whether roller skates are covered under the concept *wheeled vehicle,* the judge is not dealing with a determinate, value-neutral concept that simply needs to be unpacked; rather, deciding what that concept is to mean involves additional acts of "normation or evaluation," and "this is a further determination of the law."[11]

In reply to Hare, Donagan objects strenuously that, although such cases are not deductively determined, they can always be decided by a form of reasoning that in no way involves an additional normative judgment: "Any British or American bench, called upon to determine whether the words of an Act forbidding the use of wheeled vehicles in a public park apply to roller skating, . . . , would normally be able to do so by the ordinary process of statutory interpretation. It is almost unthinkable that it would have to legislate under the guise of giving judgment" (71).

It is extremely important to be clear about what is at issue here, as it bears on our conception of what morality is. What Donagan is reacting so strongly to is Hare's view that applications of a legal (or moral) concept might actually transform that concept and that the very concept itself has a normative dimension. What Donagan cannot allow is the possibility that the fundamental moral concept (or any subsidiary concepts) might be relatively indeterminate and would thus be open to possible alternative interpretations relative to a context, set of purposes, or complex of interests. For this would mean that clarifying or determining a concept in a given context would require an evaluative decision. That, of course, would destroy the kind of objectivity that is the defining and motivating force of moral absolutism. If morality is to be regarded as a system of rules of the sort Donagan requires, then its concepts and rules must be absolutely fixed, and their applications must not involve new normative judgments.

Turning, then, from the legal to the moral context, Donagan immediately reiterates, in the strongest possible terms, his claim that the fundamental moral concept does indeed have this fixed and highly determinate nature, and that we do not have to make normative decisions in order to apply the concept.

> The fundamental concept of respecting every human being as a rational creature is fuzzy at the edges in the superficial sense that its application to this or that species of case can be disputed. But among those who share in the life of a culture in which the Hebrew-Christian moral tradition is accepted, the concept is in large measure understood in itself; and it is connected with numerous applications, as to the different weights of

which there is some measure of agreement. This is enough for it to be possible to determine many specificatory premises with virtual certainty and others with a high degree of confidence. (71)

Now, it may appear that Donagan has easily won the day in his attack on Hare, for he has surely described a situation that obtains, both with respect to the wheeled vehicle case and in legal reasoning generally, which is that there typically exists a relatively unproblematic core of cases falling under a law, about which there will be virtually no disagreement or contention. As Steven Winter has pointed out in his discussion of the Hart-Fuller debate, the case of roller skates and the case of a World War II military vehicle mounted on a pedestal in the park as a war memorial are easily and noncontroversially decided as not falling under the prohibition specified by the act. [12]

But the crucial questions, Winter argues, are not even being addressed in drawing this conclusion, and this gives the misleading appearance that Hart is wrong. Those key questions that must be addressed are (1) *Why* is there a stable core to most legal (and moral) concepts; that is, what do we know about cognition that explains the existence of such a core? (2) What are we to do regarding the penumbral or peripheral cases that arise beyond this core? Once these questions are asked, Hart's account begins to look much more insightful.

I will argue that the answer to the first question, concerning the proper explanation of the stable center of a moral concept, is quite different from what Donagan suggests. Contrary to Donagan's view, the concept does not simply exist with a determinate essence that can be "understood in itself." Rather, it has its meaning only in relation to a culture's shared, evolving experience and social interactions, and it is the existence of stable structures of such interactions that lends stability to the concept. In other words, the fact that there is a core to the concept is not typically a result of properties alleged to be inherent in the concept, but, instead, it is a result of continuity within the social background of a culture's shared experience by virtue of which the concept can mean what it does. I will give an example of the way in which a particular moral concept gets its meaning from its prototype structure relative to certain idealized cognitive models that are shared by members of our culture.

In answer to the second question about how we are able to treat the penumbral, problematic cases, I will suggest that prototype structure gives us ways of imaginatively extending our understanding to nonprototypical cases. Such imaginative reasoning is almost never a matter of unpacking the intrinsic meaning of a fixed concept.

I will thus be arguing that, although Donagan correctly recognizes the relatively stable core that exists for most moral concepts, the appropriate explanation of this phenomenon is not Donagan's rule-theoretical view of concepts and precepts. Instead, the stable part of a concept depends on its prototype structure and on the stability of the idealized cognitive models shared within a culture, which give meaning to its concepts and moral ideals. Consequently, Donagan's claim that our fundamental moral concept is in part "understood in itself"—and so has a fixed, determinate structure—is ultimately misleading, for it ignores the nonprototypical cases that require imaginative moral understanding and reasoning.

The Case of 'Lie': Prototype Structure and Conceptual Indeterminacy

To examine the nature of moral concepts, I want to take as an example the concept *lie,* which has been the subject of some excellent research in the last few years. According to a classical or objectivist[13] theory of category structure (as spelled out in the account of absolutism above), there must be a set of necessary and sufficient conditions the possession of which alone makes a speech act a lie. As a Moral Law theorist and an absolutist, Donagan defines the essential features of a *lie* as "any free linguistic utterance expressing something contrary to the speaker's mind" (88).

However, there is considerable evidence that the structure of the concept *lie* is far more complex than this. Linda Coleman and Paul Kay found that the category *lie* exhibits prototype effects; that is, there are certain central instances of speech acts that speakers easily and noncontroversially recognize as lies.[14] These form a core of the concept, which is then surrounded by a large number of other far less clear-cut cases about which speakers are unsure, in varying degrees, to what extent they are lies, and how we ought to assess them morally (e.g., such cases as white lies, social lies, mistakes, jokes, exaggerations, and oversimplifications). Coleman and Kay also found that prototypical lies (e.g., the ones at the center of the category, such as assuring your spouse that you haven't been gambling, when you just lost a wad betting on a Lakers/Pistons game) fulfilled all three of the following conditions:

1. the speaker believes the statement is false,
2. the speaker intends to deceive the hearer, and
3. the statement is factually false.

If none of these conditions is satisfied, then the speech act is not a lie. The less central, less prototypical instances of lying tend to be those that fulfill only one or two of the conditions. Moreover, subjects typically ranked the conditions in order of importance, with 1 being most important and 3 the least. In short, the informants in the study "fairly easily and reliably assign the word *lie* to reported speech acts in a more-or-less, rather than all-or-none, fashion; and . . . subjects agree fairly generally on the relative weights of the elements."[15]

The concept *lie,* then, does not exhibit classical (objectivist) category structure. It is not defined by a set of fixed essential features but is rather a radially structured concept, with prototypical instances making up the center of the concept and nonprototypical instances radiating out at various (conceptual) distances from the central members.[16] There is considerable internal structure to the concept, which is crucial in determining where and how we apply it.

Now we are confronted with the decisive question for the classical (objectivist) view of categorization that is presupposed by moral absolutism: How are we to explain this complex radial category structure for *lie?* The objectivist view that concepts are defined by sets of necessary and sufficient conditions simply cannot explain prototype effects. It has no way of accounting for any internal structure of a concept. Since each member of the category must possess all of the essential features, and those features are the only structure the category has, the classical objectivist theory recognizes no internal structure to a category that could distinguish one member from any other. With respect to our understanding of the category, all the members must be equal. Thus, for an objectivist, a speech act either does or does not satisfy the conditions specified by the concept *lie,* and there is nothing like an internal structure or architecture for the concept that could differentiate various kinds of lies.

However, Eve Sweetser has shown in detail that the concept *lie* does not work this way.[17] Instead, the concept exhibits prototype structure, and it functions and gets its meaning only in conjunction with certain background models of knowledge and communication that are presupposed by us in most of our mundane communicative interactions. The extent to which these background models are universal depends, *not* on any alleged a priori structure of the mind, but rather on what is shared across cultures concerning human communicative interaction.

Sweetser demonstrates this in the course of explaining an apparent anomaly discovered by Coleman and Kay. The anomaly is that, even though factual falsity is clearly the least important condition in identifying prototypical lies, it turns out that, if informants are asked informally, they typically give falsity as the primary identifying feature of lies.

The explanation of this unexpected fact is based on the existence of what Lakoff has called "idealized cognitive models."[18] An idealized cognitive model is a simplified cognitive gestalt that organizes selected aspects of our knowledge, understanding, or experience of a given domain. Such models are *idealized,* as Robert McCauley explains, in that they *"select* from among all the possible features of the stimuli those that are systematically efficacious (in more purely theoretical domains) or socially or instrumentally significant (in practical domains)."[19] As such, these models may not fit exactly any particular situation, but they capture features and structures that have proved to be important to us in our interactions with our physical and social environments. The models are *cognitive* in the sense that they are imaginative structures by which we organize and make sense of our experience, rather than being objectively existing features of external things. And they are *models* in that they provide structures or standards against which we measure and evaluate our particular experiences and judgments.

Sweetser identifies two basic idealized cognitive models,[20] one for knowledge and the other for communication, that lie behind our understanding of lying.

The Idealized Cognitive Model of ORDINARY KNOWLEDGE
1. People have adequate reasons for their beliefs.
2. Beliefs for which people have adequate reasons are true.
3. So, people's beliefs are true and constitute knowledge.
3'. Something that is false is not believed.

The Idealized Cognitive Model of ORDINARY COMMUNICATION
4. People intend to help one another (= try to help, not harm).[21]
5. Truthful information is helpful.
6. The speaker intends to help the hearer by sharing information.
6'. A speaker who knowingly communicates false information intends to harm the hearer.

These two models jointly make up a widely shared background understanding that determines much of what goes on in ordinary daily conversation. They are both obvious idealizations, since, for example, we hold all sorts of beliefs that aren't true, and we often speak without intending to help the hearer. Yet these models give us a stable set of expectations that make it possible for ordinary conversation to proceed. If we had to check up on every statement and test out the intentions of every speaker for every utterance, our suspicion would turn even the simplest daily discourse into a task of monumental proportions.

Given these two roughly sketched models of ORDINARY KNOWLEDGE and ORDINARY COMMUNICATION, it now becomes possible to explain three important characteristics of the concept *lie:* (1) the Coleman-Kay anomaly, (2) the complex prototype structure of the category, and (3) the interaction of background models and conceptual structure that makes up our understanding of lying. Sweetser treats the first two of these characteristics explicitly, and I will develop the argument for the third, which is crucial both to my critique of moral absolutism and to my elaboration of an alternative account of moral understanding.

First, the anomaly: Why should people informally tend to regard the factual falsity of a statement as the primary identifying feature of a lie, when factual falsity is ranked by them as the least important of the three conditions for prototypical lies? The answer depends on seeing how the concept *lie* is understood only in relation to the social and epistemic conditions embodied in the two idealized cognitive models. In the idealized situation set up by these models, according to 3' above, that which is false is not believed. So, factual falsity entails lack of belief (which is the second most important condition for prototypical lies). According to 6' above, giving false information harms and deceives the hearer. So, falsity entails intent to deceive (which is the most important of the three conditions for prototypical lies). What we discover, then, is that *within the idealized world established by the models* that govern most of our communicative interaction, the third and least important condition (i.e., factual falsity) actually entails the other two more important conditions (i.e., falsity of belief and intent to deceive). In this way the commonplace definition of a lie as a false statement can serve as a shorthand for the prototypical cases of lying (provided, of course, that the two relevant idealized cognitive models are in place as background conditions).

The second important result of Sweetser's analysis, which is unavailable to any objectivist view of concepts, is an explanation of the prototype structure of the concept *lie*. The details of this structure have been worked out by Sweetser, Lakoff, and Winter, so I will give only a couple of illustrations. Notice that candidates for nonprototypical lies (such as *white lies, tall tales,* and *social lies*) and for nonlies (such as *oversimplifications, jokes,* and *mistakes*) are all cases that fail to fit, in varying ways and to varying degrees, the conditions set forth in the idealized cognitive models of knowledge and communication. Take, for instance, *white lies* and *social lies.* These are cases that fall short or differ from the conditions specified in the idealized cognitive model of ORDINARY COMMUNICATION. Both are lies, but they constitute deceptions in situations where truthful information is not necessarily very important (*white lies*) or socially helpful (*social lies*). *White lies* are cases where the statement is not egregiously false and where it does little or no harm; hence, we speak of a "little white lie." In the case of a *social lie,* not telling the truth might even serve the purposes of social interaction and community.

Jokes and *kidding,* on the other hand, are not lies at all, for they occur outside the situations in which information is being exchanged, and so there exists no prior expectation that truthful information is at issue. *Oversimplifications* and *exaggerations* are more difficult borderline cases. They may not actually run contrary to the truth, yet in some cases they give false or misleading information. Still, they can often be quite useful, insofar as they present us with selected, highlighted features of a situation. So, whether we regard these as lies, and how we understand and judge their reprehensibility, will depend on the context in which they occur and the assumptions in place at the moment (such as the idealized cognitive models of ORDINARY COMMUNICATION and ORDINARY KNOWLEDGE, and our purposes in saying what we say, and how we say it).

Finally, there is a third, and for our purposes most important, consequence of the radial structure of the concept *lie* and its dependence on idealized cognitive models for its meaning. This is that the concept itself is evaluative, so that its application is always a normative act. For the moral absolutist the concept *lie* cannot itself be evaluative or value-laden. It is regarded, instead, as purely descriptive—it states the conditions that are necessary and sufficient for making something a lie. Defining *lie* and identifying cases as lies does not, on this view, require normative acts. This, I take it, is Donagan's point against Hare when he insists that no additional acts of "normation or evaluation" are required to decide what counts as a *wheeled vehicle* under the act forbidding such vehicles in the park.

In order to see more clearly what the absolutist view misses, we need only remind ourselves why lying is usually considered to be a bad thing to do. The answer is that lying is typically *harmful* to others. But notice now that the relevant notion of harm is partially specified by the idealized cognitive model of

ORDINARY COMMUNICATION. A notion of helping and harming is *built into* that model. Therefore, to the extent that our determination of what counts as a lie in a particular situation depends on the idealized cognitive model of ORDINARY COMMUNICATION, our understanding of *lie* is inextricably tied up with an evaluative notion of help and harm.

Contrary to the absolutist view, the concept *lie* is not value-neutral, it is not purely descriptive, and it is not self-contained. Its very application is a normative act. *The meaning of the concept* is inextricably tied up with at least two idealized cognitive models (of ORDINARY KNOWLEDGE and ORDINARY COMMUNICATION) that are themselves heavily value-laden. It is only by referring to these cognitive models that we can determine the moral status of various nonprototypical candidates for the concept *lie*.

As an example, consider what is known as the 'official lie'—an intentionally deceptive false statement made by a government spokesperson on behalf of the government. Do we hold the person himself responsible for lying? The answer is not clear. This is surely not a prototypical lie, for the individual is not speaking on his own behalf, but rather he is merely filling the role of spokesperson. We *expect* whoever fills the role of spokesperson to issue, from time to time, official lies. We understand this nonprototypical instance of lying only relative to a background scenario we have concerning how governments disseminate certain sorts of information and what they are expected to do in cases where important national secrets are at issue.

As a second illustration, consider a case where the Central Intelligence Agency lies to protect its agents. What about cases where the CIA refuses to acknowledge the existence of operatives or even to admit the existence of an operation that is, or has been, undertaken? Is lying to the American people about such matters wrong? Many people will say that the CIA is obviously justified in lying to insure the safety of agents or the integrity of important operations. But some of these lies that are made allegedly to avoid putting a few agents at risk at the same time affect the lives of millions of people by the way they influence international relations.

So, here we have a case where the absolutist (one who was not a fanatic opposed to any form of lying) must claim a higher moral principle or value that overrides the prohibition against lying. But this means that the nature of the reprehensibility of lying *is relative to our framing of the situation!* In other words, the concept *lie* does not possess its meaning and moral force in itself, but gets that meaning, as we have seen, from background idealized cognitive models and folk theories we have about a government's responsibilities to its people, the way international relations work, prerogatives of political authorities, and so forth.

As I have already noted, no moral absolutist need ever be daunted by this situation, for they can always claim undoubting insight into the requirements of a universal moral rationality. They could, for instance, claim that 'official lies' and 'social lies' are, indeed, lies, and then formulate other principles to specify when certain kinds of lies are permissible. But the evidence for the prototype structure of *lie* and the crucial role of idealized cognitive models seems to me overwhelming against the classical objectivist view of concepts accepted by absolutists. What the evidence shows, I suggest, is that our ordinary moral concepts are not defined 'in themselves' and that they get their meaning relative to idealized cognitive models that define communal practices.

Let us return to the heart of Donagan's absolutist argument about the concept of respect for persons. If the concept *lie* is a radial category with a prototype structure that presupposes idealized cognitive models, then how much more complex will our concept of a *person* be? In our Western moral tradition the concept *person* is the basis for our most fundamental moral principles. And what could be more complexly structured and perennially contestable than such a pivotal notion? I will take up the concept *person* later. For now, I can only suggest that the concept *person* is a radial category consisting of certain prototypical instances (e.g., sane adult white heterosexual *males*) surrounded by nonprototypical instances (e.g., females,[22] nonwhites, children, senile elderly, mentally handicapped) and fading off into borderline cases (e.g., higher primates). According to Donagan, moral reasoning consists basically in discerning which beings have the status of rational personhood and then determining what is required in order to respect them properly. To hold, with Donagan, that this concept might be "understood in itself"[23] is simply unbelievable. Such a view overlooks the complex internal structure of the concept *person* and ignores its built-in indeterminacy. It also misses the way in which our conceptions of personality, rationality, and morality are all inextricably tied up with conceptions of human flourishing (i.e., with fundamental values about the nature of meaningful and significant human activity). Far from there being a univocal concept of personhood that exists in itself waiting to be unpacked by human reason, the very concept is irreducibly complex and contestable.

For instance, what is going to define the concept *person?* Is it our material, physical being? Our biological self? Our social and interpersonal selves defined by roles? Our psychoanalytic self? Our developmental self (as in stages of life)?

Our autobiographical self? Our legal self? Our theological self? Our political self? Every one of these complex conceptions of selfhood and personality presuppose a massive background of values, folk theories, cognitive models, and so forth that give it meaning and reality. To think that *anybody* could grasp what this concept means as it is "understood in itself" is to strain credibility beyond the breaking point.

What is the animal rights debate but a fascinating set of arguments about whether it is legitimate to extend the concept *person* metaphorically to include animals whose brains are not constructed exactly like beings who we tend to regard as prototypical persons? The debate is precisely one about prototype structure and extensions to nonprototypical cases, typically by means of metaphorical principles.

Similarly, some environmentalists and ecologists are urging us to abandon our anthropocentric prejudice by extending metaphorically our concept of personhood to the level of the ecosystem of our planet. That debates such as these are even intelligible is due to the prototype structure of our category *person* and to our imaginative ability to project beyond prototypical cases to marginal ones, including even those that previously fell outside the concept. It is debates like these, over the radial structure of our most basic moral concepts, that make up the vast majority of significant moral argument.

Kinds of Conceptual Stability and Indeterminacy

Still, Donagan is correct when he claims that there will be a core of cases about which there exists virtually universal agreement within a moral tradition. These, we now see, are the prototypical or central members of a particular moral concept. This stable core of cases is the result of the stability of the context of shared values, idealized cognitive models, practices, and purposes within a culture. *It is the theory of prototype structure and idealized cognitive models that explains conceptual stability,* in a way that is unavailable to the classical theory of categories. Contrary to Donagan's absolutist view, such stability is *not* the result of a fixed, objective category structure.

In the case of the statute concerning wheeled vehicles in the park, for example, we can often decide quite easily what kinds of objects fall under the act. But we can only do this because of our shared background knowledge about such things as the purposes to which we typically put wheeled vehicles, the purposes parks serve for us, what it means to have our activities disrupted, and what current standards of public behavior are. In light of this experience and knowledge, some of which changes in a culture over time,[24] there will generally be a range of 'clear' cases where it is quite easy for us to decide what ought to count as a wheeled vehicle under the act.

For the concept of a person, however, things are infinitely more complex and messy. Here, we even have debate about our prototypical members of the category, as, for example, our current controversy concerning the 'phallocentric' and racist biases that pervade Western culture. It is now thoroughly documented (as if it weren't obvious) that women have not been granted the same prototypical status as men with respect to moral personhood throughout history.

When even our very prototypes are in dispute, we have a concept that is contestable at every point. Such is the character of our present moral confusion. Contrary to moral absolutist claims, however, it is not a confusion that could be eliminated by some good old-fashioned clear-headed reasoning about the essence of personhood. The indeterminacy (as well as the correlative determinacy) is inherent in the prototype structure of our concept *person,* and it is relative to culturally contingent, historically changing values, cognitive models, and folk theories.

To summarize the nature of conceptual stability and determinacy: Most of our moral concepts will have a relatively stable core centered around cognitive prototypes. The stability is due both to prototype structure and to the stability in our background idealized cognitive models and folk theories, and the purposes they serve in our lives. All of these together make it possible for there to be clear and unproblematic cases. However, we have seen that some of our most important moral concepts are contestable even regarding what constitutes a prototype. In the case of the concept *person,* for instance, we may be witnessing a modest transformation of its structure.

The theory of cognitive prototypes also gives us the resources to explain the nature of the problematic (peripheral or penumbral) cases that arise in our understanding of any concept. We will be able to say why those cases are indeterminate in the way, and to the degree, that they are. Their indeterminacy will rest primarily on the way(s) in which they fail to fit the idealized cognitive models and the conditions of prototypicality that make up the background by means of which the concept gets its meaning. In the case of *lie,* for example, we can see both why and how *social lies* diverge from the idealized speech situation set up by our model of ORDINARY COMMUNICATION (e.g., they do not harm, and they actually contribute to social harmony and interaction). Moreover, understanding this divergence will help us to decide whether and to what extent social lies are acceptable within certain limits and under certain circumstances.

The same situation applies to the concept *person* as to *lie*. However, the concept *person* is so vastly more complex in its internal structure, and thus in its relation to background models and values, that it becomes enormously difficult to describe the imaginative structures for extending beyond prototypical members to nonprototypical ones. These are the questions that plague us in our struggles over abortion, euthanasia, civil rights, animal rights, and our environmental responsibilities.

The fact of relative conceptual indeterminacy obviously has far-reaching implications for any account of moral reasoning, the chief of which is that, contrary to the absolutist view, moral reasoning cannot consist merely in the rational unpacking of a determinate concept. Instead, it requires imaginative extensions to nonprototypical cases.

Let us take stock of the argument so far. Understanding the prototype structure of our moral concepts makes it possible to explain both the relatively stable core of these concepts and why they have a certain relative *indeterminacy*. The indeterminacy is the result of the radial structure of our basic concepts and the fact that most of our moral difficulties arise for the nonprototypical cases. It is extremely important to get clear about the extent and depth of this indeterminacy, and to see why it is not a radical indeterminacy of the sort claimed by Rorty and various deconstructivists.[25]

In a discussion of the imaginative character of legal reasoning, Steven Winter has identified three major kinds of indeterminacy that are unavoidable whenever we apply laws to real-life situations.[26]

1. *Indeterminacy of extension.* As a result of the prototype (or 'radial') structure of some of our most important concepts, there will be a built-in indeterminacy when we try to decide how to treat nonprototypical cases within the category. It is this type of indeterminacy that I have been discussing above, where movement beyond the central, prototypical members of the category involves various degrees of divergence from the idealized cognitive models in relation to which the concept develops its structure and meaning. For example, trying to determine our moral responsibilities toward unborn fetuses is notoriously difficult because there are different ways one might possibly argue concerning whether *person* should be extended to apply to them.

In emphasizing the difficulties presented by this kind of conceptual indeterminacy, we must not overlook the equally important counterpart, which is the highly stable and determinate character of the prototypical cases. That there is such stability is sufficient to undercut any claim that all our moral concepts are radically indeterminate. Extreme relativism, or any radical indeterminacy thesis, is simply contradicted by what we are learning about prototype structure.

It is this settled core that Donagan has recognized as central to legal and moral reasoning alike, but he has overemphasized it to the extent of mistakenly underestimating the indeterminacy that arises when we consider nonprototypical cases. So, we can accept Donagan's identification of conceptual stability *as far as it goes,* but only on two conditions: (1) We must recognize that the proper explanation of this relative stability is based on prototype structure and shared assumptions concerning our idealized cognitive models and other background frames. (2) We must pay appropriate attention to the counterpart *in*determinacy that arises the farther we extend beyond the prototypical cases. This relative indeterminacy is equally present, though it is sometimes peripheral and unimportant in a particular context.

It is extremely important to notice that "lack of determinacy of extension does not connote arbitrariness of extension. Rather, there are motivating structures that constrain-but-do-not-determine both the extension of [idealized cognitive models] and their initial formulation" (1196). Once we move into what Hart calls the 'penumbra' surrounding the stable and determinate core of a concept, we are not cast adrift on an ever-changing, featureless, boundless sea. We are able to make judgments about difficult cases with at least some guidance, because we can understand in what respects our difficult case fails to fit the idealized cognitive models lying behind the concept. Or else we can examine the relation between central, nonproblematic cases and the one we are now considering. The indeterminacy here is relative—there is a range of possible interpretations for a given case, but not any interpretation will do. For example, in the case of a nonprototypical lie (such as a *white lie*), there may not be one correct moral evaluation, yet it is not open to us to ignore altogether the idealized cognitive models of ORDINARY KNOWLEDGE and ORDINARY COMMUNICATION in our assessment of the case.

2. *Indeterminacy of paradigm.* The result of the disparity between the moral absolutist model of concepts and reasoning and the way human cognition actually works is indeterminacy of paradigm. What absolutism (as a form of objectivism) requires of us cannot be satisfied, given the nature of our cognitive processes. Winter explains that, in legal matters, we are confronted with objecti-

vist expectations and demands for propositional laws and rules. But human reasoning is not just propositional and syllogistic. We have seen that our moral reasoning often depends on deep metaphoric and imaginative structures that are nonpropositional. Classical deductive logic has no place for metaphorical concepts. As Winter explains: "The rules proposed by the objectivist present themselves as propositional and syllogistic; but human rationality is neither. Propositional legal rules promise determinate answers; the imaginative and metaphoric structure of thought yields a different pattern of decision-making. This lack of fit between the professed and the experienced is perceived as indeterminacy" (1196).

Winter has described a very real dilemma many people face when they reflect on the difficulty of making wise moral judgments. Our moral tradition, based on its acceptance of the Moral Law folk theory, is fundamentally absolutist in character. Consequently, we experience ourselves as bound by a view of morality that presupposes an unrealistic classical (objectivist) view of concepts and reasoning. We are sometimes painfully aware that we do not actually think in accordance with the demands of an objectivist logic. As a result, we sometimes feel that *we* are somehow deficient, because *our* reasoning, *our* understanding, and *our* clarity do not even begin to meet up to the standards presupposed by that objectivist view. We experience this inner tension precisely because many of our concepts do not have classical category structure. *Our* concepts aren't working in the way our Moral Law folk theory assumes that they do. So, what we 'feel in our guts' is the clash between our absolutist (hence, objectivist) Moral Law folk theory and how our reasoning *actually* operates, that is, in nonobjectivist ways.

This does not, of course, relieve us of our responsibility to try to live up to our highest moral ideals. On the contrary, it is crucial to morality that we should feel drawn by our moral ideals to improvement, transcendence, and transformation —to be better persons. Only, those ideals should be psychologically real and consistent with the way our minds actually work. We needn't feel that we are failures because we can't achieve the impossible clarity, decisiveness, and logical rigor promised by moral absolutism. For moral absolutism holds up false ideals that have little to do with the realities of human cognition.[27]

3. *Substantive indeterminacy.* The historical and social contingency of our idealized cognitive models that provide the context for moral reasoning produce substantive indeterminacy. The models that underlie our moral concepts and reasoning have a sociocultural dimension that is subject to change. I have suggested, for example, that our concept of *moral personhood* is currently undergoing such

substantive change. It is perhaps possible that even what we take to be prototypical members of that category is changing.

Unless one views society as fixed in its basic structure and institutions, unless one ignores historical transformation, and unless one rejects genuine novelty, it is not possible to deny substantive indeterminacy. Morality is inextricably tied up with this transformative process. The whole point and direction of moral deliberation is intelligent, sensitive, and constructive directing of this unavoidable process of change.

To sum up: The types of indeterminacy Winter has described as coming into play whenever we apply laws to actual historical cases exist also for our moral reasoning. While these three kinds of indeterminacy certainly undermine the false absolutist ideals of objectivist concepts, values, and laws, they do not underwrite anarchy. Giving up on the possibility of One True Theory (or set of concepts, or system of rules) defining morality is not an abdication of reason. Rather, it is a recognition of the multivalent, multidimensional character of human reason.

Human experience is a complex blending of biological, cultural, economic, political, religious, aesthetic, and legal dimensions that both *influence* and *are influenced by* our values, purposes, institutions, and practices. For example, my biological nature as an organism seeking to survive in my environment (a biological value) *influences* which forms of social and political interaction I will prefer. Not all of them will equally serve my purposes. But, at the same time, the social, political, and economic practices and institutions into which I am born will *influence* the way I understand and pursue my biological goal of survival and flourishing. A society in which altruistic forms of action are prized will lead me to pursue survival in ways quite different than I might in a culture whose forms of social interaction are far more Hobbesian or Machiavellian in nature. Thus, a purpose and value that, from one perspective, seems to be a biological given is, when realized within a particular cultural tradition, actually more malleable and open-ended than it at first appears.

But it most definitely does not follow from this relative indeterminacy that reason can be replaced by arbitrary willful acts. It is stupid to think that any kind of reasoning, or any arbitrary set of principles, or any random form of action is appropriate to our moral ideals and purposes. The fact that our moral concepts and reasoning are often metaphorical and imaginative through and through does not reduce moral deliberation to an arbitrary, random play of thought. What it does is to highlight the fallibility of reason and the unlikelihood of our ever being certain, before the act, that what we are doing, and the reasons we are doing it,[28] will turn out to be for the best.

Beyond Rules to Principles and Ideals

I have been mounting a sustained critique of what I have been calling absolutist and objectivist 'rule theories' of morality, that is, of views that limit morality to a system of universal moral laws discoverable by human reason. My claims so far are that such views represent an impoverished view of human reason and presuppose an objectivist view of concepts that is incompatible with what we are learning about conceptual structure. Moral Law theories tell part of the story, but they leave out some of the most important dimensions of our moral reasoning. Later, I will also consider the inadequate picture of the self and its actions that is presupposed by absolutism (as a form of objectivism). Morality conceived as a system of laws is simply too narrow and too unimaginative to capture most of what goes on in our moral experience. It ends up ignoring just those imaginative dimensions of our reasoning and deliberation that are the key to our moral understanding.

The mistake is to peel off a specific law from its embodiment in the historically developing moral experience of a people. Whatever moral laws there are have their meaning and usefulness only within the horizon of an evolving moral tradition. The mistake is thus to divorce the law from its experiential origins within a particular historical, political, social, economic, and psychological context.

My contention is that there cannot be any set of definitive laws or rules capable of doing what Moral Law theories claim for them. Since our concepts and reason don't work this way, Moral Law theories can only give us illusory ideals that could never be met and that are inconsistent with the nature of human reason. To the extent that there are any determinate, useful rules, they will apply non-controversially only to cases lying at the stable core of the relevant concepts. But in the penumbral or peripheral cases that occupy us in so much of our moral deliberation, the 'rules' are not enough. They can only serve as summaries of the developing insight of our moral tradition, and they cannot stand alone, independent of the shared experience that makes up that tradition.

Moral Law theories, in short, get something right and something wrong. What they get right is that the reflective dimension of moral deliberation requires intellectual principles and ideals that we sometimes attempt to encapsulate in the form of laws or determinate rules. There must be principles that make it possible for us to rise above mere habit and to reflect critically on our own assumptions, commitments, and values. Without such a reflective dimension, there would be no possibility of self-transcendence, no creative transformation of a situation toward some end, and no morality.

Moral Law theories go wrong when they assume that all morality can be reduced to the following of rules (whether consciously or by habit). It is critical to distinguish *rules* (as understood in Moral Law theories)—which are supposed to tell you how to act—from general *principles*—which are summaries of our collective moral insight. The crucial distinction I have in mind was made by Dewey, who understood rules as ready-made, fixed precepts that become divorced from their origins in concrete situations and are then 'applied' to new situations according to an objectivist model of cases being 'brought under' laws.

Principles, on the other hand, are crystallizations of the insights that emerge out of a people's ongoing experience. As such, they provide ideals that establish standpoints from which to view and evaluate our experience and our proposed actions. For Dewey rules have a much more immediately practical function as technical guides, while principles hold up imaginative ideals for reflecting on our lives, goals, values, and actions. Dewey summarizes: "*Rules are practical; they are habitual ways of doing things. But principles are intellectual; they are the final methods used in judging suggested courses of action.* The fundamental error of the intuitionalist is that he is on the outlook for rules which will of themselves tell agents just what course of action to pursue; *whereas the object of moral principles is to supply standpoints and methods which will enable the individual to make for himself an analysis of the elements of good and evil in the particular situation in which he finds himself.*"[29]

The point here is not to raise up a rigid distinction between rules and principles. Dewey's point is rather that, no matter what we call them, there are intellectual principles that have an important bearing on our moral deliberations. However, they must be seen, not as recipes for action, but as reminders of what one's tradition has found, through its ongoing experience and reflection, to be important considerations in reflecting on past actions, courses of action open to us, and the choices of people we regard as possessing practical wisdom.[30] Dewey continues, "A moral principle, such as that of chastity, of justice, of the Golden Rule, gives the agent a basis for looking at and examining a particular question that comes up. It holds before him certain possible aspects of the act; it warns him against taking a short or partial view of the act. It economizes his thinking by supplying him with the main heads by reference to which to consider the bearings of his desires and purposes; it guides him in his thinking by suggesting to him the important considerations for which he should be on the lookout."[31]

This account of principles gives us a very different view of the kind of reflection that lies at the heart of morality. It is not, as Moral Law theories suppose, a matter of bringing new cases under already established, fixed, and highly determinate rules (laws). It is a far more imaginative and exploratory enterprise, in which we try to imagine the large-scale implications of taking certain values, principles, and commitments as primary. Hard-core Moral Law theories are motivated by a desire to avoid the ineliminable indeterminacy and uncertainty inherent in such imaginative exploration. But the fact is that this cannot be done, at least not if one wants to remain open and sensitive to the complexities and evolution of human experience.

Moral principles are thus abstract intellectual tools that we employ as we try to work out our problematic lives. In this Deweyan sense, the 'Golden Rule' is not a rule, but rather a general principle that can be part of our basis for reflecting on which actions are preferable among those available to us. Moral principles of this sort were formed as appropriate to certain kinds of situations, to certain kinds of problems, for which they are well fitted. But because our experience develops and changes, new problematic situations will arise that were not even contemplated when those tools were first formed. A principle like the Golden Rule is not meant to tell us what exactly to do in this or that situation.

And so new problems and situations will require of us either the alteration of our tools, or perhaps even the development of new ones that are only loosely related to the old tools.[32] For example, the emergence of new technologies, such as recent reproductive technologies, has created new moral problems and situations that neither existed nor were even imagined when certain 'standards' of sexual, familial, and biomedical practice were gradually formulated in our moral tradition. To assume, without critical examination, that our traditional concepts and standards must 'fit' these new cases in some way is merely to deny the possibility of change in the character of our experience. But events such as the development of in vitro fertilization and genetic engineering have confronted us with possibilities that might actually require us to revise our concepts of personhood and our assumptions about what is 'natural' in the reproductive process.

This tool analogy has its own particular disadvantages, but it correctly emphasizes the adaptive nature of our moral reasoning in light of the constant evolution of human experience. It is precisely where our habits, and the rules that encode them, are ill-adapted to our hitherto unforeseen problems, newly emerging purposes, and evolving technologies that we need intelligent moral reflection. Such reflection must be an imaginative exploration of possible courses of action in search of ways to enhance the quality of our group existence, thereby making it possible for us to function in the face of problematic and indeterminate situations. My allusions to the imaginative character of such moral reflection and deliberation have become increasingly more prominent as my criticism of moral absolutism has developed. What is needed is a constructive account of the nature of this imaginative activity that I am claiming as the basis for an alternative to moral absolutism (and, as we will see, to moral relativism, too).

The Impoverishment of Reason:
Our Enlightenment Legacy

According to moral absolutism, reason is defined by an abstract structure that stands above and transcends any particular instance of reasoning in actual historical contexts. Rationality is viewed as Universal Reason—a fixed, transtemporal structure that in no way depends on the nature of our bodily experience nor on the social contexts, historical events, or cultural practices in which it is manifested. The absolutist moral ideal presupposes a Universal Reason which, when it functions 'correctly,' issues in universal standards for assessing the morality of our thoughts, plans, goals, and actions.

Nowhere in this account of moral reasoning is there *any* place for moral imagination. Absolutism conceives reason metaphorically as essentially a *constraining force* that is realized in sets of *restrictive laws*. But we have seen, on the contrary, that our moral understanding and reasoning are fundamentally imaginative, involving conceptual metaphor, image schemas, and prototype structure for concepts. Such imaginative moral deliberation is an open-ended constructive process by which we explore values and possibilities for action that are latent within our present situation. Describing this process as the application of moral laws to situations simply cannot capture most of what is really going on here. It is our moral imagination that permits us to rehearse dramatically various projected courses of action, so that we may investigate the morality of the options available to us within particular circumstances. Moral self-knowledge thus requires us to understand how our moral concepts, our framing of situations, and our reasoning about what to do are *all* based on various forms of imagination.

Consequently, while the dominant absolutist Moral Law tradition in the Western world recognizes the existence of imaginative acts, its basic assumptions require the almost total exclusion of imagination from the structure of practical reason. I have argued that this view is motivated by the mistaken fear that the inclusion of imaginative structures as essential to moral reasoning would be disastrous, insofar as it would introduce an ineliminable openness and indeterminacy into our moral deliberations.

Absolutists, therefore, find it necessary to banish imagination disparagingly to the domain of moral psychology. They construe *moral psychology* as an empirical discipline that studies such things as the nature of various cognitive processes involved in our moral deliberations. *Moral philosophy,* as they define it, is a rational inquiry concerned solely with how we *ought* to reason and act, rather than with how we *do,* in fact, reason and act. Moral philosophy is thus supposed to give us the standards by which we can judge our actual reasons, motives, and actions. Moral Law theories therefore tend to assume that moral psychology is relatively unimportant, or even irrelevant, to moral theory.[1]

Notice, however, the obvious point that any moral theory will necessarily assume that its view of concepts is correct, that its view of reason is correct, and that human beings can actually do what morality requires. This means that moral theory must at least be compatible with moral psychology, that is, with our empirical understanding of conceptualization, reasoning, motivation, personal identity, and so forth. Nevertheless, our Moral Law folk theory and many of the moral philosophies that presuppose it are not, as we have begun to see, consistent with what the cognitive sciences are telling us about the human mind. One major consequence of this is that Moral Law theories almost totally disenfranchise moral imagination.[2]

In this chapter I want to ask how it is that our tradition has come to regard moral reasoning in a way that tends to exclude precisely that imaginative capacity which a reflection on our moral experience would reveal to be indispensable. How did we come to have such an impoverished view of human reason and moral understanding? Human beings develop in an evolving environment where their physical setting, sociopolitical institutions, and communal relations are typically in a process of very gradual change, though one that is infrequently punctuated with moments of more radical and rapid transformation. To adapt to such a changing complex of physical, interpersonal, and cultural interactions requires imagination, the ability to transform and adjust our categories, social relations, and institutional commitments. We really must be innovators, if we hope to meet in an intelligent way the demands of these various sorts of change that confront us daily in all aspects of our lives. We must decide which attitudes, traits of character, human goods, and actions serve our purposes and aims within communities that represent continuing and developing moral traditions. This will involve critically scrutinizing our own purposes and values, as well as imaginatively envisioning alternative perspectives and possibilities for human flourishing.

So, it is at least initially puzzling as to how our tradition, especially since the Enlightenment, has come to think of morality as *not* being a matter of *imagina-*

tive rationality. In order to underscore the need for a theory of constructive moral imagination, let us examine the prejudices that conspired to exclude imagination from moral reasoning. The most prominent constriction of reason occurs in Enlightenment moral theory, which presupposes the Moral Law folk theory, and which is the basis for most of our contemporary views about morality.

I shall focus, in particular, on Kantian rational ethics and on its antagonistic counterpart—utilitarianism—because they are chiefly responsible for the inadequate view of reason and moral agency we have inherited in the present century. The chief problem with Kantian rationalism is that it leaves us with far too abstract a conception of reason, while utilitarianism gives us far too reductionistic a conception of reason. *Both* views err in giving us one-dimensional pictures of rationality. I want to emphasize that my concern is not merely with Enlightenment moral *philosophy* as such, but rather with our shared Moral Law folk theory, upon which that philosophy is based. The key point is that it is the view of reason built into the Moral Law folk theory that is impoverished.

Kantian Abstractionism

In "The Diversity of Goods,"[3] Charles Taylor explains how it transpired that the two great exemplars of Enlightenment moral theory—Kantian formalism and utilitarianism—were able to convince themselves that they represented the very *essence* of reason, and hence were universally valid moral philosophies.

Taylor points out that Kantian rational ethics and utilitarianism alike rest on a fundamental assumption that we, as westerners sharing what I am calling the Moral Law folk theory, are very likely to regard as a moral absolute and as the key to the superiority of the Judeo-Christian moral tradition. That assumption is a principle of the universal attribution of moral personality to every human being; namely, "in fundamental ethical matters, everyone ought to count and all ought to count in the same way. Within this outlook, one absolute requirement of ethical thinking is that we respect other human agents as subjects of practical reasoning on the same footing as ourselves" (130).

This foundational belief in the universal moral status of each and every person dates at least as far back in our tradition as the Judeo-Christian idea that, because each of us is created "in the image of God," we are all equal from a moral point of view. What makes us equal is that each of us supposedly possesses an essential human reason by which we can discern moral laws and govern our actions in accordance with them. That is, we all stand equally under the same moral laws, and so have the same duties toward ourselves and others. As rational, all are due equal respect as moral agents.

The ideal of universal moral personality is so constitutive of our Moral Law tradition that one can hardly imagine it as other than an absolute moral principle built into the very essence of practical reason in its moral dimension. And this is exactly what Kant, and virtually everyone else in the Judeo-Christian moral tradition, does assume. Kant's categorical imperative, in each of its several (metaphorical) formulations that we examined earlier,[4] is precisely this very ideal of equal moral status regarded as issuing categorically from practical reason,[5] as if the principle of universal moral personality were, in fact, a *formal principle of reason itself!*[6] To be captivated by Kant's brilliant analysis of our moral tradition is to become convinced that this principle *just is* the core of morally practical reason. As Taylor explains, "Because this principle seems to flow so naturally from our cultural values, we tend to put it on a different level—to erect it into an absolute principle of *any* moral reasoning. . . . We might even talk ourselves into believing that it is not a moral principle in any substantive contestable sense at all, but some kind of limiting principle of moral reasoning" (131).

But the fact is that what we have come to regard as this 'universal,' 'formal,' 'limiting' principle of reason (i.e., the principle of universal moral personhood) is only one among many possible principles, values, goods, and ends we might reasonably come to embrace. It just happens to be the foundational principle for *our* moral tradition. But to say that it is foundational for *our* tradition does not make it a formal principle of *reason itself*. It simply means that our tradition is built upon it and upon the corresponding conception of practical reason that it requires. Saying this, obviously, does not make it part of the essence of reason.

To see that our principle of universal moral personhood is not necessarily built into the essence of human reason, it helps to remember that it is certainly not a principle that everyone has at all times and in all places assented to. For example, it was surely not affirmed in classical Greece, nor does it seem to be acknowledged as foundational in India today.[7] Richard Shweder and Edmund Bourne note the copious anthropological evidence that reveals the highly parochial nature of our Western conception of moral personhood. They observe that, all over the world, "the folk believe that specific situations determine the moral character of a particular action, that the individual person per se is neither an object of importance nor inherently worthy of respect, that the individual as moral agent ought not to be distinguished from the social status she or he occupies, that, indeed, the individual as an abstract *ethical* and *normative* category is not to be acknowledged."[8]

To insist that it is of the 'essence' of reason to assert this principle is, therefore, merely to privilege one set of values and goods over others and to forget that we are doing so. There is no non-question-begging way to argue for *any* essential definition of reason. This need not, however, prevent us from giving our reasons for holding one conception of rationality as superior to another. As Rawls, following Quine (who followed Dewey), has noted, our conception of reason is but one dimension of a complex moral viewpoint in which each part must be balanced and blended with the other parts (such as one's conception of human nature, one's reflectively derived moral principles, and one's considered moral intuitions).[9]

My point here is not to criticize this principle of universal moral personality. It is a central principle for me as much as it is for anyone else, and I am deeply committed to living by it. What I am criticizing, following Taylor, is the mistaken assumption that this principle does constitute the essence of morally practical reason, or, even worse, that it is somehow a *formal* principle of reason. Instead, this view of practical reason is but one of several possible competing views, each of which ranks one set of values over all others. There is no value-neutral reason, and to embrace one conception of practical reason is to privilege one value over other competing values.[10]

Taylor makes this crucial point by setting out four alternative values that would entail four different conceptions of highest goods, and therefore four different correlative notions of morally practical reason.

1. *Personal integrity.* What matters most is to live a life that expresses what one regards as important, admirable, noble, and desirable. While such a view of meaningful human existence might in some cases recognize the principle of universal moral personality, it need not necessarily rank that principle as higher than any of a number of alternative goods or values.

2. *Christian agapē.* One's fundamental purpose is to become a medium of God's love for humanity, a conduit by which that love is expressed in this world. Clearly, a life so lived might forgo any claim to be counted as equal to every other and to be counted always in every situation that affects one's life. Certain forms of charity might actually require one to put the welfare of another before one's own welfare, and thus to ignore the principle of universal moral personhood.

3. *Liberation.* Our aim ought to be, above all else, to enhance the dignity of human beings by making it possible for them to direct their own lives. While such

liberation might seem to be dependent on the principle of universal moral personality, since dignity requires respect for each person, it is quite possible that privileging liberation above all else might occasionally justify discriminatory actions in which every person is *not* counted as one. Such discrimination would be explained, for example, as a means to the greater good of freeing and empowering the oppressed.

4. *Economic rationality.* As in utilitarianism, the goal of maximizing overall utility for the society as a whole could also justify discriminatory judgments that fail to honor the principle of moral personality. It might be argued that situations arise in which a person may be treated in a discriminatory fashion to produce a greater good for society as a whole.

Taylor calls such potentially conflicting values "languages of qualitative contrast" which specify alternative goods and their corresponding conceptions of rationality: "These are the qualitative distinctions we make between different actions, or feelings, or modes of life, as being in some way morally higher or lower, noble or base, admirable or contemptible. It is these languages of qualitative contrast that get marginalised, or even expunged altogether, by the utilitarian or formalist reductions. I want to argue, in opposition to this, that they are central to our moral thinking and ineradicable from it" (132–33).

Any conception of practical reason is itself value-laden. We can stipulate a narrow definition of practical reason, as when we identify its essence with the principle of universal moral personality or with some other principle of qualitative contrast. Or, as Taylor proposes, we can give a far richer account of practical reason that includes some or all of these diverse values and goods in a way that precludes any single criterion of moral evaluation. But what we cannot do is to supply a value-neutral conception of morally practical reason. Whatever our conception, it will involve value judgments[11] that are not themselves either self-evident or absolute.

The Normative Dimension of Reason

This point about the value-ladenness of any conception of reason is fundamental and merits further consideration. Carol Gilligan's work on moral understanding and reasoning shows some of the ways in which our very conceptions of reason, morality, and human well-being are inextricably interrelated and interdefined.[12] There is no antecedently existing pure reason from which we then deduce our conception of morality and human flourishing. Rather, each is defined relative to the others. As an extended illustration of this crucial point, let us consider some of Gilligan's examples of potentially competing values and conceptions of moral reasoning.

Gilligan's work is well-known as arguing that the most influential studies of moral development, such as Lawrence Kohlberg's famous projects over the last three decades,[13] have focused almost exclusively on but *one form of moral reasoning*. In this chapter, my interest is not so much in Gilligan's critique of Kohlberg, but rather in the way her examples of moral reasoning reveal the normative dimension of any view of practical reason. Gilligan argues that the form of moral reasoning Kohlberg observed in his male subjects is by no means characteristic of all, or even most, moral reasoning. Gilligan takes Kohlberg's work to show that most males do operate with a logic of individual rights and universal rules of conduct. However, Gilligan's own studies showed that her female subjects more typically approached situations with a morality focused on care, responsibility for others, and communal cooperation.

> But just as the conventions that shape women's moral judgment differ from those that apply to men, so also women's definition of the moral domain diverges from that derived from studies of men. Women's construction of the moral problem as a problem of care and responsibility in relationships rather than one of rights and rules ties the development of their moral thinking to changes in their understanding of responsibility and relationships, just as the conception of morality as justice ties development to the logic of equality and reciprocity. Thus the logic underlying an ethic of care is a psychological logic of relationships, which contrasts with the formal logic of fairness that informs the justice approach. (73)

Gilligan is careful not to draw the distinction between modes of moral reasoning strictly along gender lines, though it appears that men and women have traditionally been socialized into these different attitudes and perspectives. The key point is to recognize that we are dealing here with two very different ways of approaching moral problems, two different conceptions of practical reasoning, and two different foci of moral attention. A morality of rights, rules, and justice-as-fairness requires a procedure for calculating what is *due* to each individual in a situation, and thus determining the right rule to follow. A morality of care, relationships, and cooperation seeks a way to preserve and enhance relationships and community in the face of conflict and competing interests.

These two different modes of reasoning can be seen in Gilligan's juxtapositions of male and female responses to situations. A subject from one of Kohlberg's early studies who is now an adult male responds to the question, "What does the word morality mean to you?" as follows: "Nobody in the world knows the answer. I think it is recognizing the right of the individual, the rights of other individuals, not interfering with those rights. Act as fairly as you would have them treat you. I think it is basically to preserve the human being's right to existence. I think that is the most important. Secondly, the human being's right to do as he pleases, again without interfering with somebody else's rights" (19).

Here is an example of a morality of rights and rules, with its attendant logic of noninterference. It is defined by the fundamental metaphors of the Moral Law folk theory: A RIGHT IS A RIGHT-OF-WAY to move in an unimpeded fashion along an action-path toward some purpose-destination. Where you have a right-of-way, others have duties not to obstruct your metaphorical movement along this action-path. JUSTICE-AS-FAIRNESS is a balancing of rights among all persons according to the logic of the SOCIAL ACCOUNTING metaphor. According to the other basic metaphor for rights in which A RIGHT IS A LETTER OF CREDIT (an IOU), each of us is *owed* the same rights, insofar as we are all equal members of a moral community. Within this SOCIAL ACCOUNTING framework, each of us can *calculate* what is due us as rational agents, that is, what our rights are. If we each keep 'within' our rights, and if we each thereby refrain from interfering with the rights of others, then we can realize a balance of mutually respected rights to perform certain actions for our various purposes. This provides the basis for our 'liberal' ideal of morality.

But now contrast this rights-and-justice approach to that of an adult woman in one of Gilligan's studies who is answering the question, "Is there really some correct solution to moral problems, or is everybody's opinion equally right?"

> No, I don't think everybody's opinion is equally right. I think that in some situations there may be opinions that are equally valid, and one could conscientiously adopt one of several courses of action. But there are other situations in which I think there are right and wrong answers, that sort of inhere in the nature of existence, of all individuals here who need to live with each other to live. We need to depend on each other, and hopefully it is not only a physical need but a need of fulfillment in ourselves, that a person's life is enriched by cooperating with other people and striving to live in harmony with everybody else, and to that end, there are right and wrong, there are things which promote that end and that move away from it, and in that way it is possible to choose in

certain cases among different courses of action that obviously promote
or harm that goal. (20)

There is a different locus of moral reasoning here. Unlike the previous example, it is not a calculation of rights, duties, and obligations according to universal rules. Instead, it is a logic of cooperation, of figuring out how to work
together—to be responsible to and for others—in the presence of conflict. The
best course of action is determined by what is required to preserve certain relationships and to promote the growth of harmony and community. The fundamental defining metaphors here are those of TIES and LINKS with other people. With
the maintenance of relationships as primary, it might actually be necessary to
forgo something to which, from the perspective of a morality of rights and justice, one has a right or entitlement.

Consequently, one can envision numerous situations of daily life in which
these two modes of reasoning—a logic of rights versus a logic of care and
responsibility—would come into conflict. In such cases it is not a question of
having two different types of reasoning for two different types of situation, but
rather of having two different moral logics for the *same* situation.

The crucial point is that many, if not most, people will have both of these competing sets of values and their corresponding notions of reasoning that they will
bring into play in a given situation. Most of us do not live exclusively by one such
set of values or the other. We have *both* of them, as well as others, woven together
in our complex moral understanding. The inherent tension among these competing logics is part of what makes ordinary moral deliberation so difficult. It is typically not a solution to adopt only one such logic to the total exclusion of every
other, for that would impoverish our moral reason and make us far less able to do
the best thing in a given situation.

This inescapable conflict of goods and moral logics can be seen more clearly in
the responses of two eleven-year-olds to the question, "When responsibility to
oneself and responsibility to others conflict, how should one choose?" The boy,
Jake, answers,

> You go about one-fourth to the others and three-fourths to yourself.
> ([*Question*]: Why?)
> *Jake:* Because the most important thing in your decision should be
> yourself, don't let yourself be guided totally by other people, but you
> have to take them into consideration. So, if what you want to do is
> blow yourself up with an atom bomb, you should maybe blow yourself

up with a hand grenade because you are thinking about your neighbors who would die also. (35–36)

Jake claims to know just what to do and how to *calculate* the right answer ("one-fourth to the others and three-fourths to yourself"). You have a right to put yourself first, so long as this is compatible with the rights of others. You must not infringe on their freedom in certain specified ways. You must, therefore, figure their rights *into the equation* ("take them into consideration") as you seek the correct balance of rights.

Eleven-year-old Amy responds with a somewhat different mode of evaluation that stresses responsibility to others:

Amy: Well, it really depends on the situation. If you have a responsibility with somebody else, then you should keep it to a certain extent, but to the extent that it is really going to hurt you or stop you from doing something that you really, really want, then I think maybe you should put yourself first. But if it is your responsibility to somebody really close to you, you've just got to decide in that situation which is more important, yourself or that person, and like I said, it really depends on what kind of person you are and how you feel about the other person or persons involved.
([*Question*]: Why?)
Amy: Well, like some people put themselves and things for themselves before they put other people, and some people really care about other people. Like, I don't think your job is as important as somebody that you really love, like your husband or your parents or a very close friend. . . . but if it's somebody that you really love and love as much or even more than you love yourself, you've got to decide what you really love more, that person, or that thing, or yourself.
([*Question*]: And how do you do that?)
Amy: Well, you've got to think about it, and you've got to think about both sides, and you've got to think which would be better for everybody or better for yourself, which is more important, and which will make everybody happier. (35–36)

Superficially, both Jake and Amy engage in a form of calculative reasoning in which they must weigh various factors to determine the correct outcome. But the crucial differences emerge in what they take as relevant to the calculation. Jake sees it as principally a question of balancing rights. Amy's reasoning differs in three major ways.

1. She begins by framing the entire issue as one that is relative to the context ("it really depends on the situation"). For her there is no one right answer independent of one's circumstances, commitments, and relationships. That is why she argues that you must always consider *with whom* you have relevant relationships and *how important* those ties and commitments are to you. Jake tends to see the issue more one-dimensionally, as a question of rights alone.

2. From the very start, Amy's primary concern, the first issue she mentions, is that of *responsibility to others* ("If you have a responsibility with somebody else, then you should keep it to a certain extent"). The locus of the deliberation is commitments and ties to others within a community. Whatever calculations are done, they must take into consideration the full range of factors that arise from our identity as bound up in interpersonal relationships.

3. I think it is also important to compare the length of Jake's and Amy's responses to the same question. Quite strikingly, Jake's answer is direct and short. There is a right thing to do, and there is a single criterion for deciding what that is ("Because the most important thing in your decision should be yourself"), according to a logic of rights. Amy's response appears to ramble and be indecisive, precisely because it recognizes the pull of many different factors. It acknowledges a complexity based on multiple goods and values. Amy thus sets out a larger number of factors that must be considered and balanced out in deciding what is best. Situations, as she sees, are complex and confusing, and they require subtle discriminations among competing goods.

I want to emphasize three major implications of these examples of different modes of moral evaluation. First, what we have here are two different forms of moral reasoning, both of which could reasonably lay a claim to our commitment in one and the same situation. Neither one is more (or less) a part of some antecedently existing essence of practical reason. Instead, each one tends to define a different conception of moral reason, what we might call a different moral logic. The idea of a Universal Reason, with its own essential structure, from which all morality stems, misses the fact that our core notions of reason, right, and good are mutually interdefined. None is ontologically or epistemologically or logically prior to any other.

Second, it is quite frequently the case that our moral dilemmas will stem from the difficulty of balancing and harmonizing these *and other* competing moral logics that make up the complex moral understanding of a single person. We cannot reduce one logic to another, nor can we always rank them hierarchically to avoid conflict. None of these conceptions, therefore, can lay claim to being *the* essence of reason.

Third, each of these competing views involves a different set of underlying metaphors, image schemas, and metonymies that define and constrain our reasoning. The logic of rights and rules is defined more typically by metaphors of PATHS, OBSTACLES, RIGHTS-OF-WAY, NONINTERFERENCE, DEBTS, LETTERS OF CREDIT, and so forth, while the logic of care and responsibility for others is defined by metaphors of TIES, LINKS, COMMUNITY, HARMONY, and so forth. The relevant conceptions of moral reasoning are metaphorically constituted.

To summarize: Amy and Jake do not so much represent 'female' versus 'male' modes of reasoning as they represent competing moral logics, values, and conceptions of reason that confront anyone who is sensitive to the complexities of human situations. Many of our moral dilemmas result from our feeling the contrary pull of competing frameworks, each of which lays a claim on us that we cannot escape. Moral absolutism is simply blind to the complex imaginative structure of human reason and even to the existence of valid alternative interpretations of a given situation. It impoverishes our conception of moral reason by presupposing an impoverished view of moral imagination.

The fact that our most fundamental concepts of reason, right, good, and so forth are interdefined undermines the Kantian rationalist assumption of a pure practical reason. Such a view requires us to accept some form of essentialism concerning the nature of reason. But essentialism, along with all allegedly a priori claims about the nature of reason, has come to be increasingly untenable in light of a long history of criticism and argument from Dewey to Wittgenstein, Quine to Putnam, Derrida to Rorty. The idea that there exists a method for distinguishing analytic from synthetic judgments, propositions, or sentences, and that the analytic component gives us insight into the structure of rationality as such, has been discredited more thoroughly than any other logical positivist dogma.[14]

Within such an anti-essentialist context, Taylor's central point can be summarized as follows: Any sort of Kantian formalism or similar rationalist ethics will be founded on the mistaken assumption that it has insight a priori into the nature of practical reason. Such a program will take a principle that is absolutely fundamental for our particular moral tradition (e.g., the Moral Law folk theory) and regard it as a formal principle of reason itself. This error leads to the privileging of one set of values (and one corresponding conception of reason) over all others. It gives rise to the un-self-reflective assertion that the value *it* privileges is actually a formal principle built into the essential structure of rationality. It is only because the favored principle is formulated at such a high level of abstraction that it comes to seem as though it is nothing but a formal principle. One result of this abstractionism, as Taylor points out, is that we come to ignore the historical context out of which the principle emerged: "What is really going on is that some forms of ethical reasoning are being privileged over others because in our civilisation they come less into dispute or look easier to defend. . . . In a similar way, we have been manoeuvered into a restrictive definition of ethics, which takes account of some of the goods we seek, e.g., utility, and universal respect for moral personality, while excluding others, . . . largely on the grounds that the former are subject to less embarrassing dispute" (139–40).

Kantian formalism, as the exemplar of all rationalistic moral philosophies, thus desiccates our moral reason by abstraction. It formulates one abstract principle, and one principle only, as the formal structure of morally practical reason itself, and thereby excludes all other values as either of lesser importance or even as standing outside the domain of moral philosophy altogether.

Utilitarian Reductionism

Whereas Kantianism impoverishes reason by its excessive abstractionism, its chief Enlightenment rival, utilitarianism, does so by a corresponding reductionism. To put it crudely, utilitarianism reduces reason to economic, means-ends, technical rationality as the sole criterion for moral evaluation. It narrows our reason so drastically that it excludes most of what is significant in our ordinary moral deliberations.

Utilitarianism was motivated by the Enlightenment hope that ethics could be made scientific. This was predicated on the belief that reason had achieved sufficient self-reflectiveness so that we could at last discover a scientific criterion for the moral evaluation of every conceivable situation. That criterion—the principle of utility—was supposed to be the ultimate principle of human behavior stemming from a truly scientific study of human nature.

Bentham defined the principle of utility as "that principle which approves or disapproves of every action whatsoever, according to the tendency which it appears to have to augment or diminish the happiness of the party whose interest is in question."[15] More generally, utilitarianism is the view that a given act or rule is right to the extent that it maximizes the good of human beings. According to the version known as 'act' utilitarianism, what one compares in moral deliberation are the total consequences of the alternative acts open to the agent. 'Rule' utilitarianism compares the consequences of following certain universal rules, rather than calculating the good produced by a given act.

The key concept of 'the good' can be defined either hedonistically (as in Bentham's identification of good with pleasurable feeling), eudaimonistically (as in Mill's focus on happiness and well-being), or in other ways (for instance, Moore's exclusive attention to the enjoyment of certain states of mind, such as the experience of beauty and friendship). Utilitarianism is distinguished from individualistic or egoistic hedonisms by its insistence that the good to be maximized must be that of the entire community of persons who are in any way affected by one's actions.

The essential unifying feature of all versions of utilitarianism is the *calculation* of utility. Moral reasoning is reduced to a MORAL ARITHMETIC, that is, to acts of adding and averaging what is taken to be an objectively quantifiable good, commodity, or property of an object or situation. Such a moral calculus is most notoriously evident in Bentham's dream of a rigorous procedure for assigning values to relevant variables and then summing up the expected utility of any given action. Bentham indicates the appropriate mathematical procedure as follows:

> To take an exact account then of the general tendency of any act, by which the interests of the community are affected, proceed as follows. Begin with any one person of those whose interests seem most immediately to be affected by it: and take an account,
> 1. Of the value of each distinguishable *pleasure* which appears to be produced by it in the *first* instance.
> 2. Of the value of each *pain* which appears to be produced by it in the *first* instance.
> 3. Of the value of each pleasure which appears to be produced by it *after* the first. This constitutes the *fecundity* of the first *pleasure* and the *impurity* of the first *pain*.
> 4. Of the value of each *pain* which appears to be produced by it after the first. This constitutes the *fecundity* of the first *pain,* and the *impurity* of the first *pleasure*.
> 5. Sum up all the values of all the *pleasures* on the one side, and those of all the *pains* on the other. The balance, if it be on the side of pleasure, will give the *good* tendency of the act upon the whole, with respect to the interests of that *individual* person; if on the side of pain, the *bad* tendency of it upon the whole.[16]

Bentham goes on to specify other rules of calculation, but those listed above are sufficient to indicate the unabashed confidence with which his program, founded on the metaphor of MORAL ARITHMETIC, was first put forward. At last, morality was to be grounded on the sure foundations of objective scientific and mathematical procedures. All ambiguous, indeterminate, and highly suspect metaphysical and theological concepts and principles that had populated traditional moral theory would be swept away forever, to be replaced by the certain determinations of a progressive scientific program.

This halo of scientific objectivity and rigor (coupled with its adherence to a version of the principle of universal moral personality) has sustained utilitarianism's appeal in our common understanding long after it has ceased to be a defensible position. It is simply enough, by way of criticism, to call the bluff of those who continue to assume, without argument or example, that such calculations are even *possible*, much less useful, in actual situations. As Donagan has pointed out, "The difficulty is not that it is impracticable for him to calculate what productive actions open to him would have the greatest utility but that the calculation itself has no definite solution."[17] There is nothing scientific about any of this whatsoever, for there is no scientific calculation possible, given our present lack of knowledge of causal connections and our inability to decide in any satisfactory way where to terminate our consideration of the indefinitely long chains of effects issuing from a given action. Furthermore, utilitarianism requires us to be responsible for the outcome of joint projects that depend upon the cooperative action of other agents over which we have no control. And it would require of us a psychologically impossible awareness of all the actions available to us at a given moment that might positively affect the well-being of others.[18]

These, and other, objections are well-known.[19] My purpose is not to rehearse such criticisms. Rather, I am concerned with understanding how utilitarianism leads inescapably to a reductionistic view of reason as mere *calculation*. In its quest for the one, absolute, scientific criterion of morality, utilitarianism lost touch with the rich, complex, and varied character of human moral reasoning. In order to sustain even the pretense of scientific objectivity, utilitarianism had to adopt a set of absolutist concepts and assumptions the likes of which have seldom been witnessed together in one place. The result is an utterly one-dimensional view of reason as 'economic rationality,' a merely calculative reason that focuses exclusively on determining the most efficient means to pregiven ends.

Taylor has given an exquisite summary of many of the absolutist assumptions underlying utilitarian rationality: "We have here the model of a human being who is clairvoyant about his goals, and capable of objectifying and understanding himself and the world which surrounds him. He can get a clear grasp of the mechanisms at work in self and world, and can thus direct his action clear-sightedly and deliberately. To do this he must resist the temptations offered by the various comforting illusions that make the self or the world so much more attractive than they really are in the cold light of science" (133–34).

Here we find moral absolutism in a nutshell. Moral agents are rationally transparent individuals who possess desires that they understand completely. They have complete knowledge of their ends, which are regarded as completely determinate, fixed, and given in advance of their moral deliberations about means to these ends. They have all the relevant knowledge, both of themselves (their instincts, motivations, wants) and of the mechanisms of causality in the external world. Moreover, their reason is a calculative capacity for algorithmically processing this massive body of relevant knowledge.

I take it as evident that these assumptions wear their implausibility on their sleeves. We have already seen what is wrong with most of these absolutist views. Here I want only to emphasize just how restrictive and reductionistic utilitarian rationality really is. In its attempt to specify a single, universal scientific criterion, utilitarianism is forced to make so many falsifying and distorting assumptions, and to so restrict the purview of rational deliberation, that it reduces human reason to pseudomechanistic calculation. It is certainly no surprise, therefore, that it banishes imagination from the scene altogether, as representing everything to which objective reason is opposed. There can be no place for imagination in any view that convinces itself that moral reasoning is just 'doing numbers.'

Where Has Reason Gone?

It would be a mistake to suppose that either the abstractionist or reductionistic views of reason just described are somehow Enlightenment artifacts that we *truly enlightened* souls have transcended and can look upon with amusement as illusions of an earlier age. On the contrary, the models I have sketched are based on the folk theory of Faculty Psychology and of Moral Law that are presupposed by a great deal of contemporary moral, social, political, economic, psychological, and educational theory.[20] They are *our* models, whether we know it or not, and they influence the way we conceive of morality and reason about what we ought to do. They are inextricably tied up with, and definitive of, absolutist thinking and all forms of moral objectivism. We must overcome them if we are going to develop models of reason that have even a chance of capturing the complex, evolving, and imaginative character of actual human meaning, cognition, and reason.

Absolutism is motivated by a quest for certainty. It draws its appeal from the universal human need for security, control, and order. Moral absolutism thus seeks principles valid for all people, at all times, and in all historical contexts. It assumes that moral laws come out of an allegedly essential structure of rationality. It seeks a single unified criterion (or small set of hierarchically ranked criteria) for the moral evaluation of all actions.

In setting out its fundamental notions, absolutism thus wants to avoid having to rely on any concepts or principles that are tied to historically contingent embodied human subjects, practices, institutions, or cultural contexts. Consequently, it must define the domain of morality so as to exclude values or principles whose meaning and force are context-dependent in any but the most general way. Absolutism thus assumes that the polysemy, multivalence, and multidimensionality that characterize our conceptualization of a particular situation must be *reducible* to a list of the most general and abstract features shared by all situations 'of the same kind.'

Furthermore, absolutism requires that any alternative language of qualitative contrast must either be reduced to the language of the allegedly privileged formal principle, or be relegated to the level of a mere personal preference or subjective choice. For example, someone who unreflectively accepts the principle of universal moral personality as constituting the essence of practical reason cannot allow the values of Christian *agapē* equal status with the privileged principle. To preserve the supremacy of the principle of universal moral personality would typically require the strategy of claiming that *agapē* is not actually a moral requirement or obligation but is rather a personal preference or choice of lifestyle permitted within the constraints of rational morality. In this way the alternative value is recognized while not being granted status as competing with one's fundamental moral principles.

What this absolutist orientation denies is the existence of genuine irresolvable moral conflict—conflict among competing conceptions of goods, justice, and reason. But, as Martha Nussbaum has argued so eloquently,[21] life presents us with conflicting obligations that cannot be hierarchically ordered by some univocal universal principle. Antigone has very real duties both to her family and to her *polis*, neither of which can be explained away and neither of which can be subordinated to any other. And yet she must act and accept responsibility for what she chooses. The moral realm is not a homogeneous domain unified by a single overarching criterion for assessing the merits of all competing views. Instead, as Taylor observes,

> many people find themselves drawn by more than one of these views, and are faced with the job of somehow making them compatible in their lives. This is where the question can arise whether all the demands that we might consider moral and which we recognise as valid can be coherently combined. This question naturally raises another one, whether it is really appropriate to talk of single type of demand called 'moral.'
> . . . The really important question may turn out to be how we combine in our lives two or three or four different goals, or virtues, or standards, which we feel we cannot repudiate but which seem to demand incompatible things of us. (134–35)

The fact that our moral concepts are defined by various kinds of imaginative structure (such as image schemas, prototype structure, and metaphor) points the way toward a far richer account of moral reasoning than that bequeathed to us by our Enlightenment forebears. The kind of rationality we need in such a case is one that is imaginative through and through. Our task as moral agents cannot be merely to discover the right rule for a particular case, *the* rule that supposedly specifies 'the right thing to do,' because the nature of the case might well preclude such a possibility, insofar as genuine moral conflict of goods, values, and obligations exists. What we need in such cases is a cultivated moral imagination for exploring the various courses of action open to us, for rehearsing possible relationships and forms of action, and for doing our best to harmonize our often conflicting values and conceptions of reason. We need to determine both what courses are, in fact, open to us (i.e., we need the imagination to project possibilities for action) and also what it would mean for us to pursue one course of action rather than another (i.e., to explore imaginatively the implications of each projected course).

Our most pressing task, then, is to elaborate a satisfactory and workable theory of imaginative rationality. Such a theory must include a view of imagination adequate to the tasks that we, as evolving, self-reflective moral agents, encounter in our daily lives. Our account of moral reasoning must also be compatible with what empirical psychological studies have revealed about the nature of persons, about psychological motivation, and about human reason. That brings us to the question of what it means to be a person capable of moral agency.

What's Wrong with the Objectivist Self

We have seen some of the damage that moral absolutism inflicts on our picture of human reason, either by excessive abstraction (as in Kantian-style rational ethics) or by extreme reduction (as in the utilitarian means-ends conception of reason). We have seen how defining rationality as having an essential, fixed, ahistorical nature that can be specified by a set of rules or laws governing morally correct willing leaves no place for the central role of imagination in moral deliberation. Absolutism's restriction of reason to the narrow role of a 'constraining force' leaves no room for the creative, exploratory dimension of rational deliberation.

But the damage done by absolutism doesn't stop with its impoverished conception of reason. It extends even further to an equally problematic correlative view of the self. In this chapter I want to set out and criticize what I shall call the 'objectivist' view of the self that is presupposed by the Moral Law folk theory. I will show that it cannot give an adequate account of moral personality, because it cannot account for the way in which the moral identity of a person is an ongoing, culturally and historically situated, imaginative process of thought and action. In the next chapter I will argue that we can properly understand the identity of moral agents (and their actions) only within a narrative context of the sort that moral absolutism regards as mostly irrelevant. I will suggest that the historical, narrative process by which moral agents formulate and continually revise their moral identity is incompatible with the objectivist metaphysics and epistemology that underlies our Moral Law folk theory.

Our Objectivist Folk Model of Moral Personality

The Moral Law folk theory that defines a large part of the Western moral tradition presupposes an 'objectivist' model of moral agency. It is a model of humans as 'rational animals' who have a dual nature, part bodily and part mental. Our bodily side, which is the source of our needs and wants, seeks always to satisfy its own animal desires. From the point of view of persons as *animals,* their desire is held to be conditioned by their bodily makeup, character traits, and prior experiences.

If we were nothing but brute animals, then morality would be a mere illusion, since we would in fact be nothing more than conditioned organisms driven by our strongest urges and desires to pursue ends we perceive as satisfying our self-interest.

We alone in the animal realm, however, possess *reason,* which not only tells us how best to realize our ends (means-ends rationality) but also specifies what ends we ought to pursue (moral reason). Our will (as practical reason) can cause actions under the guidance of rational principles, rather than merely as the result of contingent natural causes. Our will is thus held to be rational and free, in the sense that it can *choose* to act (it is free) and it can do so on the basis of principles given to it by reason (it is rational).

According to this objectivist view of the self, therefore, the problem of morality stems from the fact that our animal desire is not intrinsically rational. Will must be strong to resist the force of desire, whenever desire or passion goes against what reason demands. Moral reasoning is viewed as rationally determining the appropriate moral law for a particular situation and then summoning the willpower to act as reason dictates.

The picture I have just sketched constitutes a folk model of moral personality shared by virtually all members of our common moral tradition. It involves a set of related assumptions about the nature of the self, reason, motivation, action, and deliberation, which roughly define our sense of morality. Not everyone in our tradition will hold every part of this objectivist folk model of the self. Within a theologically based ethics, for example, determining the right course of action is conceived as a matter of human reason grasping the dictates of divine reason. By contrast, in a strictly rationalist ethics human reason is regarded as autonomous, that is, as giving moral laws to itself rather than relying on external divine authority. Yet both views share the same objectivist folk model insofar as they both accept the central role of an essential, transcendental reason that issues moral laws.

Like all folk models, the objectivist model of moral personality (and reason) seldom operates at the level of our conscious reflection. So, while few people could articulate the model explicitly, most people nevertheless act in terms of the model, as, for instance, when they experience their bodies as sources of blind desires that need to be brought under the guidance of reason.

There is something profoundly misleading about the objectivist folk model of the self. It gives us an erroneous picture of ourselves as metaphysically bifurcated creatures who inhabit two radically distinct worlds (i.e., the mental and the physical) that can never be fully harmonized. It has left us with a woefully inadequate view of human identity that tends either toward an extreme dualism or toward reductionism. It defines moral personhood without reference to the social relations and cultural roles that form such a large part of our personal identity. And it has no place for imagination in its account of moral reasoning.

In order to see what's wrong with this objectivist conception of the self, let us consider more deeply its chief features and how it is motivated.

The Objectivist Folk Model of the Self

1. *The essential, rational self.* For objectivism the moral agent must be some kind of quasi-object with a fixed, determinate nature. The self may be seen as a physical object of sorts (as in a materialist metaphysics) or it may be a transcendental subject (as in idealist metaphysics), but in either case it is regarded as having an unchanging nature that it shares with all other creatures of its kind.

The distinguishing essence of human beings is their reason. Rationality has an essential, fixed structure that can be specified as a set of logically related principles. As Alan Donagan has argued, within this traditional view, being rational is following those laws that come from the essence of reason: "Thus a moral law or precept of the form 'Actions of kind K are (are not) contrary to reason,' may be analysed as 'Practical reason itself—that is, anybody's practical reason, provided that no error is made—prescribes that action of kind K may not (may) be done.' That an action is contrary to reason, or not, is therefore a fact about it, by way of being about what practical reason prescribes with regard to it."[1]

It is because reason has an essence that there can be a 'fact' about what principles it prescribes when it is functioning correctly. That is what it means to claim that certain principles 'come out of' or 'issue from' reason. Thus, moral absolutism claims that moral objectivity is based on the existence of certain objective facts about what reason prescribes, when it works correctly. As Donagan explains, "The elementary deliverances of common morality are therefore true or false according to the realist, or correspondence, theory of truth. They are true if and only if practical reason, functioning without error, would make certain prescriptions."[2]

To sum up, moral absolutism (as a form of moral objectivism) defines people by their essential rationality, that is, by their possessing practical reason, which has an essential structure that issues various practical and moral principles.[3]

2. *The ahistorical self.* If our moral personhood consists in our possessing practical reason, then our essence as moral agents is not changed by our historical circumstances. Individual people, of course, will change over time in all sorts of

ways, and so their empirical identity is bound to evolve. According to objectivist metaphysics, however, an individual's essential rationality *does not change*. Our core rationality remains fixed, no matter how much our personal identity changes. Moral objectivism can offer the comfort of a stable moral identity, but only by ignoring the possibility of evolution in our moral personality.

3. *The universal self.* If the self is defined by its rational essence, then every moral agent will possess that same essential nature. As moral agents, we are all equal by virtue of the fact that we all possess practical reason. On this view, acting morally is regarded as a matter of extracting ourselves from our particularity and realizing our shared, universal rational nature, by virtue of which we constitute a universal moral community. Kant's "realm (or kingdom) of ends" is an idealization of just such a universal community of rational beings (as ends-in-themselves) and their particular subjective ends (*F*, sec. 2).

The universal, rational self is not limited solely to rationalistic ethics. It is foundational for the Judeo-Christian moral tradition, and it is also basic to utilitarianism, which regards all moral agents as equal by virtue of their rational essence.

4. *The self bifurcated into reason and desire.* In his critique of the 'liberal psychology' that underlies modern (i.e., Enlightenment) moral and political theory, Roberto Unger has identified three fundamental principles of psychology that define the conception of the self.[4] The first principle "states that the self consists of understanding and desire, that the two are distinct from one another, and that desire is the moving, active, primary part of the self. The mind machine, by itself, wants nothing; desire, unaided by understanding, can see nothing. This might be called the principle of reason and desire" (39). Unger is describing the basis for a fundamental, unbridgeable split in our modern conception of the self. Reason or understanding is regarded as that calculative part of the self whose purpose is to seek a true description of the world and to formulate principles. Desire, by contrast, "is the faculty by which the self determines the objects of its appetites and aversions" (39). Desire motivates us—it moves us toward objects and states of being that would satisfy our interests and wants.

The problem of the split self is thus that calculative reason seems unable to move us to action, while the desire that moves us to action is not intrinsically rational. The problem is how to get these two sides together.

5. *The atomic, individual self.* According to this picture of the self as split into a rational part and a bodily, passionate part, people's needs and desires arise only from their bodily nature, their animality. Hence, people are the source of their

own ends. Moreover, rationality and freedom are inherent, essential properties of individual people. Therefore, people are atomic individuals—social atoms—in the sense that they are the source of their own ends and of the rationality and freedom to realize those ends. These inherent, essential characteristics are alleged to be in no way either defined by or dependent on other human beings.

Unger observes that this atomistic conception of persons underlies Enlightenment 'liberal psychology,'[5] which presupposes an atomistic conception of knowledge. He identifies the empiricist "principle of analysis" according to which "there is nothing in any piece of knowledge that cannot be analyzed back into the elementary sensations or ideas from which it was composed and then built up again from those sensations and ideas" (46). When applied to our knowledge of society as a whole, this principle of analysis treats society as nothing more than a sum of its individual, atomic members, who are what they are in themselves. Thus, their particular relations, histories, commitments, and institutional involvements are viewed as wholly external relations.

It is not at all surprising, therefore, that the fundamental question of liberal political theory is to explain why essentially free individuals would or should ever join communities in which they would have to give up part of their freedom to a sovereign or ruling group to which they become subject.[6] If we are essentially individuals possessing identities in ourselves without reference to our social relations, then the state becomes an artificial union that imposes constraints on individuals' freedom. If what we essentially are is rational, atomic, self-interested desiring animals, then our social and communal relations will be seen as *extrinsic* to our nature and to our identity as moral agents. As Hobbes saw, such atomic individuals would only submit themselves to restrictions on their liberty if forming into social units somehow seemed to them to serve their individual purposes, interests, and ends.

There is no such thing, on this view, as a public, universal interest that is partially definitive of the individual's being. Consequently, "when all interests are viewed as either private and subjective themselves or as combinations of subjective and private interests, no activity can be seen as the expression of a universal interest whose realization demands a universal knowledge of society. A fractured social existence can only produce a fractured knowledge of the social order" (48).

6. *The self as separate from its acts.* An atomic, essential self exists and has its identity, then, entirely independent of the actions it performs, the ends it sets for itself, or the social arrangements it may enter into. It simply is what it is *in itself.* Consequently, an objectivist view of this sort denies that a person's moral

identity—that which makes her a moral agent—is established tentatively through her ongoing acts and intentions, through her interpersonal relations, and through her historically and culturally situated experiences.

Kantian rationalism perfectly illustrates this isolation of the self from its actions and ends. Kant claims that our common moral understanding correctly recognizes that the self can have moral value in itself, regardless of its actions—it is good simply on the basis of its good willing, rather than because of what it is able to bring about through its action.[7] Kantianism thus divorces that which makes a person capable of morality (i.e., the self of moral agency) from the ends he realizes, the actions he performs, the *way* he performs them, and the personal relations he enters into. Bernard Williams observes that "Kant started from what in his view rational agents essentially *were*. He thought that the moral agent was, in a sense, a rational agent and no more, and he presented as essential to his account of morality a particular metaphysical conception of the agent, according to which the self of moral agency is what he called a "noumenal self," outside time and causality, and thus distinct from the concrete, empirically determined person that one usually takes oneself to be."[8] Kant's "noumenal self" is perhaps slightly extreme in the way it isolates the self of moral agency from a person's empirical identity. But his view is quite representative of the objectivist Enlightenment view of the self as possessing its essential freedom and rationality *in itself,* independent of its social and cultural interactions.

What's Wrong with the Objectivist Self

There are two general kinds of problems with the objectivist conception of the self that is presupposed by our Moral Law folk theory.

1. *The split self.* The most obvious problem for such a bifurcated view of moral personality is how these two distinct faculties of reason and desire could ever be brought together as a basis for rational willing. Faculty psychology assumes distinct and functionally independent faculties or capacities. If the two parts of the self really are distinct and different in nature, then how can desire heed the call of reason, since our passionate self is, by its very nature, nonrational? And how can reason experience the urgings of desire, since reason is not bodily in the way passion is?

There have been two basic strategies in Enlightenment moral theory in response to this problem. One response is emotivism, the view that reason and desire *cannot* be brought together, and that morality is almost entirely a matter of desire or feeling alone. As I will argue below, emotivism is not actually a solution to the bifurcated self. It merely presupposes the split self and then tries to locate morality entirely within the nonrational realm of feeling. It takes morality out of the realm of reason altogether and thereby makes it impossible to mount a rational critique of any morality.

The other response to the bifurcated self has been to claim that reason must somehow be united with desire to produce a reason that is truly practical. This is the Kantian rationalist strategy. Kant asserted, but could not prove, that reason is practical. He showed that our entire moral tradition rests on the assumption that reason *can* move us to action. But he argued that the metaphysical nature of the split self makes it impossible to explain how reason can be practical in this way. This has led Unger to observe that Kant's solution is no solution at all: "Kant proposed a solution whose virtue was to show that no solution was possible, unless the terms of the problem were redefined. Think of man, he said, as if he were a citizen of two kingdoms, a natural realm of causal determination and a moral realm of freedom. We assume he is the former because we want to explain the world, and that he is the latter because we want to justify conduct. But the relation between the two assumptions, desire as determined fact and as arbitrary choice, remains forever a mystery" (43).

Consequently, the bifurcated self has remained a chief source of major problems within modern economic, political, social, and moral theories. If you start with a dichotomous view of the self, you will never overcome the metaphysically split identity of moral agents. You will never be able to explain how reason could influence desire, or even how there could be an urge to bring desire into conformity with reason in the first place. If the two really are distinct in nature, then how could the pull of conscience arise at all? Reason would simply dictate what it dictates, and desire would simply want what it wants, and the two would never meet.

The source of the problem is the mistaken assumption that desire is always nonrational, arbitrary, and subjective. If desire really were nonrational, then rationalizing it (i.e., getting it to submit to reason), as moral objectivism requires, would be nothing more than an act of 'power' or 'force' on the part of reason; hence, the origin of the reason-as-constraining-force model of rationality.

As we will see, the only way to deal with the problem of the split self is to deny the split in the first place.

2. *The atomic, rational ego.* The second major problem is that objectivism regards the self as having a fixed, ahistorical, self-contained essence that is independent of its ends, acts, or relations. It supposes that we might somehow ana-

lyze this essential rationality to determine *the* principles of morally correct willing. I shall argue that what is missing in this picture of moral personality is the way the self is both expressed in and constituted by an ongoing temporal process of activity and social interaction. There is not some static 'thing' that the self just *is* or *ought to be,* which determines what a moral agent ought to do. Rather, one's identity as a moral agent (i.e., one's moral personality) changes and is shaped by one's way of deliberating about and pursuing one's ends and purposes.

The crux of the problem is that the view of the self required by objectivism is incompatible with what psychology tells us about the development of self-identity in *actual persons.* Tying moral personality to a universal rationality leaves no room for the role of our particularity, as manifested, for example, in the relationships, commitments, and affections that are a major part of our identity. It leaves no role for the way in which our identity is, in part, socially constructed. Human beings do not have their identity solely on the basis of their being atomic rational egos. Rather, our identities emerge and change over time in and through complex social interactions and relations.

As Owen Flanagan has argued, an atomistic view of the self is utterly incompatible with what we know about human development.

> But given that we are not in the dark about the psychology of identity formation, what are we to make of the fact that our selves are not only socially formed but, in certain respects, constituted by both our contemporaneous social relations, roles, practices, and activities and certain ancestral roots and connections as well? Of what normative consequence is seeing oneself as an "encumbered self"?
>
> One implication looks to be this. If our identities are primarily emergent, relational products rather than pure self-creations, it follows that gaining accurate self-understanding will involve seeing oneself nonatomically.[9]

We are creatures in process, evolving selves whose identities are tied up with social relations and are affected by historical contingencies. I want to argue for a self-in-process, that is, a self that is neither completely alienated from, nor completely submerged in, its acts, but has instead an identity that is both revealed in and transformed by its experience as it develops over time. It is this temporal, transformative process that moral objectivism cannot abide, because such a process would deny the static essence objectivism needs as the locus of moral agency.

We ought not underestimate the importance of objectivism's failure to account for self-identity. As Dewey saw, "it is not too much to say that the key to a correct theory of morality is recognition of the *essential unity of the self and its acts,* if the latter have any moral significance; while errors in theory arise as soon as the self and act (and their consequences) are separated from each other, and moral worth is attributed to one more than to the other."[10]

In the remainder of this chapter and in the next I am going to develop a view of self-identity that does justice to our nature as socially, culturally, and historically constituted beings. It is a view that sees people as defined, not just by rational properties they possess in themselves, nor just by their social and communal relations, but rather by an identity that emerges in, and evolves through, the interaction of individual and social factors.

Modern Manifestations of the Objectivist Self

Before I turn to my constructive account of moral self-identity, I want to give more substance to my charges about the failure of moral objectivism. In the twentieth century the objectivist folk model of the self shows up most strikingly in two major moral philosophies, namely, emotivism and Kantian-style rationalism. Since both of these views have exercised a profound influence on contemporary moral theory, it is important to see how they each give us empirically inadequate conceptions of the self. I shall give a brief account of each theory which focuses on what is mistaken about their respective models of persons.

EMOTIVISM

Emotivism is the view that moral judgments and evaluations are not based on reason, but are only expressions of emotion or attitude. Alasdair MacIntyre argues that emotivism is the chief source of the moral chaos we are experiencing today, as evidenced by the absence of any universal rational standards for adjudicating competing moral claims. He observes, correctly, that if all moral judgments are "*nothing but* expressions of preference, expressions of attitude or feeling,"[11] then there exists no common rational basis for moral community, nor any rational basis for criticism and evaluation.

1. *Hume's emotivism: the traditional interpretation.* The philosophical presuppositions of emotivism are perhaps most elegantly expressed in the work of David Hume. Morality is based, not on reason, but on feelings. The argument is simple: Hume assumes the objectivist bifurcation of reason and desire. Because reason is concerned solely with the determination of the truth and falsity of state-

ments, it can have no motive force to induce action. Instead, either it explores relations among our ideas (as in mathematics and logic), or it examines matters of empirical fact (to see whether our ideas and statements are grounded in, and correspond to, aspects of our experience). Desire, on the other hand, stems from our passions and appetites, which, being bodily, can *move us* to action. Hume draws the conclusion that only feelings or passions can provide the basis for morality: "Since morals, therefore, have an influence on the actions and affections, it follows, that they cannot be deriv'd from reason; and that because reason alone as we have already prov'd, can never have any such influence. Morals excite passions, and produce or prevent actions; Reason of itself is utterly impotent in this particular. The rules of morality, therefore, are not conclusions of reason."[12]

We see in Hume the disturbing consequences of the Enlightenment separation of reason and desire. Reason is reduced to calculation and description. In morals it can serve to calculate probable effects of our actions. In this role, it is a form of technical and 'economic' rationality, determining the most efficient means to some pregiven end. Once it has performed this preliminary stage-setting work, however, it must give way to the main players—our strong feelings—that either incline us toward, or drive us away from, the action(s) about which we are deliberating. Reason is insightful but impotent; passion is dynamic but blind: "Nothing can oppose or retard the impulse of passion, but a contrary impulse. . . . Reason is, and ought only to be the slave of the passions, and can never pretend to any other office than to serve and obey them" (2.3.3.415).

Emotivism's mistake is to assert the split self—the bifurcation of reason and desire—and then to put morality outside reason. On its account, one either does or does not feel the sentiments of approval or disapproval for a contemplated action. Reason is not practical, because by itself it cannot move us to action. Morality has nothing to do with objective qualities of action or character, but only with our feeling response (our moral sentiments) when we contemplate such actions or states of character. In Hume's terms, "when you pronounce any action or character to be vicious, you mean nothing, but that from the constitution of your nature you have a feeling or sentiment of blame from the contemplation of it" (3.1.1.469).

Hume believed that he had saved morality from mere subjectivism by arguing that the moral sentiments could be shared and cultivated. Morality was not, Hume insisted, merely a matter of what *I* happen to feel, as opposed to what *you* might happen to feel. He asserted, instead, that there are universal sentiments and that the sentiment of sympathy is the basis of morals. Because this sentiment is alleged to be universal, morality is supposedly saved from solipsism and subjective relativism. And because the sentiment of sympathy is other-regarding, morality is supposedly saved from egoism.

Hume's, and emotivism's, chief mistake is to separate reason from desire absolutely and thereby to render reason, so narrowly construed, to be nearly irrelevant to morality. He is forced to conclude that, "as reason can never immediately prevent or produce any action by contradicting or approving of it, it cannot be the source of moral good and evil, which are found to have that influence. . . . Moral distinctions, therefore, are not the offspring of reason. Reason is wholly inactive, and can never be the source of so active a principle as conscience, or a sense of morals" (3.1.1.458).

Annette Baier has pointed out that this received view of Hume as archetypal emotivist grossly oversimplifies and distorts Hume's real project, which was to articulate a far richer conception of reason as passionate, social, and expansive.[13] Baier shows masterfully how Hume criticized a narrow, calculative model of reason, in order to develop a view of reason as a power of judgment that is socially situated and cultivated: "The *Treatise* used reflection first to destroy one version of reason, then to establish the sort of customs, habits, abilities and passions that can bear their own moral survey. It thereby reestablished a transformed, active, socialized reason to a 'likeness of rank, not to say equality' with sovereign moral sentiment."[14]

Baier's reconstruction of Hume's view of moral reasoning overthrows the traditional picture of him as a reductive emotivist. Her account of Hume as supplying a conception of reason melded with sentiment and cultivated by social interaction ought to chart the course for all future explorations of his moral theory.

Nevertheless, the fact remains that it is the *traditional* interpretation of Hume that has typically underwritten contemporary versions of emotivism. Hume's legacy to date has been the emotivism described above, and so it is still fair to take the received version (if not Hume's true theory) as at least accurately setting out certain basic assumptions about reason that underlie objectivist and emotivist moral theories.

2. *Twentieth-century emotivism.* Emotivism in the twentieth century turns out to be not a whit better than the traditional interpretation of Hume's theory, and in most cases it is far less elegantly expressed. All of its forms rest on a thoroughly mistaken and discredited view of language that tried to divide all meaningful utterances into one of two types: those that make descriptive truth claims, and those

that express attitudes or emotions. The class of descriptive statements was further subdivided into two basic types: *logical truths,* statements whose truth depends only on formal logical relations (i.e., the laws of logic); and *empirical statements,* which describe states of affairs in the world and are therefore true or false empirically, depending on whether they correctly represent the way things actually are in the world. Since it was thought that ethical utterances were neither logical truths nor empirically verifiable statements, they were by default relegated to the domain of expressive discourse.

A. J. Ayer's classic formulation of logical empiricism in *Language, Truth, and Logic* (1936) is grounded entirely on just such a dichotomous view of the self and of the functions of language. Ayer dispenses with moral judgments as follows:

> We begin by admitting that the fundamental ethical concepts are unanalysable, inasmuch as there is no criterion by which one can test the validity of the judgments in which they occur. . . . We say that the reason why they are unanalysable is that they are mere pseudo-concepts. The presence of an ethical symbol in a proposition adds nothing to its factual content. Thus if I say to someone, "You acted wrongly in stealing that money," I am not stating anything more than if I had simply said, "You stole that money." In adding that this action is wrong I am not making any further statement about it. I am simply evincing my moral disapproval of it. It is as if I had said, "You stole that money," in a peculiar tone of horror.[15]

In what must surely be regarded as the nadir of moral theorizing in this century, morality has been reduced to a nonrational expression of feeling. Just as the self has been split metaphysically into reason and desire, so language is split into the descriptive and expressive components, and meaning is split into the cognitive and emotive components. Statements of moral approval or disapproval are thus analyzed by Ayer as nothing more than emotional exclamation marks attached to descriptions of actions. In other words, for Ayer, saying that some action is bad or immoral amounts to simply describing the action with a certain tone of disapproval in your voice. The 'moral' element is the feeling of disapproval you have when you contemplate that action.

What's wrong with Ayer's view, and with all emotivism, is its fragmented view of the self, in which the rational and emotional parts have nothing whatever to do with each other. Reason is impoverished, emotion is impoverished, and there is no role for imagination. So conceived, there is no basis for rational critique in morality.[16] Consequently, once the emotive character of moral judgments has been established, there is nothing further for moral philosophy to do, since there can be no constructive work for reason in ethics. Ethics is reduced to metaethics, an inquiry into the logical and semantic status of moral utterances.

3. *Moore's intuitionism as the context of emotivism.* The emotivist assumption of a bifurcated self and the denial of any serious role for reason in morality is by no means an idiosyncratic position. In fact, it makes perfectly good sense in the context of the view of morality that came to dominate twentieth-century ethics as a result of the publication in 1903 of G. E. Moore's *Principia Ethica*. Moore almost single-handedly instituted the conception of moral philosophy as nothing but metaethics, and the unfortunate effects of his drastically narrow conception of the subject still plague philosophy today.

Without going into Moore's view in detail, it is useful to examine the way his work set the stage for denying reason an important place in morals. Despite his vehement championing of logical thought, careful analysis, and rigorous argumentation, Moore succeeded in virtually excluding reason from normative ethics. And, once rational argument was banished from normative debate, it was no surprise that emotivism arose as its logical successor.

Our question is, How was it possible for a view that insisted so strongly on philosophical rigor to end up disenfranchising reason within ethics? In *Principia Ethica* Moore boldly asserted that we could, at last, set ethics on a sure path if only we would learn to ask the right kinds of questions and would cease to concern ourselves with misleading and unanswerable questions. The proper questions for ethics were supposed to be of two different kinds: "What kind of things ought to exist for their own sakes?"[17] (in other words, What is good in itself?), and "What kind of actions ought we to perform?" (viii, i.e., What actions are right?).

It all seemed so clear and easy when stated in this way. One had only to find out what is good in itself (first question) and then to define 'right' as that action which is productive of the most good in the situation (second question). Questions of the second kind, that is, questions about what actions were right, were questions that could be answered because they required only causal knowledge of what actions were most likely to produce which effects. This was means-ends rationality, and such knowledge was held to be empirical. Questions of the first kind, about what is good in itself, were alleged to be questions about which "no relevant evidence whatever can be adduced: from no other truth, except themselves alone, can it be inferred that they are either true or false" (viii).

But this view of knowledge created a terrible predicament. The one and only subject matter of ethics, the good, turned out to be a subject for which no argument, rational discussion, or mustering of evidence was deemed relevant. 'Good,' on Moore's view, was an undefinable term: "If I am asked 'What is good?' my answer is that good is good, and that is the end of the matter. Or if I am asked 'How is good to be defined?' my answer is that it cannot be defined, and that is all I have to say about it" (6). Moore called 'good' a "non-natural property," that is, a property attaching to certain objects independently of their perceivable ('natural') properties. Some things and states were intrinsically good, and others were not, but you couldn't determine which were which by any survey of the natural properties of the thing or state in question. Hence, 'good' was held to be indefinable, since it could not be broken down into a set of natural properties possessed by some object or state of affairs. You either saw (intuited) that some state was good, or you did not.

The alleged indefinability of 'good' did not either logically or actually prevent Moore from proceeding to say a great deal about the good, so long as he avoided the dreaded "naturalistic fallacy," the fallacy of trying to define 'good.'[18] Moore concludes that any well-bred English gentleman who seriously reflects on this question will recognize that the good consists of certain valuable states of consciousness, "which may be roughly described as the pleasures of human intercourse and the enjoyment of beautiful objects. No one, probably, who has asked himself the question, has ever doubted that personal affection and the appreciation of what is beautiful in Art or Nature, are good in themselves" (188–89).

J. M. Keynes, in his moving story of the overwhelming effect that Moore had on the Bloomsbury 'Club,' has entitled this substantial normative part of Moore's view his "religion": "Nothing mattered except states of mind, our own and other people's of course, but chiefly our own. These states of mind were not associated with action or achievement or with consequences. They consisted in timeless, passionate states of contemplation and communion, largely unattached to 'before' and 'after'. . . . The appropriate subjects of passionate contemplation and communion were a beloved person, beauty and truth, and one's prime objects in life were love, the creation and enjoyment of aesthetic experience and the pursuit of knowledge."[19]

I do not deny the importance and goodness of such states of consciousness, but I think it is quite important to be critical of what is going on here from a social-psychological standpoint. In retrospect, it seems fairly obvious that Moore was doing nothing more than espousing the values and interests of his particular social and economic class (and of his local and historically situated aesthetic views), while at the same time claiming that they were timeless truths, grounded in the essential nature of things.

This is a clear paradigm of the kind of uncritical and unreflective self-affirmation that Charles Taylor discusses in "The Diversity of Goods." We affirm our principles and values as issuing from reason itself (or, in Moore's case, the nature of value itself), and we forget that our very conception of reason is itself just one more value among alternative values. And, since everyone in Moore's group shared similar values, argument and evidence were neither needed nor, if Moore was right about goodness as an indefinable nonnatural property, even possible. Either you did or did not experience the correctness of Moore's assertions. Either you did or did not see that certain states of consciousness possessed the nonnatural property of being good. Keynes, with obvious sarcasm, has described the process: "How did we know what states of mind were good? This was a matter of direct inspection, of direct unanalysable intuition about which it was useless and impossible to argue. In that case who was right when there was a difference of opinion? . . . In practice, victory was with those who could speak with the greatest appearance of clear, undoubting conviction and could best use the accents of infallibility. Moore at this time was a master of this method."[20]

Looking back, it would appear that Moore's intuitionism was an unfortunate episode in moral theory. By claiming that empirical evidence about who we are and how we function is simply irrelevant to the fundamental questions of moral philosophy, Moore initiated a serious decline in ethics (and in value theory generally) in this century, from which we are only beginning to recover. Quite simply, he so impoverished and marginalized reason that its only role in ethics was the determination of efficient means to ends and of probable causal connections. As G. J. Warnock has summed it up, Moore leaves us with a realm of *sui generis* indefinable moral qualities about which reason can say nothing. We are confronted with "a vast corpus of moral facts about the world—known, but we cannot say how: related to other features of the world, but we cannot explain in what way: overwhelmingly important for our conduct, but we cannot say why."[21]

Ironically, in spite of all the talk about a timeless realm of moral properties, what we find here is a stage set for moral relativism. For if we cannot reason about the good, then we are each thrown back upon our own, possibly idiosyncratic, sense of values, Moore's insistence on rigorous analysis notwithstanding. If you don't see that a certain state of affairs is good, then no amount of reasoning by me can logically compel your assent, for morality is ultimately not a matter of reason. MacIntyre is therefore correct in tracing a single thread of relativism from Moore's intuitionism, at the beginning of the century, to contemporary emotivism, which assumes the bifurcation of reason and desire, and relegates morality to emotions.[22] The unifying thread in this development is the denial of any role for reason (other than means-ends technical reasoning) in our moral deliberation and evaluation. We are left with no commonly shared rational means of adjudicating disagreements in moral matters. And all of this stems from the separation of reason from desire, that is, from a bifurcated, disunified self.[23]

KANTIAN-STYLE RATIONALIST ETHICS

Kant's view of the self. The second major set of objectivist orientations in contemporary ethics, those falling loosely within a Kantian model of moral theory, are equally committed to the split between reason and passion or desire.[24] As we saw earlier, Kantianism centers on the importance of pure moral willing. Kant argued that such a will—a will good in itself—is one that is free, and thus not causally determined by any aspect of its empirical being, such as feeling, sensation, or desire for an object. As a fact of human existence, such a good will exists *in* the world (insofar as we are embodied creatures), but it must not be *of* the world, that is, it must not succumb to the enslaving ways of the flesh. Bodily desire, and everything associated with it, is conceived as *external* to the moral self (i.e., as heteronomous). The self as moral agent is regarded essentially as a rational will, that is, as practical reason. Consequently, any motivation or desire rooted in our bodily experience is branded by Kant as a source of heteronomous causality that undermines our proper moral autonomy, defined as "that property of [will] by which it is a law to itself independently of any property of objects of volition" (*F*, 440).

Kant could secure autonomy of the will only by positing a metaphysical realm beyond, and not subject to, the empirical realm of natural causality. But this creates for Kant an obviously bifurcated self, a self that is somehow supposed to inhabit two metaphysical realms that are radically distinct, namely, a realm of natural causal necessity (where our bodies reside) and a realm of freedom (where our reason resides). Kant was never able to explain how these two utterly different domains—one governed by laws of natural causality and the other by rational laws of freedom—could possibly interact, as they must if morality is not a mere illusion.[25] He leaves us with reason inhabiting one metaphysical realm (of freedom) while our bodies, our empirical selves, inhabit the other realm (of nature).

No explanation is possible for how desire can fall under the commands of reason, nor how reason can have the motivating power of desire. In his introduction to Kant's *Religion within the Bounds of Reason Alone* John Silber traces Kant's attempts to find a place for a reason permeated with desire. In the *Foundations* Kant captured the notion that we are only fully free to the extent that we act morally, thereby realizing our true rational nature. But this entailed the problematic result that we could never hold a person responsible for immoral heteronomous acts (since they would then not be acting freely). So, in the *Critique of Practical Reason* Kant makes the apparent advance of dividing will into two aspects (*Wille* and *Willkür*), the former constituting the 'rational,' law-generating side of will and the latter consisting of our embodied capacity to make choices. In this way, will has both a rational side and a side tied up with our sensuous desire.

This additional splitting of the will simply repeats the bifurcation problem at a different level. It creates the "dismaying consequence that a person is still a person in possession of his freedom even if he rejects the law. Thus the law no longer appears to be related to the will as a condition of its being. The categorical imperative seems to resolve itself into a hypothetical one: if one wishes to be moral he must obey the moral law."[26] This move would entail that the moral law is not binding on us merely by virtue of our nature as rational beings. Such a consequence is disastrous for Kant's view that being a rational creature places us under categorical moral obligations.

Rawls's detranscendentalized Kantianism. Present day Kantians have dealt with these problems of the split self in various ways. Some, like Donagan, have insisted that Kant's view of practical reason is roughly correct and that, although Kant was much too causally deterministic about the natural realm, he was essentially correct in recognizing an irreducible metaphysical tension in the concept of a moral agent.[27]

Other Kantians, among whom John Rawls is the most prominent, have admitted that certain of Kant's metaphysical and epistemological claims are indefensible and must be revised in light of recent developments in philosophy. Rawls rejects both Kant's essentialism and his belief in absolute, transcendent rational foundations. Thus, whereas Kant can be seen as having reconstructed the Judeo-Christian moral tradition by detheologizing and rationalizing it, Rawls may be seen as transforming Kantianism by detranscendentalizing it, stripping away its most problematic metaphysical assumptions.[28]

Rawls's task, then, is to reconstruct Kantian liberal theory "within the scope of an empirical theory."[29] In place of Kant's ultimate metaphysical and epistemological assumptions Rawls claims to substitute conceptions of reason and moral personality that are not metaphysical, but rather are to be defined as the result of debate and rational agreement. No part of the theory is taken as an absolute foundation, and there is no reliance on self-evident truths or conditions on principles: "The search for reasonable grounds for reaching agreement rooted in our conception of ourselves and in our relation to society replaces the search for moral truth interpreted as fixed by a prior and independent order of objects and relations, whether natural or divine, an order apart and distinct from how we conceive of ourselves. The task is to articulate a public conception of justice that all can live with who regard their person and their relations to society in a certain way."[30] Rawls produces a theory in which a conception of the person, a conception of a well-ordered society, a view of reason, a set of moral principles, and a group of reflectively considered judgments about particular situations must all be balanced and made coherent, without any one aspect being immune to criticism or revision. "Justification is a matter of the mutual support of many considerations, of everything fitting together into one coherent view."[31]

I embrace Rawls's general conception of the reflective empirical nature of moral theory that eschews all reliance on essences, self-evident truths, analytic propositions, and a priori principles. But the question before us now is whether he has provided a satisfactory conception of the self and moral personality that avoids the problems inherent in the moral objectivist view that has been dominant since the Enlightenment. Can he be anti-essentialist and antimetaphysical, still produce a liberal theory, yet avoid the atomic and bifurcated self that seems definitive of the Enlightenment conception upon which liberal political theory is grounded?

I want to suggest that Rawls comes as close to pulling off this feat as one can, but that he does not fully escape the objectivist conception of the self that he inherits from the Enlightenment. Rawls thinks he can preserve the fundamental insights of our liberal moral and political tradition without succumbing to its metaphysical assumptions. Let us see whether this is true.

It is important to note that Rawls repeatedly reminds us that he is offering a theory of *justice,* and that a theory of morality would require, perhaps, some different or additional assumptions. He also makes it clear, however, that one could extend the structure of his theory to elaborate a theory of morality. So, I am proceeding on the assumption that the conception of the self would not be substantially different in a theory of morality, as contrasted with a theory of justice.

Just what *is* Rawls's conception of the self? Michael Sandel has argued the 'strong' reading, which presents Rawls as being unable to overcome the metaphysical assumptions of his Enlightenment heritage. He sees Rawls as Kantian in his insistence on the "primacy of justice" and the "priority of the self." Sandel argues that, for Rawls's Kantian conception, "justice is not merely one important value among others, to be weighed and considered as the occasion requires, but rather *the means* by which values are weighed and assessed. It is in this sense the 'value of values,' so to speak, not subject itself to the same kind of trade-offs as the values it regulates."[32] This primacy of justice has as its correlative notion the "priority of the self," for, as Rawls says, "each person possesses an inviolability founded on justice that even the welfare of society as a whole cannot override."[33]

Now in Kantianism it is the moral agent's metaphysical status as a *free, rational* creature that justifies the alleged priority of the self. As the basis of moral autonomy, freedom is the necessary presupposition of morality. Therefore, the self (as free moral agent) achieves a priority that requires that it must always be treated as an end-in-itself, and never merely as a means.[34]

Rawls, however, cannot follow Kant's strategy of positing a noumenal realm of transcendental subjects wholly beyond experience, who, as free and rational beings, are the source of moral value. To make such ontological assumptions would contradict Rawls's antimetaphysical and anti-essentialist commitments. Nevertheless, he does follow Kant in claiming that it is our capacity to make choices in a principled manner that defines our being. Consequently, the view of the self that is embodied in the conception of the 'original position' (from which the principles of justice are chosen) is one that stresses the *free choice* of ends, rather than any particular set of ends chosen.

Rawls thus rejects any sort of teleological view where 'the good' is first specified in terms of desired ends, and then 'the right' is defined as that which maximizes the good. Instead, right is defined prior to and independent of the good. Determining right action becomes a matter of choosing which rational principles are going to guide one's actions. It follows, on this deontological view, that "it is not our aims that primarily reveal our nature but rather the principles that we would acknowledge to govern the background conditions under which these aims are to be formed and the manner in which they are to be pursued. For the self is prior to the ends which are affirmed by it."[35]

On the face of it, this 'self prior to its ends' seems to be precisely that atomistic agent that we have been criticizing as a product of Enlightenment metaphysics. It is what Sandel calls a 'voluntarist' notion of moral agency, where whatever it is that constitutes a self as a moral agent or person does not, and cannot, change in and through the experience of various ends. Such a view would appear to rule out the conception of a self-in-process which could serve as the object of our ongoing quest for moral self-knowledge. Sandel explains that the voluntarist self can ask but one question, What ends shall I choose? but not Who am I? since the latter question presupposes that the identity of the self is not already given prior to our experience of various ends.[36]

Rawls has responded directly that Sandel's 'strong' interpretation does not necessarily follow from the view of the person set forth in *A Theory of Justice*.

> The description of the parties may seem to presuppose some metaphysi-
> cal conception of the person, for example, that the essential nature of
> persons is independent of and prior to their contingent attributes, in-
> cluding their final ends and attachments, and indeed, their character as a
> whole. But this is an illusion caused by not seeing the original position
> as a device of representation. The veil of ignorance . . . has no meta-
> physical implications concerning the nature of the self; it does not imply
> that the self is ontologically prior to the facts about persons that the par-
> ties are excluded from knowing.[37]

If correct, Rawls's response avoids the obvious inconsistency of claiming a fixed, atomic self while at the same time espousing his thoroughgoing rejection of metaphysical assumptions.

Owen Flanagan has argued at length that Rawls is not committed to an atomic self, and that most of Sandel's communitarian requirements concerning personal identity can be met within a Rawlsian framework.[38] He lists four principles built into Rawls's theory in various ways that present social, communal, and historical dimensions of people's identities: (1) the principle that self-respect and self-esteem depend partly on being respected by others whom one respects; (2) the idea of fellow-feeling, both for one's contemporaries and for future generations; (3) the fact that personal flourishing depends in several ways on living in a community; and (4) the idea that certain basic human goods (e.g., love, friendship, self-respect) require forms of social union among people. Flanagan has thus answered virtually all of the communitarian objections by a careful reading of what is required, as well as what is open as a possibility, within Rawls's theory.

However, this still leaves us with the question of whether, in light of Rawls's conception of the nature of a moral theory, he can avoid making at least some metaphysical commitments. In particular, does the very structure of his theory require a self defined prior to its ends or any relations it might enter into? It seems clear that the very fact that he must be committed to some conception of a person entails at least minimal metaphysical assumptions. That explains why Rawls immediately backs away from his denial of metaphysical commitments to the weaker claim that, although there may be some metaphysical presuppositions, "perhaps they are so general that they would not distinguish between the distinctive metaphysical views . . . with which philosophy has traditionally been concerned."[39]

Are Rawls's metaphysical assumptions about the self really innocuous? Among his assumptions are that moral agents are (1) free and equal rational beings that (2) have a 'sense of justice' (i.e., a capacity to formulate and act from a conception of justice) and (3) have a capacity to form a conception of their rational advantage and to pursue it as good. Is Rawls's conception of equality neutral to all metaphysical systems? Of course not, as he well recognizes, for it is certainly not affirmed by many non-Western ethical systems, such as Hinduism.

Even if we were to regard these fundamental attributes of moral personhood as metaphysically innocuous, however, Sandel does seem to be correct in observing that, as a form of liberal Enlightenment theory, Rawls's theory inherits the view that the self as moral agent is defined independent of the ends *it chooses*. This is the crux of Rawls's notion of the priority of right over good. In other words, the principle of right action or justice must be specifiable independently of any particular conception of the good, any end one might choose, or any attachments one might have.

At the level of constructing the theory, Rawls's view requires a (relatively) fixed rational agent as chooser of principles. And, at the level of action based on the theory, Rawls's view needs a chooser who *decides* which ends to adopt and pursue. But what if, as Sandel urges, our moral personhood is inextricably linked to the ends we pursue? Sandel calls this a 'cognitivist' view of moral personality, where one's identity as a moral agent is defined as developing over time through one's deliberations, choices, and actions: "For the self whose identity is constituted in the light of ends already before it, agency consists less in summoning the will than in seeking self-understanding. The relevant question is not what ends to choose, . . . but rather who I am, how I am to discern in this clutter of possible ends what is me from what is mine. Here, the bounds of the self are not fixtures but possibilities, their contours no longer self-evident but at least partly unformed."[40]

The Self in Process: The Unity of the Self and Its Actions

A historically situated self of the sort Sandel is describing develops as a continuity of an ongoing process. We find ourselves (as presently formed) thrown into evolving situations not entirely (or even chiefly) of our own making, in which we pursue all sorts of ends, some tied to bodily desires, others to personal attachments and institutional involvements, others to socioeconomic conditions, and still others to principles we think we have 'chosen.' For a self so conceived, morality is never simply a matter of willing correctly in accordance with some conception of practical reason. Rather, we come to regard a certain course of action as right or wrong, beneficial or harmful, enlightening or deluding, in and through our working out in thought and action just what it is that we *are* pursuing as an end. Morality defines the arena of commitment, reflection, and engaged exploration of possible actions in which the self struggles continually both to *find* and to *form* its identity within the mass of ends it finds itself pursuing.

To put this less obscurely, people do not have preestablished, fixed identities on the basis of which they then make choices from among a range of possible goods. Instead, our evolving identity emerges in and through the ends we come to seek, the relationships we establish, and the way others come to regard us. In a sense, we grope around for our identity, which is never a fixed or finished thing. It changes over time, while preserving some degree of continuity with our previous identities. That is why we can always be surprised by discovering new things about who we are, why we do what we do, and how others see us.

To sum up: The issue of whether or not Rawls has avoided substantial metaphysical assumptions about the nature of the self is a difficult question, which he has not, by his own admission, adequately addressed.[41] What remains undeniably clear, nonetheless, is that the Enlightenment (liberal) political tradition out of which Rawls's view emerges *does* present us with an atomic, bifurcated self. Consequently, Sandel's summary of his criticism of Rawls, while it may miss Rawls's intent and while it may be answerable in Rawlsian terms, does a nice job of capturing what is basically wrong with the objectivist conception of the self.

> For Rawls, reflection 'on the kind of beings we *are*' rather than on the kind of desires we *have* is not a possibility, first because the kind of beings we are is antecedently given and not subject to revision in the light of reflection or any other form of agency, and second, because Rawls' self is conceived as barren of constituent traits, possessed only

of contingent attributes held always at a certain distance, and so there is nothing *in* the self for reflection to survey or apprehend. For Rawls, the identity of the subject can never be at stake in moments of choice or deliberation. . . , for the bounds that define it are beyond the reach of the agency—whether voluntarist or cognitive—that would contribute to the transformation.[42]

The key point here—a point that is absolutely crucial for any adequate theory of moral personality—is that the self (i.e., that which constitutes moral personality) *is* at stake in moments of choice and deliberation. Human beings are not fixed quasi-objects that have an independent prior identity and *then* go about making choices from which they are distanced. We are, rather, beings in process whose identity emerges and is continually transformed in an ongoing process of reflection and action. Our actions express who we are, and they may also transform who we are at the same time. It is primarily this historical-temporal dimension of the self that objectivism cannot tolerate, for objectivism can find absolute principles of morality only by adopting a radically idealized conception of a fixed, universal self whose identity rests entirely in its capacity to choose ends and means. Correlatively, objectivism of this sort requires a corresponding fixed reason that can supply principles static and general enough to have the appearance of being universally applicable.

I am suggesting that what we need is an understanding of moral deliberation as being also an activity of self-understanding, critical self-reflection, and self-formation. In Sandel's words, "We must be subjects constituted in part by our central aspirations and attachments, always open, indeed vulnerable, to growth and transformation in the light of revised self-understandings."[43]

The central theme of this chapter is that neither emotivism nor Kantianism, which share objectivist assumptions about the nature of the self and which underlie much contemporary moral theory, can offer us an adequate conception of moral personality and self-identity. I take it as obvious, and have not, therefore, argued the case, that utilitarianism also shares this impoverished view of the self, when it defines the moral agent as an atomic, self-interested, means-ends reasoner who calculates what will produce the most good. What we need, instead, is an account of the self as both related to its ends (by way of possessing them) and yet distanced from its ends (so as to retain its individual existence). The self cannot *be* its ends, but then again it cannot be indifferent to or wholly distinct from its ends.

Dewey saw that our choices both express and re-form our self-identity.

> Now every such choice sustains a double relation to the self. It reveals the existing self and it forms the future self. That which is chosen is that which is found congenial to the desires and habits of the self as it already exists. . . . The resulting choice also shapes the self, making it, in some degree, a new self. . . . In committing oneself to a particular course, a person gives a lasting set to his own being. Consequently, it is proper to say that in choosing this object rather than that, one is in reality choosing what kind of person or self one is going to be. Superficially, the deliberation which terminates in choice is concerned with weighing the values of particular ends. Below the surface, it is a process of discovering what sort of being a person most wants to become.[44]

A self-in-process, which is what each of us is, is a self that is continually both searching for its identity (i.e., trying to find itself in its ends, actions, feelings, moods, attitudes, experiences) and is contemporaneously trying to form itself in accordance with its imaginative ideals of what it might be. Moral deliberation is primarily a matter of the way in which our imaginative ideals inform our exploration of possibilities for acting within a morally problematic situation. Therefore, in order to understand the nature of moral personality, we must consider more carefully the nature of human actions, their connection to the formation of the self, and their intimate relation to imaginative moral ideals. That is a task I now take up by examining the narrative context within which the self as moral agent develops.

The Narrative Context of Self and Action

The Narrative Character of Selfhood and Agency

In the previous chapter we examined what is wrong with the Enlightenment view of the person (as moral agent), as it has come to underlie most of modern moral theory. On that objectivist view moral agents are free and equal rational beings who by nature seek to maximize their satisfactions in accordance with their perceived self-interest. They have a separate faculty of desire that stands subject to the judgment and control of the faculty of practical reason. The self (as this free autonomous being) is defined prior to its ends and independent of the contexts it comes to inhabit. As free, a moral agent can choose which, if any, contextual features it will allow to influence its deliberations. Thus, the moral agent purports to choose freely what aspects of its physical, social, and cultural environment it will permit to have an effect on its actions.

Human beings are not at all like this. We are far more socially constituted, far more historically situated, and far more changeable than objectivism allows. The self is defined not only by its biological makeup as a physical organism, but also by its ends, its interpersonal relationships, its cultural traditions, its institutional commitments, and its historical context. Within this evolving context it must work out its identity.

As MacIntyre observes, our historical situatedness imposes considerable restrictions on who we can become: "In life . . . we are always under constraints. We enter upon a stage which we did not design and we find ourselves part of an action that was not of our making."[1] Say, for example, that a child is born into and raised within a particular family. She finds herself thrown into the role of a daughter, a role that involves social constraints she did not make and perhaps cannot alter. And no matter how much she may try to rebel against that particular role and her particular history, her very act of rebellion, her attempt to cast off that unwanted role, and her attempt to forge a new one all presuppose the prior existence of a socially defined role of 'daughter' within that cultural setting. Consequently, the decisions she makes are *always* framed within, or played off against, a highly complex, radially structured category of 'daughter.' In many of the mundane actions she performs, the fact of her being a daughter may be relatively unimportant, having few or no practical consequences. But, however much her role as daughter may recede into the background, it is nevertheless still part of the setting within which she acts.

No matter how 'free' I am, *I* (as a male) cannot adopt the role of radical lesbian separatist, any more than I can make it not the case that I have the family I have. Even if I should decide to 'disown' my family and should cease to communicate with them, part of my present identity is still inextricably tied up with them. To deny or repress this part of my identity would be a form of self-deception. I may try to create new roles, or to transform old ones, but I can do this only within a context that includes my family history and thereby constrains my possibilities in highly determinate ways.

Such constraint is not, however, absolute. It is a crucially important fact that these constraints on our identity are somewhat flexible. Each of us is living out a developing story over which we have a measure of control, however small, in forming our character. For instance, while I cannot *now* avoid being a father, there is a great deal of latitude in how I can live out or take up that role. The range of possibilities for realizing the role of 'father' is broad and diverse: the family patriarch, the sole breadwinner, the househusband, the derelict and irresponsible father, the father who abandons his family, and so forth. It is this flexibility in the way we may creatively play out our lives that is the basis for social change on a large scale.[2] If we are imaginative enough, committed enough, and courageous enough, we may actually find it possible to transform our roles, social practices, and cultural values in creative ways. Large-scale change of this sort is rare, but there are such cases: Gandhi's use of nonviolent resistance in India, Martin Luther King Jr.'s assault on racism, Susan B. Anthony's struggle for voting rights.

The 'self,' then, develops its identity by inhabiting characters embedded within socially shared roles and by creatively appropriating those roles, even to the point of coauthoring new ones. I stress coauthoring, because all of this imaginative exploration of possibilities is carried on in and through complex social interactions in which practices and forms of relationship are communally constructed. As a result, I can only come to know who I am, and discover who I might become, by seeing how it is that I play out various roles and inhabit various characters, or create new characters by an ongoing process that is never completed during my lifetime or beyond. I am *not* reducible to the roles I internalize, but neither do I have an identity utterly independent of those roles.

In this chapter, I want to examine generally the way in which the identity of a self and its actions are always dependent on imaginative frames, of which 'role' is but one instance. I will argue that, since we develop through time, that is, since the identity of the self is always a continuity of an experiential process over time, any adequate understanding of moral agency must recognize its temporal character.

Human beings are imaginative synthesizing animals. Every one of us is continually about the vital business of weaving together the threads of our lives. In order for us to have coherent experiences, to make any sense at all of what happens to us, to survive in our environment, and to enhance the quality of our lives, we must organize and reorganize our experience from moment to moment. In previous chapters we have seen some of the imaginative resources we have for this basic synthesizing activity that makes it possible for us to have any sort of understanding of our world and of ourselves. These resources include image schemas, prototype structure of categories, semantic frames, and conceptual metaphor and metonymy. These imaginative mechanisms make up a large part of our *understanding,* by which I mean, not just our beliefs, but rather our bodily, imaginative, socially constructed way of being in and inhabiting a world.

I now want to explore another form of imaginative synthesizing activity that brings *time* into the fabric of our lives. I will pursue Paul Ricoeur's suggestion that *narrative* provides the most comprehensive structure for grasping the temporal dimension of our moral selfhood and action. My view of action and selfhood as implicating narrative settings entails that *any adequate theory of morality will have to explain the central role of such narratives and other imaginative structures in moral deliberation.*[3] A central task for any moral theory, therefore, must be to understand how we narratively construct our lives and how our deliberations are framed by those narratives.

It is extremely important for my argument to stress the broad sense in which I will be using the term 'narrative.' *Prototypical* narratives are linguistic stories we tell to others and sometimes write down in words. They constitute spoken or written texts. I am going to raise the question of how far it is legitimate and useful to extend metaphorically the notion of narrative from explicit linguistic texts down to the level of broad (narrative) synthesizing structures within our very experience itself. I am going to argue that such a metaphorical extension of the term is not only legitimate but necessary, if we are to understand both our moral self-identity and the moral dimensions of the actions we perform. When I speak of the narrative or prenarrative structuring of our experience, therefore, I am using the term in this metaphorically extended sense.

It most definitely does not follow from this use of 'narrative' that every experience is a 'text' in the sense of a linguistic entity. We have seen already that there are nonlinguistic, nonpropositional imaginative structures in our experience (e.g., image schemas and conceptual metaphors) that are constitutive of our understanding. So, the narrative context of selfhood and action does not turn everything into a linguistic text. However, my sense of narrative does indeed entail that we are fundamentally interpretive animals in virtually everything that we do.

MacIntyre describes the narrative context of our self-understanding and our action as follows:

> man is in his actions and practice, as well as in his fictions, essentially a story-telling animal. He is not essentially, but becomes through his history, a teller of stories that aspire to truth. But the key question for men is not about their own authorship; I can only answer the question 'What am I to do?' if I can answer the prior question 'Of what story or stories do I find myself a part?' We enter human society, that is, with one or more imputed characters—roles into which we have been drafted—and we have to learn what they are in order to be able to understand how others respond to us and how our responses to them are apt to be construed.[4]

MacIntyre regards a moral agent as a character in, and coauthor of, an enacted experiential narrative. An agent is born into a web of narratives, and he or she must define their own end (*telos*) by means of a narrative quest. MacIntyre sees the ultimate human *telos* as this very activity of questing for narrative unity, and thereby pursuing some notion of the good. Actions, in turn, can have identity and meaning only within the context of such socially constructed narrative complexes.

As Owen Flanagan has pointed out, MacIntyre's suggestion that every meaningful human life must necessarily strive for various kinds of narrative unity is probably too strong a claim to be asserted without qualification.[5] Some lives involve discontinuities that undermine any possibility of an overarching narrative unity, yet they are not without moral significance, and we do not regard the person involved as lacking an identity. Flanagan cites the example of St. Augustine's conversion as a radical rupture in the unity of his previous life. Still, as we shall see, the quest for at least a loose narrative structuring of our experience is very basic to our being human. I thus want to examine the validity of MacIntyre's strong thesis concerning the narrative character of self and action.

MacIntyre's view entails that any adequate moral theory must give a central place to narrative (as a structure of our experience, and not merely as storytelling). I will argue that such narratives provide the broadest and most relevant descriptions of the meaning of an action and, therefore, that they are crucial to our assessment of its moral import. However, narratives make use of other imaginative framing devices (e.g., prototype structure, conceptual metaphor) which often give us perfectly adequate descriptions of a situation without rising to the level of narrative unity. Consequently, there may be an appropriate description of an action that is not obviously narrative. *That* description, however, will be embedded within ever more comprehensive frames, the ultimate of which will be a narrative. I will argue that an adequate moral theory must acknowledge the way we try to construct narrative unities that give us the means to criticize our present situation, explore avenues of possible action, and transform our identity in the process.

A Hooker's Tale

I begin with the more modest claim that human beings try to understand and justify themselves by constructing broad narrative contexts within which they locate their identities. We tend to see our lives, and those of others, narratively. We continually reinterpret and revise our narrative self-understanding. To see what I mean by 'narrative self-understanding,' consider the following true story.

She is a hooker, explaining how she first began to turn tricks for money. She is relating part of her life story, not just telling a story, but trying to reconstruct the narrative of her actual lived experience. Most important, she is explaining herself and her actions from a *moral* standpoint, trying to justify herself through a narrative.

> I was about fifteen, going on sixteen. I was sitting in a coffee shop in the Village, and a friend of mine came by. She said, "I've got a cab waiting. Hurry up. You can make fifty dollars in twenty minutes." Looking back, I wonder why I was so willing to run out of the coffee shop, get in a cab, and turn a trick. It wasn't traumatic because my training had been in how to be a hustler anyway.
>
> I learned it from the society around me, just as a woman. We're taught how to hustle, how to attract, hold a man, and give sexual favors

in return. The language that you hear all the time, "Don't sell yourself cheap." "Hold out for the highest bidder." "Is it proper to kiss a man good night on the first date?" The implication is it may not be proper on the first date, but if he takes you out to dinner on the second date, it's proper. If he brings you a bottle of perfume on the third date, you should let him touch you above the waist. And go on from there. It's a market place transaction.

Somehow I managed to absorb that when I was quite young. So it wasn't even a moment of truth when this woman came into the coffee shop and said, "Come on." I was back in twenty-five minutes and I felt no guilt.[6]

What is going on in this passage is the most existentially significant kind of rational storytelling one can engage in—giving a narrative account of one's life. This woman is trying to explain to another, and thereby to understand for herself, who she is, why she came to be where she is today, and how things work in her world. Most important, she is trying to justify herself morally in terms of the values and practices of her culture. She is trying to construct a narrative explanation that will be morally acceptable in her social and cultural setting.

I regard this account as a model of what each of us does every day—we live out narratives in our lives, we reconstruct them for our self-understanding, we explain the morality of our actions at least partly in terms of them, and we imaginatively extend them into the future. A brief examination of the hooker's tale illustrates the fundamentally narrative and imaginative character of our moral understanding and deliberation.

The first major point to emphasize is that this woman's narrative explanation is a response to some problem, uncertainty, loss of clarity, or lack of coherence in her situation. Moral reasoning is purposive. It is directed toward resolving indeterminate situations, solving problems about how to act, and justifying those actions to others. What count as appropriate standards of moral reasoning emerge in a context-dependent fashion relative to such purposes. The prostitute wants to justify her actions, to explain how certain things have happened to her, and to retain a sense of self-worth in the telling. Therefore, she must select appropriate details and order them in ways fitted to her purposes and the standards of narrative explanation sanctioned by her community and culture.

The fundamental form of such explanation is narrative. This does not mean that every time we engage in moral deliberation we are either calling up or telling ourselves stories. In our mundane moral deliberations we typically draw on a wide range of resources that are not overtly narrative. Sometimes we recall previous situations where we acted well or poorly that are similar to our present one, and so we use those as models to guide us (e.g., "Last time I was in a mess like this, I did X, when I should have done Y, so now I should do . . ."). Sometimes we try to imagine how those we regard as exemplary moral characters might act in our situation ("What would *she* do if she were in my shoes?"). And sometimes we consult conventionalized moral precepts or principles ("Lying never turns out to be for the best"). But in each of these cases there are broader narrative frameworks in the background which make it possible for us to grasp the meaning, importance, and relevance of a particular exemplar, anecdote, or principle. This is the basis of Richard Eldridge's suggestion that it is primarily through narrative that we begin to give concrete meaning to our moral principles and to understand how they might be relevant to the kinds of situations in which we find ourselves caught.[7] When we employ principles, then, or when we refer to various moral frameworks, images, or ideals, we do so always relative to an implicit, tacit narrative. I will give more substance to this central claim as we proceed.

This leads to a second major point—that both the order of narration and the principles of selectivity for relevant details are established within a culture. This sets up a range of constraints on what can count as moral reasoning and explanation, that is, of what stories one can live out and relate with plausible moral justification. Consider the order and sequence of the hooker's narrative, and the way she brings into her account just the right explanatory considerations at just the right points in her story.

1. *Time.* She starts by locating the episode in time relative to her entire life span ("I was about fifteen, going on sixteen"). She was very young, which is a crucial fact bearing on the extent to which we hold her responsible for her judgments and actions.

2. *Location.* Next, she establishes the spatial setting ("in a coffee shop in the Village"). The moral ambience of a Greenwich Village cafe is entirely different from that of the lunch counter in the Greensboro, North Carolina, Woolworth's, which is entirely different from a doughnut shop in Indianapolis. *Where* we find this young woman sets the entire tone for what follows.

3. *Extenuating circumstances.* Then, immediately, the initiating action (her friend rushes in, surprises her, and offers the chance for fifty bucks: "I've got a cab waiting. Hurry up"). The implications are, first, that she is forced into a quick decision without the opportunity for deliberation and, second, that the 'real'

choice was made by another who bears the responsibility for initiating the sequence of events.

4. *Action sequence*. After this there follows the rapid-fire sequence of events in succession: coffee shop, cab, trick, cab, coffee shop—a balanced structure that peaks with the ill-fated deed, and ends at the coffee shop where it began. She is carried along on the cresting wave of events which, though it brings her back to where she started in a spatial sense, actually deposits her in a moral space far removed from where she began.

5. *The moral*. Finally, the moral: "It wasn't traumatic because my training had been in how to be a hustler anyway." Training, habituation, and cultural role are used, once again, as extenuating circumstances. In only a few short lines of narrative we have been swept, as she was, from an innocent cup of coffee to an explanation of a life of prostitution.

Now the stage is set for a more general explanation and moral justification, which is nothing more than an elaboration of the 'argument' of the first paragraph of her account. She takes up again the various extenuating circumstances one by one.

1. *Sociopsychological conditioning*. She gives a more abstract account of the social and psychological cultivation of women in America as an explanation of her particular situation. The 'logic' is quite clear. This specific case (the woman's first trick that led to prostitution) is seen as merely an instance of a general pattern that controls the lives of all women, namely, "We're taught how to hustle, how to attract, hold a man, and give sexual favors in return."

The fundamental pattern or model here is metaphoric—SEX IS A MARKET TRANSACTION, which is related to the broader cultural metaphor LOVE IS A MARKET TRANSACTION. Though he doesn't call it metaphoric, Thomas Merton has analyzed the nature of this metaphorical framework, its pervasiveness in our society, and the ways in which it undermines the possibility of genuine love.[8] According to the concept of LOVE AS MARKET TRANSACTION, people are not persons, but 'products.' We are all engaged in trying to 'sell' ourselves, which requires packaging and advertising. We do not give ourselves to others. Instead, we 'make deals.' No 'deal' is final, for it lasts only as long as it is 'profitable.' Moreover, it is only reasonable for us to look constantly for more and better deals. Love becomes a mechanism for the satisfaction of instinctive needs, rather than a form of self-transcendence. Finally, life is a 'marketplace,' and love is 'free enterprise.'

Both the LOVE IS A MARKET TRANSACTION and SEX IS A MARKET TRANSACTION metaphors carry implicit narrative structure within them, insofar as they are spelled out narratively. We are protagonists entering into the arena of a highly competitive marketplace. We are in search of certain satisfactions, because we find ourselves in need. We must struggle with others (antagonists) for scarce resources and prized goods. We must use our wit and cunning to accomplish our ends. We enlist the aid of others along the way. We may come to moments of self-discovery, reversal, or triumph. In this way, the hooker calls up a narrative framework presupposed by the SEX IS A MARKET TRANSACTION metaphor.

2. *Development.* The explanation then shifts back in time, quite naturally, to the woman's youth. Now we are given a developmental narrative, which is another of our culturally accepted modes of explanation. It was at that early stage of her development that the practice of hustling was inculcated in her. We are to understand that her first trick at age fifteen was actually only one more manifestation of what she had been taught as proper for a woman. It is one of our culturally shared assumptions that age may excuse. We do not expect the young to be fully responsible, nor to have the requisite experience and wisdom to make the best choices about the conduct of their lives.

3. *Unanticipated events.* From there we move to the description of a *surprise* event. The woman is sitting innocently and unprepared over her coffee, when her friend rushes in and wisks her away to an event that radically changes her future. It all happens so suddenly ("I was back in twenty-five minutes"). Without sufficient time for moral deliberation, one cannot be held responsible for clear-headed judgment. Had she had more time to think things through, it might have been different.

4. *Economic conditioning.* However, we see immediately that, even if she did have more time, it might not have been any different. For there were even stronger influences than age and chance acting upon her. As a woman, she was subject to an overwhelming economic conditioning. One could not expect her to resist such an all-pervasive and long-term conditioning in hustling. Here she calls into play a widely held behavioristic model that regards us as animals determined by the particular complex of conditioning forces that act upon us. The behaviorist model is an example of a scientific and philosophical theory that works its way into popular culture and comes to serve as a folk theory for the explanation of action.

The woman makes her moral defense forcefully in terms of this behaviorist system, as she lists various conditioning forces to which all women are allegedly subject ("Don't sell yourself cheap," "Hold out for the highest bidder"). This is followed immediately by a statement of the accepted sequence of sexual expectations sanctioned by society: "The implication is it may not be proper on the first date, but if he takes you out to dinner on the second date, it's proper. If . . . on the third date, you should . . ." First date, second date, third date—the sequence builds up a kind of pressure, or, more accurately, a kind of *debt* that one ought to repay with sexual favors.

This pattern of interactive behavior is modelled on a business transaction. She is receiving goods and is expected to return goods of equal value, though of a different kind. We live in a society grounded on capitalist principles in which buying and selling are economic institutions. There is virtually nothing we will not sell, including power, fame, status, religion, political office, our name, and our honor. So, when the woman concludes that prostitution is for her just a "market place transaction," she further explains how she can keep her self-respect while turning tricks. It does not touch her. She is simply selling a service, like a massage, or a haircut, or a manicure. There was but ever so slight a difference when she moved from the economic transaction of dating (where she is paid in gifts, food, and entertainment) to the economic transaction of prostitution (where she is paid in cash, food, and entertainment). In the remainder of her narrative, therefore, it is not surprising that she devotes considerable attention to explaining how she kept her self-respect by regarding herself as engaged in a business transaction.

How ought we to regard the moral relevance of this woman's account? Is this merely a piece of after-the-fact rationalization, exemplary material for psychological and sociological study? Or is she doing *what we all do,* namely, constructing her life in an ongoing narrative process that is highly constrained by her culture, but that leaves room for making it *her* story? The objectivist retort is that her story is nothing but narrative rationalization that is irrelevant to a moral evaluation of her actions. A proper evaluation would supposedly require measuring her conduct by the principle that even she ultimately recognizes (namely, that selling sexual services degrades humanity in one's own person). Even more, the hooker comes to regret the drug dependency that she acquired in her effort to avoid facing up to the reality of what she is doing. So, the objectivist can acknowledge the importance of a full narrative account of the hooker's situation, but only as it seems useful for self-understanding and therapy. Moral principles are alleged to have their meaning and force independent of such narrative contexts, relying only on descriptions of actions as being of one *kind* or another, and thereby as falling under this or that principle in certain specifiable ways.

The fact that we do sometimes call up general rules in evaluating or justifying actions of various kinds can make it seem as though this is the essence of moral reasoning. After the fact, for instance, it is relatively easy to point out why the hooker shouldn't have acted as she did, and we might summarize our reasoning by saying that what she did was dehumanizing and degrading, and that she violated her moral integrity. But the merely apparent adequacy of this model of moral reasoning is an illusion, or so I shall argue, that is fostered by our forgetting that morally adequate descriptions of actions usually involve narrative contexts, that we cannot assess character independent of narrative setting, and that we can almost never decide (reflectively) how to act without considering the ways in which we can continue our narrative construction of our situation.

My view, then, is not that we don't have moral principles, but rather that such meaning, relevance, and guidance as they offer depends ultimately (though perhaps not always immediately) upon the narrative settings in which they have emerged and to which they are being applied. I will suggest that only within this fuller narrative context can we understand what the hooker (or anyone) has done, who she is, why she acted as she did, and how we ought to evaluate her character and behavior. Our final judgments, and her self-judgments also, may well accord with the pronouncements of an objectivist argument. But the difference lies in the way we came to those judgments and in the way we will regard the character of her action. Furthermore, it is crucial to see that *we ordinary humans* understand, deliberate, and evaluate within such narrative contexts, even though we are seldom aware of this. I want to examine the way our moral self-identity and the nature of our actions are situated within a narrative process that we actually live out in our developing lives.

The Experientialist Self

Human beings exist in and through time. Our character, our identity, emerges gradually over time and typically develops through various stages. Change over time is so important that ceasing our ongoing adaptation can lead to intellectual, aesthetic, social, spiritual, or moral disintegration, or, in extreme cases, even to bodily death. Moral deliberation is that dimension of this complex adaptive process which concerns the development of our character, the nature of our relations to others, and our ability to discern constructive solutions that realize possibilities for meaning and well-being in our interdependent lives. Morality thus pervades all aspects of our experience, and it cannot, therefore, be compartmentalized as merely one independent, self-contained component of our lives.

The conception of the self and of moral personality presupposed here has little in common with the objectivist self, that self defined as an individual metaphysical entity with an essential rational nature that issues in universal moral rules. Objectivism treats the self as existing and having its identity, both temporally and metaphysically, prior to its actions. It treats the self as retaining its essential structure—as rational will—regardless of the contingent acts it performs and the historical situations it inhabits.

In sharp contrast, the nonobjectivist, or experientialist view (as I shall call it), regards the person as a self-in-process. A person is never merely the brute physical organism of the body, nor is the person a metaphysically distinct spiritual substance utterly independent of, yet lodged in, the body. Rather, we exist as complex, self-transforming biological organisms in interaction with our physical, interpersonal, and cultural environments. Although most of these interactions occur beneath the level of self-conscious awareness, they are the basis of our inhabiting a world that is at once physical, social, and cultural. We inhabit this world both as beings who are *constituted by* sedimented cultural practices, institutions, and meanings, but also as *constituting* beings who can gradually transform dimensions of these preexistent, inherited structures of meaning and action.[9]

This experientialist view of the self is not nearly so abstruse or esoteric as it might sound. It is simply an account of what the least bit of reflection reveals about our identity: (1) We know that we are embodied creatures—our bodies are the locus of our concrete situatedness in the world. They are the site of our interactions, perceptions, relationships, and projects. (2) But we are not merely the material stuff of our bodies, for we are organisms, that is, we are incredibly complex organic unities with emergent properties that are possible only when certain levels of organization are achieved, and only within certain ecological settings. (3) We are imaginative (and, thereby, self-transforming) beings, for we can go beyond the givenness of our past experience by reflecting on our situation and developing novel organizations. In other words, we are creative at the level of organism-environment interactions, as we must be if we are to adapt to the continual change that characterizes our world. (4) However, our modest self-transcendence is not based on an allegedly radical freedom of a spiritual substance known as the free will. Instead, our freedom is the constrained freedom of a physically and culturally situated self-consciousness. We can transform our experience, but only within limits marked out by our biological and cultural being. There are general constraints imposed by the nature of our bodies and brains, by the symbolic systems we have inherited, and by contingent possibilities for action that are available to us at a particular point in history. These options constitute a horizon of possibilities spreading out around each of us. As we pursue selected options, the actions we take thereby open up new situations that change the contours of our experienced world. Consequently, we experience ourselves as 'in process' rather than as fixed metaphysical entities with unchanging identities.

Consider, for example, the situation of an Afro-American woman in the American South of the 1950s. On the one hand, the idea that she possesses a radical freedom is ludicrous. If anything, she appears to be utterly imprisoned by her physical, cultural, and historical identity. She is genetically a female with black skin. She is born into a socioeconomic condition that rigidly constrains the extent to which she can improve her situation materially and socially. She speaks a language that presupposes a conceptual system that recognizes only certain sorts of distinctions, categorizations, and connections. She finds herself under the authority of a political system that in fact, if not in principle, denies her the right to vote and excludes her from a broad range of privileges available to whites and members of different socioeconomic classes. The roles she can apparently play out are well-defined and, for the most part, highly limiting. For her, the idea of radical freedom is a cruel joke.

On the other hand, she is not without the resources to transform her situation and her identity in ways that reveal the measure of her modest freedom. There is latitude in the way she can live out and develop every role she inherits or adopts. She can develop certain of her physical and intellectual attributes and thereby open up for herself a range of possibilities for what she can experience and who she can become. She has the imaginative capacity to envision an identity that she might develop within the options open to her. She can introduce novel organizations in her interpersonal relations. She can perhaps muster the courage to sit at the front of the bus where 'Whites Only' are allowed, or to sit at the lunch counter reserved for whites alone. 'Free' acts such as these, in conjunction with collaborative sustained acts of a similar sort by other people, can sometimes lead to the sorts of radical social and political change that fools us into thinking that we have more freedom than we do, in fact, possess.

In short, this woman is *constituted* by forces, institutions, and historical circumstances beyond her control, and she simultaneously *constitutes* her identity by certain sorts of restrictedly free acts. That is the kind of limited, situated freedom we all possess.

If a moral agent has no fixed essence and no absolute inner core of being, then how does the self come to have an identity at all? The answer requires an explanation of the relation of the self to its actions, for, to recall Dewey's requirement, "the key to a correct theory of morality is recognition of the *essential unity of the self and its acts*."[10] This crucial relation is not simple or obvious. The self is both *related to* its acts (the acts are *mine*), and yet it is also *distanced from* them to a certain extent (I am not merely my acts).

An experientialist view takes the self and its acts as interwoven into a basic experiential process, and it thus regards the identity of the self as an emergent structure of an experiential process—a process of physical, interpersonal, and cultural interactions. That is, the self is not merely some object or substance, but rather an identity of an interactive process that characterizes and gives unity to a sequence of developing, related experiences.

I am going to explore the hypothesis that a person's identity as a moral agent is inextricably tied up with her quest for synthetic unity in her life, the most comprehensive form of which is narrative. In the hooker's tale we have already seen some of the primary ways in which both a person's identity and the nature of her actions are partially defined by imaginative structures and frames, chief among which is narrative.

Before spelling out my understanding of narrative structure as a mode of synthesis, I want to emphasize two important limits on my view of narrative. First, I am not taking 'narrative' as merely a story one tells as a way of organizing a prior, completed experience. Nor am I taking it as merely a linguistic form of fictional presentation. Narrative in my sense is not merely linguistic and textual. Rather, I shall argue that *narrative characterizes the synthetic character of our very experience,* and it is prefigured in our daily activities and projects. The stories we tell emerge from, and can then refigure, the narrative structure of our experience. Consequently, the way we understand, express, and communicate our experience is derived from and dependent on that prior narrative structure of our lives. And yet, because we are imaginative narrative creatures, we can also configure our lives in novel ways.

Second, although the particular descriptions of actions that we give will often not involve explicit narrative, they make use of various imaginative resources (e.g., image schemas, conceptual metaphor, and metonymy) for developing coherence and synthetic unity through a temporal sequence of events. I will argue, nevertheless, that our understanding of those action sequences and situations typically presupposes a mostly tacit narrative background. There is a narrative (or, at least, protonarrative) structure to experience, to our identity, and to action, which is the basis for our concern with verbal narratives that constitute the most pervasive mode of rational explanation we have.

To sum up, experience is *synthetic* all the way down, and narrative is our most comprehensive form of synthetic understanding. My hypothesis is that we cannot understand moral reasoning unless we place it within its proper narrative context and realize its narrative dimensions. Moral absolutism (as a form of objectivism) assumes that we can get definite descriptions of actions and agents in terms of concepts that can be brought under moral rules independent of context. I will argue that this account misses the temporal, historical character of our experience, which is organized at the highest level by narrative structure. Making judgments of the morality of an intention, action, or character requires that we first understand the narratives that frame the situation. To sum up, *only within a narrative context can we fully understand moral personality (the self) and its actions. The unity of the self and its acts is, in the broadest context, a narrative unity.*

The Cognitive Basis for the Narrative Construction of Meaning

Most of the myriad acts we perform every day, from picking up coffee cups to reading the newspaper to playing games with our children, are done for some purpose or other. Most of the time, we pursue these purposes with little or no conscious reflection or awareness, for the acts we perform are mostly routine. Nonetheless, the purposive element is almost always present, because we are constantly directing our energies toward realizing goals that are means to our more comprehensive goals of survival and flourishing. Virtually all of our actions, therefore, are situated within larger projects that jointly constitute the pattern and direction of our lives. These projects emerge from our individual and communal histories, which set out for us a range of activities that are meaningful and available to us at a given moment.

We strive for unity in our lives by situating our present acts within our history and by projecting ourselves into a future that somehow partly blends together our multiple understandings, values, and purposes. We spend an enormous amount of time and energy trying to construct significant unities in our lives, thereby minimizing the fragmentary, isolated, and insignificant episodes of our existence. It is through this evolving process that we both express our selves as presently formed and also transform ourselves as we stretch out toward our future.

Once we have managed our most basic project of survival, we immediately pursue apparent goods that we think will enhance the quality of our lives. Beneath all of this striving is our search for meaning in our lives, however we might define it, and however misguided we might sometimes be about what will really give our lives meaning and value. Our quests for physical gratification, sexual satisfaction, wealth, vocational success, fame, respect, moral or spiritual purity, and so forth, are all either subsidiary to, or partially constitutive of, our quest for meaningful, valuable lives.

What is it that distinguishes disconnected, unrelated, and episodic events falling randomly into sequences from meaningful actions? The answer is the synthetic unity supplied by cognitive models, metaphors, frames, and narratives— the overarching ordering that transforms mere sequences of atomic events into significant human actions and projects that have meaning and moral import. Every one of us is actively plotting our lives, both consciously and unconsciously, by attempting to construct ourselves as significant characters within what we regard as meaningful life stories.[11]

Owen Flanagan observes, however, that we don't do this *all* the time and that some of our lives are more disjointed than unified.[12] But we nevertheless do see ourselves at least minimally in roles that fit within broad narratives, and we do try to find *some* unity within our lives, and thus to make some sense of them. Even when 'sense making' is not our primary occupation, we pursue some measure of synthetic unity in our experience, just by virtue of our acting to pursue goals. As a result, we come to understand and evaluate the morality of our character, intentions, and actions within the context of imaginative models and frames that give partial syntheses to our manifold and variegated experiences. Our cultural and individual narratives are the broadest synthetic structures we have for making sense of our lives.

I want to explore the origin and nature of narrative structure in our lives. My hypothesis is that narrative unity emerges through the various kinds of imaginative synthesizing activity by which we achieve coherence within a temporal sequence of events. The stories we find ourselves living out and telling to ourselves and others can be meaningful to us precisely because of the way they make use of imaginative cognitive processes and models that make it possible for us to have any coherent, unified experience at all.

My argument, which is already underway in this and earlier chapters, has the following form: (1) We are basically beings in process, synthesizing creatures, whose bodies locate us within a world that is at once physical, social, moral, and political all intertwined. (2) We are situated within a tradition and culture that supplies a stock of roles, scripts, frames, models, and metaphors that are our way of having a world, understanding it, and reasoning about it. (3) Moral judgments occur within this biological-cultural background and make use of these imaginative tools (e.g., as when the hooker appropriates the SEX IS A MARKET TRANSACTION metaphor in framing her experience). (4) As the most comprehensive synthesizing process, narrative plays a role in organizing our long-term identity and in testing our scenarios in making moral choices.

In order to see how narrative comes to play such a formative role, let us now consider briefly some of the ways in which narrative structure makes use of imaginative devices in our experience. In his exploration of the role of narrative meaning in legal reasoning Steven Winter has given an outline of some of the cognitive structures that underlie prototypical narratives.[13] Following Ricoeur, Winter notes that in order for an account of events to become a story it must pass beyond being a mere succession of events in serial order to become a "configuration."[14] What is required is a synthesis of parts into a unified whole with a certain structure, one which, as Aristotle was first to note, "has a beginning, middle, and an end" (*Poetics* 50b).

This beginning-middle-end structure is an instance of an even more basic recurring imaginative pattern—the SOURCE-PATH-GOAL schema[15]—that structures much of our bodily movement and perception, and that is present in our understanding of temporal processes (via the metaphor of TIME IS A MOVING OBJECT[16]). The SOURCE-PATH-GOAL schema consists structurally of a starting point, a contiguous series of intermediate points, and an end point. This image schema underlies the structure of stories that typically *start* at some point in time, *move through* a series of more or less connected intermediate events, and *end* with some culminating event. The pervasive SOURCE-PATH-GOAL schema is evident in Ricoeur's description of prototypical story structure: "To *follow* a story is to *move forward* in the midst of contingencies and peripeteia under the *guidance* of an expectation that finds its fulfillment in the 'conclusion' of the story. . . . It gives the story an '*end point*,' which, in turn, furnishes the *point of view* from which the story can be perceived as forming a whole. To understand the story is to understand how and why the successive episodes *led* to the conclusion."[17]

The SOURCE-PATH-GOAL schema is operative on at least three levels in stories. First, stories often involve actual physical journeys of characters from a starting point, along a path, toward some destination. Second, we *follow* the story itself metaphorically along its path, as it proceeds from start to finish. Third, via the PURPOSES ARE DESTINATIONS metaphor, we can understand all purposive activity metaphorically as movement (physical or mental) directed toward a goal (physical or abstract), according to the following mapping:

The PURPOSES ARE DESTINATIONS Metaphor

Motion in Space		*Purposive Action*
Physical starting point	$\longrightarrow$	Initial state
Motions along a path	$\longrightarrow$	Intermediate states
End point (physical)	$\longrightarrow$	Final state/goal

The PURPOSES ARE DESTINATIONS metaphor has as specific instances the LONG-TERM PURPOSEFUL ACTIVITIES ARE JOURNEYS and LIFE IS A JOURNEY metaphors. In chapter 2 we saw how the LOCATION part of the EVENT STRUCTURE metaphor is based on the SOURCE-PATH-GOAL schema. Any temporal process can be understood metaphorically as movement along a path, with stages of the process corresponding to points along the path. If PURPOSES ARE DESTINATIONS (and thus purposeful activity is a form of journey), then LONG-TERM PURPOSEFUL ACTIVITY IS A JOURNEY is one specific instance of the general EVENT STRUCTURE metaphor. Since living a life is a long-term purposeful activity, too, life can be understood metaphorically as a journey along an abstract metaphorical path toward a final destination. What all three of these forms of purposeful activity have in common is that they are each metaphorical extensions of the SOURCE-PATH-GOAL schema, according to the following hierarchical structure:

Movement through space from point A to point B.

$\downarrow$

Purposive action (either physical or nonphysical)

$\downarrow$

Long-term purposeful activity

$\downarrow$

Living a life

There is thus an inheritance hierarchy[18] established here, in which each 'higher' level metaphorical system (e.g., LIFE IS A JOURNEY) inherits the image-schematic structure of the levels below it (e.g., LONG-TERM PURPOSEFUL ACTION IS A JOURNEY).

We can now explain one reason why narrative is an eminently appropriate mode of explanation for human action. All forms of action (from mundane tasks, to large-scale projects, to life plans) can be understood metaphorically as journeys. The basis for the isomorphism across each of these domains is the SOURCE-PATH-GOAL schema. Therefore, between different forms of purposeful activity, on the one hand, and narrative as journey, on the other, there is a structural isomorphism—they each involve the SOURCE-PATH-GOAL schema elaborated metaphorically to cover all forms of temporal process. The SOURCE-PATH-GOAL schema, by means of various metaphorical mappings, relates patterns in domains of experience as diverse as physical travel, long-term purposeful activity, following the connection of episodes, and grasping the character's intentional states and actions.

Moreover, as simple as the SOURCE-PATH-GOAL schema is, it has sufficient internal structure to determine the structure of prototypical stories. Given the parts of the schema, that is, starting point, intermediate path, and end point, we can use what we know about journeys to fill out our model of narrative.

1. Whenever there is movement along a path there must be something that moves. In typical stories it is a person in pursuit of some end, either by a physical journey or by an intellectual or spiritual quest (a metaphorical journey). This literal or metaphorical traveller is often the protagonist of the story.

2. Travellers cannot make journeys unless certain enabling conditions are met. These conditions may be material (use of a vehicle, sufficient fuel, money), or they may be social (cooperation of others, permission to take a certain route). Metaphorical travellers (or protagonists) must, therefore, have their own resources (material, psychological, or intellectual), and they are subject to various enabling conditions (of a psychological, social, institutional, or political sort).

3. Travellers may encounter obstacles that must be overcome if their journey is to proceed. One will either be turned back by the obstacle, go around it, or overcome it by force. Such obstacles can be actual physical objects or persons, or else they can be (metaphorically understood) states of character or social or legal constraints.

4. Thus, there arises an *agon*, a struggle or conflict, around which the narrative turns. The story comes to its fulfillment by the way this *agon* leads toward a resolution of some sort, or fails to achieve a resolution we have come to expect.

What I have been describing is the basic mapping that exists between the three domains of spatial movement, journeying, and story structure, based on the underlying SOURCE-PATH-GOAL schema as follows:

The STORIES ARE JOURNEYS Metaphor

Spatial movement	*Journey*	*Story*
Moving object ⟶	Traveller ⟶	Protagonist
Initial conditions ⟶	Enabling conditions ⟶	Setting
Starting point ⟶	Point of departure ⟶	Beginning
End point ⟶	Destination ⟶	Conclusion
Obstacles ⟶	Difficulties ⟶	Antagonist/difficulties
Interacting forces ⟶	Conflict ⟶	*Agon*

The SOURCE-PATH-GOAL schema is thus the basis for our sense of stories as both literal and figurative journeys. And it is the isomorphism between the obstacle or difficulty (in the journey model) and the *agon* (in the story structure) that becomes crucial in the relevance of narrative to moral deliberation, since our moral dilemmas typically arise as conflicts with our experience.

The role of the *agon* in narrative also typically involves an image schema for BALANCE. A story will often begin with an initial situation characterized by a balanced, harmonious state, either the psychological state of the protagonist, family harmony, or a balanced social or political order. But this balance is soon upset, creating a deep tension. Something is lacking emotionally, romantically, occupationally, politically, or religiously. Or perhaps certain forces (natural, psychological, political) fall out of balance. Strife, tension, loss of meaning, dissolution of institutions, and spiritual malaise may follow. The story develops around attempts to restore the initial harmony or to forge some new harmony that restores the normative BALANCE.

In combination, the SOURCE-PATH-GOAL and BALANCE schemas provide the basic structure of prototypical narratives. Nonprototypical narratives are, for the most part, metaphorical variations of these underlying image-schematic structures. For instance, in narratives of psychological struggle, certain character traits of the protagonist that undermine his or her psychological health, well-being, or fulfillment may be the (metaphorical) 'antagonist.'

We can also explain nonprototypical stories where there is no resolution of conflict, or where the story seems to 'go nowhere.' Stories without a resolution leave us frustrated and unsatisfied precisely because we bring to any story expectations established by the prototypical cases in which there *are* resolutions. Unresolved stories are those that lack an *end point* on the metaphorically interpreted SOURCE-PATH-GOAL schema. Stories that 'go nowhere' are stories that lack *any path at all*. They are experienced as frustrating because they conflict with our expectations for SOURCE-PATH-GOAL structure in narrative development, and in action generally.

I have sketched only an idealized model of the structure of prototypical stories. It is constructed out of certain simple image-schematic structures, such as SOURCE-PATH-GOAL and BALANCE. I have mentioned only these two, but there are others, such as schemas for COMPULSIVE FORCE, ATTRACTION/REPULSION, CENTER/PERIPHERY, CYCLIC ACTIVITY, that are the basis for metaphorical and metonymic mappings that give rise to variations on prototypical story structure.

The main point of this section has been to examine some of the imaginative elements (e.g., image schemas and metaphors) that make up prototypical narratives, in order to see how and why narrative provides the most comprehensive synthesizing structure for our life experiences. This does not mean, of course, that we can't understand situations or reason about them unless we explicitly call up some narrative framework. As I acknowledged earlier, we have all sorts of imaginative framing devices (e.g., idealized cognitive models, metaphors, metonymies, scripts) for making sense of our experience that do not rise to the generality of narrative unity. Still, these imaginative resources are themselves typically situated within the context of overarching narratives, which keep the episodes of our mundane existence from being isolated, unrelated events. To the extent that our lives are not merely a series of disconnected, atomic events, with no larger coherence to give them meaning, there must be something that ties the events of our lives together in a significant synthesis.

My claim is that most of this synthesizing activity is done by imaginative structures and that narrative structure provides the most comprehensive synthetic unity that we can achieve. This is not to deny that our lives are shot through with gaps, disjunctions, reversals, fractures, and fragmentations that constitute what Ricoeur calls the 'discordance' of human existence. Yet we *strive* for meaning, coherence, and narrative unity, even if it is never fully attainable. In Ricoeur's terms, both narratives and human lives have a "discordant concordance," an ineliminable tension that resists our attempts to construct a total unity and harmony.

Our striving for narrative unity establishes the moral arena in which our character, thoughts, and actions acquire moral import. What makes narrative so unique and indispensable for moral reasoning is that it alone captures the full significance of two crucial dimensions of human life. (1) Narrative supplies and reveals the themes by which we seek to unify the temporal, historical dimension of our existence, and without which our lives would be a meaningless jumble of disconnected events. (2) Narrative can illuminate purposes, plans, and goals, which are the forms by which our lives have some direction, motivation, and significance for us. There is no other cognitive-experiential structure that blends these two basic dimensions of human existence. Consequently, while we can capture certain aspects of our experience via concepts, models, propositions, metaphors, and paradigms, only narrative encompasses both the temporality and the purposive organization at the general level at which we pursue overarching unity and meaning for our lives.

We might suppose, for example, that we understand a certain situation solely via a 'restaurant' script, evaluating our actions relative to the appropriate behaviors specified by that scenario. We might suppose that we evaluate the hooker's actions solely in terms of moral precepts, such as "Never degrade your humanity by using yourself merely as a means only to some satisfaction." We might suppose that discovering a basic metaphor (e.g., SEX IS A MARKET TRANSACTION) would be sufficient to understand the moral dimensions of a particular situation. But such suppositions are mistaken.

On the contrary, in each of these cases, the meaning and relevance of the script, principle, or metaphor depends ultimately on a larger narrative setting. The SEX IS A MARKET TRANSACTION metaphor, for instance, does not carry its moral import encapsulated within it, like the content of a container. Its moral significance depends on its role in the trajectory of a life in quest of a certain kind of narrative unity or coherence. We can neither understand nor judge the hooker's life outside the context of the narrative of her strivings. Similarly, the principle prohibiting the use of oneself merely as a means to some end has meaning and force in a particular situation only because it serves as a kind of summary of an ideal we have of a well-lived life that realizes certain values and sustains certain forms of community. So, behind, beneath, and surrounding the various imaginative devices we use to make sense of our lives lies a narrative framework or a cluster of developing narratives. Narratives are the means for configuring our lives, and they undergo from time to time various transformations[19] or refigurations through our individual and communal acts.

The Narrative Structure of Human Action

Narratives can embody our moral ideas and can give us the means for exploring possible actions within concrete day-to-day situations that make up the moral fabric of our lives. Our earliest encounter with explanation comes in the form of stories told to us by our parents. From the beginning we must learn how to construct our own story fragments in response to our parents' questioning of our actions. "*How* did *that* happen?" screams Dad, as the goldfish flops wildly on the wet carpet, and the four-year-old's mind searches frantically for a story that concludes with a flopping goldfish yet doesn't implicate her. In one *Calvin and Hobbes* cartoon Calvin explains to his mother that he couldn't possibly be expected to have cleaned his room, because he just returned from a state in which his body suddenly became larger than the whole earth. But this won't answer Mom's 'why' question ("Why haven't you cleaned your room?"), because it doesn't conform to the rather strict (overly strict according to Calvin's way of thinking) forms of narrative that Mom and Dad deem appropriate.

We thus make our first struggling, halting attempts at rational explanation by constructing narrative unities out of our confusing experience, in response to the recurrent who, what, when, where, why, and how questions that haunt us throughout our childhood and into our adulthood.

As Paul Ricoeur has argued, such explanatory stories are both elicited and supported by the narrative character of human action itself.[20] What is it, Ricoeur asks, that distinguishes a mere physical *event* from a human *action?* His answer is that what we regard as prototypical actions are distinguished structurally from mere events insofar as they bring into play a conceptual network consisting of the following features:

1. *Goals*. Actions are directed toward goals, which ordinarily consist of events or states we desire to realize. These goals are occasionally fixed, determinate situations that we can consciously form a conception of prior to our acting. More often, however, they are ill-defined, are not wholly conscious, and become determinate only in and through our action. In other words, most of the time we become clear about our goals, if we ever do, through a gradually dawning awareness that our dispositions and actions are moving us in a certain direction, toward a certain end that emerges slowly and partially over the course of a sequence of actions.

Goals are values for us. They take on an importance to the extent that we are willing to muster our resources toward realizing them. They depend on our interests, both conscious and unconscious. They have moral implications for our lives and the lives of those around us.

2. *Motives*. Actions are motivated, which is to say that we can partially explain them by giving *reasons* why they were performed. Motivations need not be consciously or reflectively present in order for us to act, but there can be neither action nor explanation of action without reference to them. The very notion of action carries with it implicitly the possibility of 'giving an account' of what we

have done and why we have done it. It does not follow from this, however, that we can always, or ever, fully plumb the depths of our motivations. What is going on in our unconscious is usually so complex and so hidden, fragmented, or repressed that we are hardly ever likely to grasp it reflectively.[21]

3. *Agents*. Both the motivations and the goals that figure in a given action are those of the agent of that action, the person whose action it is. The act is *her* deed, so that she becomes responsible for it and some of its effects on other agents. The agent's identity emerges in and through her actions, but is not identical with them. It is, rather, that which gives those actions a measure of unity and an identity as *hers,* or *his,* or *mine,* or *ours.* Here again, caution is necessary, for we cannot discount notions of agency that go beyond the individual subject (as in "Something bigger than both of us is at work here"). However, since we take humans as prototypical agents, conceptions of nonhuman agency will be metaphorical extensions from prototypical human agency.

4. *Contextual circumstances*. Actions are embedded within morally significant contexts that determine their character. The idea of a 'basic action'[22] as a morally neutral atomic unit of behavior is highly suspect. Of course, there is something fundamental about our *bodily* movements, since they are the locus of our actions in the world. We can identify those movements by physical descriptions, such as 'flipping the light switch.' That is why we describe thousands of daily acts with such simple phrases that allow us to understand perfectly well what is being talked about.

Bodily movements, taken by themselves, however, are very seldom actions. They are typically identifiable as actions only within some context that gives them a specific character. Even the smallest, most trivial mechanical acts get their meaning and relevant description from the larger frames in which they are embedded. Those larger contexts, in turn, have moral dimensions that color our simplest physical acts. 'Flipping the light switch' is thus not an irreducible smallest unit of unmediated behavior. Notice that it can be broken down further into constituent parts, such as muscle contractions or even neural firings. The 'basicness' of an action depends on what we can perceive, how our bodies work, how we interact with things, and what our interests and purposes are. We understand these supposed simple acts only because we presuppose a much larger context in which they get their point, purpose, and meaning.

Therefore, even though we can speak of the act of flipping the light switch, we only flip light switches within larger frames that supply the relevant human description of the act, such as "turning on the light to surprise an adulterous spouse," "shedding more light on the workbench so that we can repair the broken skateboard," "providing an enlightening example in a seminar on action theory," or "flipping the switch because we are bored and it is something to do." Moreover, we understand these longer descriptions within larger and larger embedded contexts. In this way almost all action is social, because the meaning of any action implicates socially constructed frameworks, symbolic mediation, and communal practices.

5. *Interaction with others.* Frequently our actions involve others, with whom we either cooperate or struggle. They become either allies or antagonists in courses of action that can have significant moral consequences.

6. *Meaningful existence.* No matter how routine or trivial an action may seem, it is always part of a larger project, namely, the agent's attempt to live a meaningful, fulfilled life. Even acts of drudgery and extreme toil that are done just to survive are performed against the background ideal of a life that is worth living, or that we hope will become worthwhile if we can survive our present struggle. Every action is thus part of the living of a life that involves misfortune, luck, happiness, suffering, and fulfillment.

7. *Responsibility.* Because agents' actions are *theirs,* they are held responsible for many of the effects of their acting. Agents are thus considered to be *answerable* for what they do. We hold others, and ourselves, responsible because we recognize moral consequences of actions and because we feel our interrelatedness and interdependency in performing our actions.[23]

These seven structural features, which form the conceptual network of action, are not themselves intrinsically narrative. They form the synthetic basis in our experience out of which narrative structure emerges. Ricoeur calls this the "prenarrative" character of human action, or what might perhaps more aptly be called the *proto*narrative dimension of experience.

Ricoeur argues that it is the *temporal* character of human experience that calls for narrative ordering. A particular action abstracted from the flow of experience might appear to be a discrete, isolated unit that does not necessarily entail any narrative structure. But our actions are, for the most part, not atomic individual occurrences standing as instantaneous events. Rather, they are intertwined into an experiential web that develops over time. Narrative is the most comprehensive means we have for constructing temporal syntheses that bind together and unify our past, present, and future into more or less meaningful patterns. Ricoeur's fundamental thesis is that *"time becomes human to the extent that it is articulated through a narrative mode, and narrative attains its full meaning when it becomes a condition of temporal existence."* [24] What the narrative does is to forge unified wholes out of what would otherwise remain disconnected sequences of mere events. These wholes emerge over time, as structures of our temporal existence. Such unification is possible only because our experience is already synthetic in its structure, with narrative being the most comprehensive form of synthesis.

MacIntyre also stresses the central importance of narrative as the fundamental form for the fullest explanation of an action. He argues that actions presuppose settings, settings have histories, and history is irreducibly narrative:

> We cannot characterize behavior independently of intentions, and we cannot characterize intentions independently of the settings which make those intentions intelligible both to agents themselves and to others.
> . . . A social setting may be an institution, it may be what I have called a practice, or it may be a milieu of some other human kind. But it is central to the notion of a setting . . . that a setting has a history, a history within which the histories of individual agents not only are, but have to be, situated, just because without the setting and its changes through time the history of the individual agent and his changes through time will be unintelligible. [25]

The crucial notion in this argument is that of intelligibility. Narratives are basic at the level of making our actions, motives, and thoughts intelligible. In particular, it is the historical character of actions and their settings that requires narrative explanation. In order both to understand our action and to give an account of ourselves to others, we must provide two kinds of historical accounts: one that traces out relevant causal sequences and another that locates our actions within the history of their settings. As MacIntyre concludes, "Narrative history of a certain kind turns out to be the basic and essential genre for the characterization of human action." [26]

The strongest objection to the central role I am claiming for narrative takes the following form: [27] Narrative may give us the most comprehensive, subtle, and detailed understanding of an action, but it is not typically a precondition for being able to grasp the morally relevant dimensions of an action. At any point in time we can acquire a kind of synchronic understanding of a situation necessary for our purposes, granted that this understanding will make use of various imaginative devices, such as idealized cognitive models, metaphors, frames, scripts, and so forth. A diachronic understanding, one that connects events through time, will require narrative, precisely because it is historical. According to this view, all we really need in order to understand the action description "I was married on September 16, 1972" would be our culture's idealized cognitive model of marriage as a social institution, plus a model of the calendrical system. Knowing about the history of this institution, about the history of me and my wife, about our families, and so forth, would be perhaps interesting, and it would give me a fuller account, but it is not necessary for understanding the action. Narrative, therefore, is not the basic form for understanding of actions.

My reply to this fundamental objection is to observe that even our most basic idealized cognitive models (for such things as marriage) presuppose, and are embedded in, narrative. Our allegedly 'synchronic' understanding is but a slice of a more fundamental diachronic development of experience. I do not deny that most of our understanding makes use of imaginative devices that are not explicitly narrative. Yet they *are* implicated in, and themselves implicate, narrative structure. I understand myself as 'bridegroom' when I call up my wedding day. But 'bridegroom' is a *role* in a narrative.

The merest understanding of what marriage means involves understanding a change of state, and so implicates the broader perspective of a life history. Marriage is a state one is naturally out of, which one enters into intentionally through institutional acts, and which one cannot easily get out of. The process of becoming married is embedded within the context of a prototypical life story: A man starts out as a bachelor who is sexually available and open to various forms of relationship. Marriage changes the nature of his relations, both to the woman who is now his spouse and to others with whom he has relationships. He is no longer available to others in the same way, and his relation to them changes accordingly. He enters into a family relationship, which often involves the rearing of children. In short, marriage typically involves a connected sequence of scenarios that are woven together into a broader narrative framework.

Moreover, the institution of marriage also has a history, which lies in the background, on the horizon, when I mention marriage in a certain year, at a certain place, in a certain culture. Marriage today in America is not what it was in the 1930s, nor what it was in England in the fifteenth century. It is not even what it was in 1972.

Finally, the fact that I mention my wedding twenty years after the fact, and you know that I am still married, brings into play a historical dimension that bears on the meaning of that event in 1972. Merleau-Ponty's point about "all our presents being present in my own present" is quite true. But this does not mean that my present understanding somehow expunges the historical and narrative dimension of things, as though a synchronic understanding could ever really extract itself from time. On the contrary, the narrative dimension of human experience is present (as horizon, background, etc.) in my own present, even though I am hardly ever conscious of this.[28]

The claim I am making is the strong one that human action is irreducibly narrative in character and that, consequently, moral theory must give a central role to the narrative structure of our experience and to the narrative form of our moral deliberations and explanations. We cannot abstract from narrative settings and hope to assess adequately the moral character of an action. In MacIntyre's words, "It is now becoming clear that we render the actions of others intelligible in this way because action itself has a basically historical character. It is because we all live out narratives in our lives and because we understand our own lives in terms of the narratives that we live out that the form of narrative is appropriate for understanding the actions of others. *Stories are lived before they are told*—except in the case of fiction" (emphasis added).[29]

Stories are lived before they are told, because our very experience is narratively structured, in the broad sense of narrative that goes beyond its linguistic and textual instances. We live out our lives narratively, even though there will always be many random, dissociated acts in our daily experience that fall outside our synthesizing strategies.

The Narrative Character of Experience

We are now in a position to consider the question of whether narrative understanding is merely an artificial and forceful imposition of a story order upon a human experience that is in itself disconnected, incoherent, and absurd. Does experience actually have a protonarrative structure that calls for narrative understanding?

To begin answering this question, I take it as obvious that it is impossible to demonstrate that life is not ultimately absurd or meaningless. It is a fact of life that we are unable to escape sequences of events that conspire, by their brutality, incoherence, and apparent senselessness, to overwhelm us with a sense of the absurdity of it all. At the same time, however, we humans are creatures who instinctively pursue meaning in our lives. We live in search of significance and fulfillment, just by virtue of our trying to survive and flourish. To go on from day to day we must plot out our lives. That is to say, we must construct narrative unities that make it possible for us to predict future events, criticize our current situation, solve (at least tentatively) certain practical problems, resolve certain indeterminacies in our present state, explore possibilities for fruitful action, and transform our identity.[30] The fact that doing these sorts of things does often make it possible for us to more or less successfully order our lives and pursue our ends, or to find a limited measure of fulfillment, means that we are not merely living an illusion, but rather creating a reality!

Radical skeptics can never be refuted on their own terms. There is neither proof nor disproof of a significant or meaningful order in our experience, and yet we cannot live our lives on any other assumption. As Thomas Nagel has observed, we cannot help but take our lives seriously. The fact that we continue to exist throws us into projects that require our commitment and attention. But, at the same time, we also cannot escape the possibility of doubting or calling into question the significance and ultimate justification of anything that we do. Nagel sums up: "We cannot live human lives without energy and attention, nor without making choices which show that we take some things more seriously than others. Yet we have always available a point of view outside the particular form of our lives, from which the seriousness appears gratuitous. These two inescapable viewpoints collide in us, and that is what makes life absurd."[31]

We sometimes find ourselves, therefore, caught between reflective doubt about, and unreflective commitment to, projects that we cannot help but take seriously, so long as we live. It is this latter form of commitment that thrusts us into the midst of ongoing narratives. As a practical matter we live narrative lives just insofar as we take anything in our lives seriously enough to go on projecting ourselves into our futures, authoring our stories.

Think of a person's life story as something that is *lived out* in concrete situations and is not merely a tale to be narrated, nor merely a linguistic entity. Life stories emerge as responses to basic situations that confront us as human beings, situations that require us to ask questions such as "Who am I?" "Why am I here?" "What should I do in this situation?" and so forth. Life stories are thus *tasks we perform in composing our lives,* and they are motivated by these sorts of pressing practical and moral considerations, partial solutions to which constitute our present identity. Consequently, living out a narrative quest is not merely optional, if we hope to make sense of our lives at all. Making *at least some* sense of our lives is something we all try to do in varying degrees and with different amounts of success and failure. Whether or not we ever verbalize our self-understanding, we will still at least minimally seek to construct our life narratively.[32]

Moral Reasoning as Narrative Exploration

I have already suggested that small children first encounter rational explanation in narrative form. For them, to explain is to tell the right story that is appropriate to the situation, one that has a chance of answering possible who, what, when, and why questions that might be put to them. Our most basic contact with rationality occurs in a culturally embedded process of story construction in response to standard sets of questions that can be answered only by a limited range of sanctioned types of narrative. Gradually we learn to fit episodes together, to select appropriate details, to construct acceptable sequences of events, and to establish the proper range of connections at the right points in the narrative. At this young age we are almost never aware that sanctioned narratives vary across cultures, paradigms, disciplines, and practices. We tend to think that we are learning *the* way to put the world together.

The stories we tell as we get older may become more detailed, more rigid, or even more devious, as we grow into our culture's forms of explanation. We may know nothing abstractly about the logical patterns of *modus ponens, modus tollens,* or the law of noncontradiction, yet we are introduced to those patterns in various highly concrete and particularized ways as we learn what sorts of structures and connections are permitted in given contexts of explanation. Above all, we are learning what it is to 'make sense of things,' to see our world as a connected and meaningful place. Our world begins to take on a certain recognizable shape as we find narrative structures that give pattern and form to most of what we experience. Not everything will fit neatly together, of course, but we must find a certain level of meaningful narrative order if we are to function physically, socially, and culturally. The possibilities for such order depend chiefly on imaginative synthesizing devices (such as image schemas, metaphors, and frames) which are encompassed within the narrative structures we inherit from our tradition.

There exists an intimate connection between life stories[33] and the structures of rationality. These stories are our most basic contact with rational explanation. The most fundamental questions I can frame about my identity and purpose are addressed through rational life stories. To live and tell such stories is to give partial answers to questions such as "What made me what I am?" "What must you know to know me?" "Why did I act as I did?" "What do I want?" and "What should I do?" *We learn the meaning of rational explanation first in the telling of our life stories.* For the most part, this is not done as a game, nor as an abstract rational or logical exercise, but rather in response to a pressing human need to know who we are, to decide how to act, to solve moral problems, and to explain ourselves to others. This is moral deliberation, moral evaluation, and moral exploration in its most basic sense. *Our moral reasoning is situated within our narrative understanding.*

Human life, then, is a narrative enterprise. Every one of us is inextricably involved in a complex narrative process by means of which we are trying to find at least some meaning and satisfaction in our lives. We want not just to survive but also to enhance the quality of our existence and to find fulfillment. This typically requires of us a great deal of imagination in the coauthoring of *our* particular narrative. Living a fulfilling life in accordance with some notion of human flourishing is one of the chief problems we are all trying to solve. We each want very badly for our particular life stories to be exciting, meaningful, and exemplary of the values we prize. Morality is thus a matter of *how well or how poorly* we construct (i.e., live out) a narrative that solves our problem of living a meaningful and significant life.

It is Dewey who, in a strikingly Aristotelian vein, best understands this view of the nature of morality.

> When we observe that morals is at home wherever considerations of the worse and better are involved, we are committed to noting that morality is a continuing process not a fixed achievement. Morals means growth of conduct in meaning; at least it means that kind of expansion in meaning which is consequent upon observations of the conditions and outcome of conduct. It is all one with growing. . . . In the largest sense of the word, morals is education. *It is learning the meaning of what we are about and employing that meaning in action.* (Emphasis added)[34]

On this view, moral deliberation is an imaginative exploration of the possibilities for constructive action within a present situation. We have a problem to solve here and now (e.g., "What am I to do?" "Who am I to become?" "How should I treat others?"), and we must try out various possible continuations of our narrative in search of the one that seems best to resolve the indeterminacy of our present situation.

We are struggling in the immediate present to make our situation more meaningful and manageable, to unburden ourselves of our felt confusion and lack of clarity. To do this, we have available to us a host of resources: ideals, people we regard as morally exemplary, cultural myths, stories of moral conflict and resolution, principles, and our sense of history. We are not seeking only to make our lives more 'meaningful,' for that could be said even of the Nazis in their quest to raise up a 'pure' people. Instead, we are trying to do the best available thing in our given situation. Some things we propose to do will, in fact, be worse, or less satisfactory, than others in this instance. Figuring out what these better things are is not typically a process of bringing cases under fixed, context-free rules. Much of the time we have to be more sensitive and subtle and reflective than that.

Dewey saw that, at bottom, what we must do is to draw on our understanding of the kinds of actions, attitudes, communal ties, and institutional commitments that have tended to expand our possibilities for meaningful, harmonious experience and fruitful human interaction in community: "Sufficient unto the day is the evil thereof. Sufficient it is to stimulate us to remedial action, to endeavor in order to convert strife into harmony, monotony into a variegated scene, and limitation into expansion. The converting is progress, the only progress conceivable or attainable by man. . . . We find our clews to direction in the projected recollections of definite experienced goods not in vague anticipations, even when we label the vagueness perfection, the Ideal, and proceed to manipulate its definition with dry dialectic logic."[35]

Let us consider a concrete example of what such ampliative and exploratory moral deliberation might involve. A fifteen-year-old finds that she is pregnant. What is she going to do? She has a moral problem *now* and needs to resolve her immediate troubled situation, which is weighing her down with a crushing force. Whatever else we may say about her situation, it cannot be understood as merely a problem of finding the right universal univocal concepts and principles under which to bring her particular case.

What she needs to do is to imagine the several possibilities open to her in her present situation—to carry out in her imagination various narrative extensions to see how her story might come out further along, depending on which course of actions she pursues. Every single one of us does this sort of imaginative projection constantly. We try to understand what it would mean to marry *this* particular person or to take *this* particular job or to give *this* particular response to our friend's criticism. So, the young woman of fifteen finds herself projecting alternative stories and trying to determine which of all these possibilities clarifies her situation best, increases meaning, and re-presents her in a manner that best expresses her sense of herself, or her ideal of what she might become.

One possible narrative extension for this young woman involves abortion.

How that option might be woven into her overall life story will depend on an enormous mass of considerations: the moral tradition within which she acquired her sense of morality, the attitudes of her family and friends, her knowledge of or prior experience with the reality of abortion, her physical and emotional well-being, the legal context within which she finds herself, her socioeconomic status, and a host of other complex, interrelated considerations.

Her immediate feelings are those of despair, anxiety, fear, uncertainty, loneliness, and helplessness. When she considers abortion, she is trying to imagine how it might transform her present feelings, what problems might be resolved, what new feelings and difficulties might then oppress her, how others are likely to regard her.

Perhaps she should take the fetus to full term. But then she has at least four possible narratives to explore: she might either marry the biological father, raise the infant herself, ask her family to assume responsibility, or choose adoption.

1. Should she marry the biological father, even if he wishes it? Is an unplanned pregnancy a good reason for marriage (which raises, of course, fundamental questions about the nature of marriage)? What are the chances for a meaningful and significant marital relation between two adolescents? Who will take primary responsibility for nurturing the infant? How will they support themselves? What will the psychological effects on the child be under such circumstances?

Notice that these perplexing questions are all relevant to the central question "What ought I to do?" (or "What is the morally correct thing to do here?"). There is not one question to answer, but rather a host of complex interrelated questions that all bear on the issue of what is best for this situation. Such questions are psychological, social, economic, political, religious, and moral all at once.

2. She might raise the infant herself, but then what will her life, and her infant's, and her family's be like? Will she finish school? If not, what are the chances for a meaningful future for herself and her child? How will she support them both? What will become of the relations she shared with her peers in what has now become a world gone by? Does she have the emotional, financial, and psychological resources to nurture her baby?

3. What if her family is willing to assume responsibility for raising her child? What sorts of burdens does that place upon their lives, emotionally, financially, and with respect to their own life plans? How will it change the whole fabric of their familial relations? What constraints will it place on their freedom? Will this be a healthy situation for the child?

4. What about adoption? Is it in *this* biological mother's and *this* infant's best interest? Does the young woman have sufficient emotional and psychological resources to be separated from her infant? What effect will this have on her family relations? It will be crucial whether or not they are supportive and loving about such an action, or whether they regard it negatively. It will perhaps matter whether or not the biological mother has any experience with adopted children.

So, the agonizing process of narrative exploration drags on as she runs over in her imagination, again and again, how she feels as she projects herself into each type of situation. There will be 'moral principles,' of course, brought into play in all of this. But they will be only one part of the relevant considerations which she must try to blend into a narrative whole.

What she really needs most here is something that the young are least likely to have, namely, mature moral imagination. As young artists of their lives, they typically do not have an experience that is broad enough, rich enough, and subtle enough to allow them to understand who they are, to imagine who they might become, to explore possibilities for meaningful action, and to harmonize their lives with those of others.

What this young woman needs, then, is not a set of rules that could tell her what to do with her pregnancy. She needs a cultivated moral imagination that can allow her to examine her present difficulties in a broader perspective, to explore how various actions might affect the lives of others as well as her own, to criticize her values and attitudes, and to glimpse possibilities for meaningful action. This ability to continue her life narrative in a constructive and life-enhancing fashion must be based on a mature, experientially grounded moral imagination, not on the existence of a set of fixed moral rules. Moral rules are often the sedimented 'wisdom' of a people. They are important and useful in our moral deliberations, but they are not sufficient unto themselves. They themselves require imagination if they are to be useful. But they are only one part of a larger picture of moral reasoning, most of which has been more or less ignored by rule theories of morality.

A Note on the Nature of Moral Theory

Theories of morality, like all theories of any sort, must deal with idealizations. Consequently, they can't be expected to take account of every minute detail of a situation, of all possible outcomes, or of every conceivable case. To ask this would be to ask too much. Theories seek generalizations, and generalizations necessarily abstract from many concrete particulars.

I have no argument with either the need for theory, the necessity for idealizations, or the crucial importance of generalization. What I am trying to do is suggest a new view of moral theory. Any theory of morality that purports to detemporalize human action (which is to say, to offer an eternal standpoint) cannot be an adequate theory of *human* morality. Humans are temporal, and ultimately narrative, creatures. It is this dimension that must be infused into moral theory. We must make use of all sorts of idealizations and imaginative models, though we want to keep them as fine-textured, flexible, and open to novelty as possible. My claim is that our idealizations, if they are to be useful, must take account of the central role of narrative in the structure of human experience.

Such a view undercuts the alleged distinction between so-called normative and descriptive theories. Every description involves norms, such as standards of what is relevant and important in a proper description. Moreover, it undermines the dream of an atemporal, eternal standpoint for evaluation. We are left with our idealizations, and we must not forget that they are tentative hypotheses, models, and principles. What we are trying to do is to weave them into a narrative that helps us resolve problematic situations and that continues our tradition while also giving us means for criticizing and transforming it.

Moral Imagination

The Need for Moral Imagination

In 1970 I was a senior in college and my draft lottery number was 37. That year of the Vietnam War the draft took all numbers up to around 260. So there was no question but that I was going to have to make what was for me the most significant moral decision of my life. I was very strongly pulled in two opposing directions— I felt the obligation to serve my country, and I felt that we had made a grave moral mistake in Vietnam.

I knew quite well the relevant arguments for both sides of this difficult question. My father, who had been a navy pilot during World War II and who remained in the reserves, had taught me that freedom is as fragile as it is precious, and that it can often be preserved only by bloody violence. He had instilled in me a sense of deep obligation to the governmental system that made it possible for us to be the citizens we were, with the rights and privileges we enjoyed.

In support of these ideals and commitments I could muster venerable philosophical arguments: Plato's prison-house insistence on our duty to obey the *polis*, which has nourished, educated, protected, and encouraged us materially, politically, and morally; the articulation by Hobbes and Locke of our obligations to defend our nation; and modern-day Kantian arguments that legitimately constituted governments may reasonably expect our service.

On the other side—the contrary view—I had, through my Lutheran upbringing, the influence of a rich Biblical tradition that offered a new vision of a form of Christian charity that would overthrow the vicious doctrine of revenge, meet cruelty with kindness, and confront evil with healing, sacrificial love. Within this context I had encountered vivid depictions of the horror and insanity of war, in such works as *All Quiet on the Western Front* and the poetry of Sassoon, Hardy, and Owen.[1] Here, too, I knew the relevant arguments, both theological and humanistic. I had read Gandhi and Tolstoy and Thomas Merton, who set forth a vision of a love capable of changing a world that seemed bent on domination, suppression, and degradation of human freedom. I was familiar with various nontheological forms of the general humanistic argument that rational creatures deserve respect, which, among other things, requires always treating other persons as ends-in-themselves, never merely as means or utensils.

All of this upbringing, moral education, and philosophical training was framed within a context defined by my personal history and life experience, and by my culturally inherited values, institutions, and practices. For instance, I had the experience of one year in the Naval Reserve Officers' Training Corps, including a two-month stint on a destroyer escort recently back from Vietnam. At the same time, I was surrounded daily by 'peace and love'—by demonstrations, marches, sit-ins, vigils, boycotts, transcendental meditation, and free love.

All of this experience. All of this education. All of this knowledge. *And I didn't know what in the world to do!* I had all of the information one could want, though even as late as 1970 it was still not completely clear what we had done in Vietnam, what we were then doing, and where it would lead. I had all the arguments, philosophical and theological, one could imagine. I had all of the moral education I could handle. I had moral ideals aplenty. I had all of the moral laws I could use, and then some. *And I couldn't decide what was 'right.'*

My problem wasn't that I had thought about this too much, becoming "sicklied o'er with the pale cast of thought." Nor was my problem one of cowardice or fear of deciding, although who can ever really be sure of their deepest motives. My problem was that I had *too many* ideals, goods, commitments, laws, arguments, and motivations, and that some of them were quite incompatible with each other. Each of my options presented itself as a good and placed on me a strong sense of obligation. I believed then, as I do today, that most of these ideals, principles, and arguments were very good arguments in their own ways. In fact, if one had a reasonable view that needed justification, there would be no trouble finding all of the sincere, honest, and rational arguments for it that one could ever hope for.

In short, I was confronted with an irreducible diversity of conflicting goods, values, and ideals, each of which pressed itself upon me with considerable moral force. And I had to choose, or else be chosen by forces beyond me.

The situation I found myself in over twenty years ago is typical of the kinds of situations all of us, from time to time, find ourselves in as we stumble through our daily lives. We run into situations where we are confronted with conflicting values, commitments, moral laws, motivations, and goals. We face a 'diversity of goods,' and we have no ultimate principle for rank ordering them. Unless we are deceiving ourselves, we see that there is no obviously 'right thing to do.' There just is not one and only one right answer, and there is no simple method for deciding how to act.

What we need more than anything else in such cases is moral imagination in its various manifestations, as a means to both knowledge and criticism. We need self-knowledge about the imaginative structure of our moral understanding, including its values, limitations, and blind spots. We need a similar knowledge of other people, both those who share our moral tradition and those who inhabit other traditions. We need to imagine how various actions open to us might alter our self-identity, modify our commitments, change our relationships, and affect the lives of others. We need to explore imaginatively what it might mean, in terms of possibilities for enhanced meaning and relationships, for us to perform this or that action. We need the ability to imagine and to enact transformations in our moral understanding, our character, and our behavior. In short, we need an *imaginative rationality* that is at once insightful, critical, exploratory, and transformative.

My central constructive thesis in this book is that a critical moral imagination of this sort ought to be the basis for our moral deliberation and self-understanding. Ideally, moral imagination would provide the means for understanding (of self, others, institutions, cultures), for reflective criticism, and for modest transformation, which together are the basis for moral growth.

What Should a Theory of Morality Be, and What Can It Do for Us?

It is time to weave together the various strands of moral imagination that we have been examining and to say explicitly why and how they change our conception of morality. What good is moral imagination, anyway, when what we really need is guidance about how to live our lives? How is having moral imagination going to tell me the right thing to do in a particular situation?

It should be clear by now that moral imagination is not going to dictate the 'right thing to do' in a given case. We have seen why the Moral Law view that there must be one and only one right thing to do in a given situation is, for the most part, mistaken. What we now see is that Moral Law theories never gave us *the* right thing to do, either. The best they could do was to formulate moral laws that seemed to work for the prototypical, nonproblematic cases. What we regard as 'moral laws' should be construed as useful rules of thumb that summarize the collective experience and wisdom of a moral tradition concerning prototypical situations. The fact that one can formulate rules for cases about which there is virtually no debate within our moral tradition does not help us deal with the real moral problems we face in our daily lives, namely, the multitude of cases for which we have no fixed set of preestablished rules, or where we experience conflicting obligations.

Nevertheless, even if we acknowledge that Moral Law theories can't actually give the useful guidance they promise, it is very difficult to get over the idea that a moral theory should give us guidance about how to act. What good is a theory of morality if it doesn't tell us what to do?

To answer this question, let us consider *scientific* theories. Do theories in physics tell us how to do physics? Do they give us methods for getting truth? Clearly not, even though some philosophers in the past have thought that they might. Yet our theories in physics do inform our approach to doing physics, and thus they do influence our practice.

Do psychological theories tell us how to be better people, or more fulfilled people, or people whose lives have more meaning? Not directly, yet knowledge of the nature of cognition, motivation, development, learning, and so forth, can have some bearing on how we live our lives. Such knowledge will not, however, give us rules for living.

Do sociological theories tell us how to behave toward other people? Not in any direct way; that is, they do not give us general laws about how to interact in groups. Yet the more sociologically well-informed we are, the more likely we are, on the whole, to understand the subtleties of group dynamics and to be more socially astute.

Moral theories are just like these other types of theory. Their purpose is not, and cannot be, to tell us the 'right thing to do' in different situations. They tell us, rather, about the nature of moral problems, moral reasoning, and moral understanding. They help us explore our moral traditions to see how they arose, what their standards of justification are, and what their limitations are. They inform us about what is common and what is different in moral traditions around the world and throughout history. They give us knowledge of the imaginative structure of our moral concepts and the reasoning we do with them.

A theory of morality, then, should be a theory of moral understanding. It should give us insight into the nature of human moral understanding, and it should thereby increase our own moral understanding. In this respect, moral theory is no different from all other types of theory, since the more we know about a given domain of experience, the more likely we are to be able to act intelligently with respect to that domain.

There is thus a dual sense in which moral theory is about moral understanding. It studies the nature of human moral understanding generally, and it also gives us a way to increase our own moral understanding. A similar duality applies to the term 'moral imagination,' too. The previous chapters have dealt almost entirely with moral understanding in the first sense, that is, with the nature of human moral understanding. My central thesis has been that our moral understanding is fundamentally imaginative in character.

We can now see that looking in detail at the ways in which our moral understanding is imaginative does have implications for how we ought to act. Just as theories in physics, psychology, sociology, and so forth, have implications for practice, likewise a theory of the imaginative structure of moral understanding can give us some very general guidance about how to live. It can have this practical value, not because it gives laws or rules for acting (which it doesn't), but rather because knowing oneself and knowing how human beings work can help one understand situations, examine problems, and work out constructive solutions.

What Is Moral Imagination, and How Does It Affect Action?

With this focus on how knowledge of the imaginative character of moral understanding bears on our own moral understanding and on our ability to act well, let us now reconsider each of the basic imaginative elements of our moral reasoning in order to determine how they ought to affect the way we think and act.

The Prototype Structure of Concepts

Many of our most basic concepts have considerable internal structure that cannot be accounted for by the classical theory of concepts as defined by necessary and sufficient features. I chose *lie* as a representative example of prototype structure, where certain members of the category are *experientially and cognitively central,* with other noncentral members related to the more central cases by various principles of extension.

I argued that, if a good many of our basic moral concepts (such as person, rights, harm, justice, love) and many of the concepts that define kinds of action (e.g., murder, lie, educate, natural, sex) have internal prototype structure, then Moral Law theories must be rejected. They are fundamentally mistaken in their view of concepts and the attendant view of moral judgment that goes along with it. Moral judgment cannot consist merely of bringing cases under laws by finding the necessary and sufficient defining features of a given situation. Most concepts simply do not map directly onto the world in the way required by Moral Law theories.

We have also seen how the prototype phenomenon explains why Moral Law theories sometimes seem to work. They 'work' for the prototypical cases—the nonproblematic ones—about which there is widespread agreement within moral traditions. What moral laws we have are precisely those that are formulated to fit the prototypical cases, the central members of a category.

Most of our reflective moral reasoning concerns, instead, the *nonprototypical* cases. But these are the very cases where the preexisting moral laws *don't* work. If we wanted to expand the rules to cover the nonprototypical cases, we couldn't do it using the rules alone, for they have no internal resources for imaginative extension. The very thing we need most in our moral deliberations is the very thing the rules can't supply.

Fortunately, what we know about prototypes *can* supply what we need to make intelligent moral decisions. There are principles of extension (e.g., metaphor) from the central to the noncentral members within a category. Often, as we will see below, these extensions are based on metaphor, such as when we understand a corporation or an entire society metaphorically as a person. Cognitive science can study empirically the nature of prototype structure and the various kinds of imaginative extension to noncentral cases.

Here are some of the chief ways in which prototypes are important in our moral deliberations:

1. They represent experientially basic types of situations. That is, given the kinds of bodies we have, the nature of our cognition, and the kinds of physical, interpersonal, and cultural interactions we engage in, certain types of situations will take on a special importance for us in our attempt to function successfully in our physical and social environments.

Paul Churchland has suggested that certain moral and social schemas are actually complex prototypes that exist as layers of "hidden" units within our neural assemblies.

> Children learn to recognize certain prototypical kinds of social situations, and they learn to produce or avoid the behaviors prototypically required or prohibited in each. Young children learn to recognize a distribution of scarce resources such as cookies or candies as a *fair* or *unfair* distribution. They learn to voice complaint in the latter case, and to withhold complaint in the former. They learn to recognize that a found object may be *someone's property,* and that access is limited as a result. They learn to discriminate *unprovoked cruelty,* and to demand or

expect punishment for the transgressor or comfort for the victim. They learn to recognize a *breach of promise,* and to howl in protest. They learn to recognize these and a hundred other prototypical social/moral situations, and the ways in which the embedding society generally reacts to those situations and expects them to react.[2]

Social and moral prototypes of this sort provide the foci of our moral experience and our moral development. We learn about justice, not as an abstract concept, but by prototypical situations of experienced fair and unfair distribution. We learn that some fair distributions of goods can be determined quantitatively, as in the dividing up of cookies, while others require temporal determinations, as in the sharing of equal time to ride the bicycle.

2. These basic prototypes carry with them the affective dimensions of the concrete situations in which they arise.[3] They thus evoke emotions, moods, erotic desire, empathy, and a host of typical affective states that motivate our actions. They carry with them their origins in our embodied, emotion-laden experience. In this way, our basic moral concepts are never pure abstractions, but are always permeated with the passion and emotion that moves us to action.

3. Prototypes are malleable and flexible. My childhood experiences of fair and unfair distribution lie at the heart of my sense of justice. But when it comes to the level of what Rawls calls fair distribution of opportunities and access to public offices, no cookie-distribution model is going to suffice. Our moral deliberations about such complex political matters of justice will require grand extensions of our primitive models of fair distribution. Our prototypes of the *bully,* the *good samaritan, fair distribution, breach of promise,* and so forth, must all undergo a series of imaginative extensions that change the meaning of those prototypes over time.

4. The meaning, point, and force of a particular prototype will also depend in part on the various narrative contexts in which it is embedded. This holds both for the way the prototype originates in an individual's experience and for the way it is developed and applied in present situations. Thus, the different narrative contexts will give rise to different realizations of a particular prototype. Breach of promise is evaluated one way within a narrative framework of lying to one's spouse about an extramarital affair, but it has a quite different significance in the context of failure to keep one's promise to an officer of a dictatorial police state. This accounts, in part, for the importance of parables, stories, and other narrative forms

in our moral development and in our knowing how we ought to behave in particular kinds of situations. They help to determine the prototype's meaning and orientation relative to a particular situation.

5. Prototypes will be the basis for whatever moral principles we have. Moral laws are typically abstractions based on cultural prototypes. Such abstracted rules have their meaning and proper application only relative to the prototype. They cannot stand on their own.

6. A central part of our moral development will be the imaginative use of particular prototypes in constructing our lives. Each prototype has a definite structure, yet that structure must undergo gradual imaginative transformation as new situations arise. It thus has a dynamic character, which is what makes possible our moral development and growth.

FRAMING OF SITUATIONS

The situations in which we find ourselves and in which we must decide how to act do not come with their one and only proper descriptions attached. *We* have to conceptualize them in a certain way. We have seen that various kinds of imaginative structure, such as image schemas, metaphors, and prototypes, are crucial in defining the idealized cognitive models we bring to situations, in terms of which we understand them. Obviously, how we frame those situations will make all the difference in the world. Consider, for example, an act in which members of a state police force break into a home and confiscate certain documents written in secret by the home owner. Framed as an invasion of privacy, we make one judgment about the action, whereas framing it as the confiscation of seditious materials in a time of national emergency might justify a radically different judgment.

Semantic frames often involve a broad range of imaginative structures, such as image schemas, various types of prototype structure, metonymy, and metaphor. As a result, they do not simply mirror some objective reality or category. Rather, they define that reality by means of imaginative structure.

Knowing about the imaginative character of frames in general is crucial to moral understanding. Knowing about the precise nature of the particular frames we inherit from our moral tradition and apply to situations is absolutely essential, if we are to be at all aware of the prejudgments we bring to situations. Knowing that there will always be multiple framings of any situation is also necessary, if we are to appreciate the nonabsolute character of our moral understanding. Not to know these things about ourselves is morally irresponsible.

METAPHOR

It appears that the chief imaginative dimension of moral understanding is metaphor. We have examined evidence showing that virtually all of our fundamental moral concepts—cause, action, well-being, purpose, state, duty, right, freedom, and so forth—are metaphorically defined, often by two or more metaphors. When it comes to our moral deliberations, therefore, we are hardly ever engaged in applying literal, univocal concepts directly to states of affairs in the world. We must give up the key tenet of Moral Law theories, that literal concepts can fit situations by virtue of objective properties of the world. Most of our moral reasoning is reasoning based on metaphors.[4]

The metaphorical character of morality has radical implications for our moral understanding. A *new set of questions* emerges that could not even have been formulated before. These are questions about the nature of the metaphorical structure of our moral knowledge. Since conceptual metaphor wasn't even recognized by traditional Moral Law theory, it couldn't conceive of such basic questions. This orientation thus opens up new dimensions of our moral understanding and requires us to rethink what moral reasoning is all about.

What follows is a list of some of the insights made possible by the recognition of the metaphoric structure of moral understanding.

1. We have a way to figure out, in detail, what the metaphors are that define our basic moral concepts. We can ask such questions as, Are there different levels of metaphor? Are they hierarchically organized? If so, how does one level depend on another? How are certain moral issues and questions generated by our fundamental metaphors?

Knowing the details of *our* metaphorically structured moral understanding is thus crucial for our self-understanding. It is one of the central ways we come to know what our values are, what they presuppose, and what they entail for our actions.

2. Metaphor analysis gives us some idea of which parts of our moral understanding might possibly be candidates for moral universals. Are certain source domains based on universal bodily experience? If so, then when they are used to understand a target domain that appears in every culture (e.g., community), they may well present experientially based cognitive universals. For example, we can determine whether the EVENT STRUCTURE metaphor is so basic to human experience that it occurs across all cultures. This is an empirically testable claim,[5] and our theory tells us how to go about testing it.

3. We can discern where cultural variation is most likely to enter into a given level of metaphorical structure. We would expect this to occur in conceptual metaphors whose source domains are not based on universal bodily and experiential structures. However, even when there are such universal bases, they are often elaborated metaphorically in different ways from culture to culture. Justice may be grounded on an image schema of BALANCE in two different cultures, but *what* gets balanced and what *counts* as balance in the two cultures may vary considerably.

4. Consequently, knowing about the metaphoric character of human conceptual systems in general, and knowing about the specific metaphors defining one's own morality in particular, will drive home the fact that there are probably no moral absolutes in any strong sense of that term. What is universal is likely to be so abstract that, when taken by itself, it places only the most general constraints on action. However, when that general principle is situated within cultural models and narratives, it may well play a role in determining very specific modes of correct behavior.

5. We have the means to determine at what level a change of metaphor (and thus a different moral understanding) might be possible. This will be a matter of how cognitively well entrenched[6] a certain metaphor system is. The more basic a conceptual metaphor is, the more it will be systematically connected to other metaphors, and the more implications it will have for our moral reasoning. It is highly unlikely that our deepest metaphors can be changed, since the resultant cognitive disruption would be extreme. This is not to deny that occasionally individuals and even cultures undergo such radical transformations, but only to note the emotional, social, and cultural costs of such large-scale change. Perhaps the imposition of Western modes of experience on non-Western peoples is the most obvious example of such catastrophic change.

When more modest change seems to be required by the emergence of novel economic, social, political, and religious situations within a culture, or within an individual's life, we can examine the system of metaphors to see what would be changed if we altered a metaphor at a particular level. I will give an example of this kind of change below in discussing change in legal reasoning as a model for moral reasoning.

6. Whenever our basic moral concepts have prototype structure, we are going to encounter many nonprototypical cases and novel cases that require extension beyond the prototype. In many cases we make these extensions via metaphor. For

example, we have a prototypical instance of the category *person* (often an adult white heterosexual male) and some sense of how persons in that sense are to be treated. Many of our moral problems stem from questions about permissible metaphorical extensions from the prototype to noncentral members, or to beings that may traditionally fall outside the category. Our moral deliberation will be about whether, for instance, certain 'higher' mammals ought to be understood metaphorically as persons, and therefore accorded certain rights.

Since our experience is never static, and since evolution and technological change introduce new entities into our lives, we are faced with novel situations that simply were not envisioned in the historical periods that gave rise to our current understanding of certain moral concepts. Metaphor is our chief device for extensions from prototypes to novel cases.

7. What we call 'lessons of life' are thus possible because of our ability to reason metaphorically. Often we learn from an experience by metaphorically extending from that particular experience to our present situation, which is not exactly the same. We grasp the metaphorical structure of the previous situation and apply it to what we are encountering now. It is the imaginative flexibility of the metaphor that makes this possible.

8. Once we see that metaphors are partial structurings of concepts, and that there are often multiple metaphors defining a single complex concept, we see that any metaphorical concept will hide as much as it highlights. Often, what is hidden turns out to be equally or more important than what has been emphasized. In looking at some of the objectivist metaphors for the self, for instance, we found that they could not capture a great deal of what is important to a person's moral identity, especially the dynamic, imaginative character of the self. Both our self-knowledge and our knowledge of alternative possibilities depend on self-critical reflection on our metaphors.

To summarize: A deep, reflective knowledge of the metaphorical nature of human understanding and of the metaphors that structure one's own moral understanding is essential for moral knowledge. Such knowledge of the metaphors we live by, as well as the metaphors other people live by, should engender a modesty about our own moral claims and a recognition of the variety of morally possible ways of living. Being without moral absolutes is not a catastrophe—it is, rather, a fact of life. Part of this fact is the recognition that metaphors are not arbitrary or unmotivated, either. There are constraints on reasoning based on metaphors, and thus we are not left with extreme subjectivism and relativism. Extreme subjectivism is avoided because there are shared bases for metaphors within a culture, and even across cultures. Extreme relativism is avoided because some metaphors appear to be grounded in universal bodily experiences.

NARRATIVE

Richard Rorty has observed that people who care about their moral self-development turn, not to philosophical texts on moral theory, but rather to novels, short stories, and plays.[7] This might seem too obvious to mention, were it not for the fact that many philosophers convince themselves and their students that books on moral theory will tell us how we ought to behave. Why is it that we turn to literary texts for our moral education? Why do we learn more from narratives than from academic moral philosophy about what it is to be human, about the contingencies of life, about the kinds of lives we most want to lead, and about what is involved in trying to lead such lives?

The key to the answer is that our lives ultimately have a narrative structure. It is in sustained narratives, therefore, that we come closest to observing and participating in the reality of life as it is actually experienced and lived. We learn from, and are changed by, such narratives to the extent that we become imaginatively engaged in making fine discriminations of character and in determining what is morally salient in particular situations. We actually enter into the lives of the characters, and we perform acts of perception, decision, and criticism. We find ourselves judging of a character that she shouldn't have done X, or wishing that he had seen a particular situation differently than he did. We want to stop the characters and tell them, "Oh, no, don't do *that!*" or "No, that's not what she meant." Just as in life, we find ourselves surprised by what happens, or disappointed in ourselves for not having seen something earlier. We explore, we learn, and we are changed by our participation in the fiction that creatively imitates life.

In two major books Martha Nussbaum has mounted an extended and quite eloquent argument for the central role of literature in our moral development.[8] Arguing for the importance of extended narratives as a basis for moral philosophy, Nussbaum makes the case that

> a whole tragic drama, unlike a schematic philosophical example making use of a similar story, is capable of tracing the history of a complex pattern of deliberation, showing its roots in a way of life and looking forward to its consequences in that life. As it does all of this, it lays open to view the complexity, the indeterminacy, the sheer difficulty of actual human deliberation. . . . A tragedy does not display the dilemmas of

its characters as pre-articulated; it shows them searching for the morally salient; and it forces us, as interpreters, to be similarly active.[9]

Narrative makes it possible for us not only to explore the consequences of decisions and commitments over an extended period of time, but also to reflect on the concrete particularities that make up the fine texture of our actual moral experience. It invites us to develop our perception of character, of what is important in a given situation, and of the subtly interwoven threads of our moral entanglements: "For stories cultivate our ability to see and care for particulars, not as representatives of a law, but as what they themselves are: to respond vigorously with senses and emotions before the new; to care deeply about chance happenings in the world, rather than to fortify ourselves against them; to wait for the outcome and to be bewildered—to wait and to float and be actively passive."[10]

Tracing out over an extended time period the consequences of various moral deliberations is therefore crucial to our moral knowledge, and it is essential for moral education. It is through sustained life narrative—through the narratives we live out and construct, and through the fictional narratives we imaginatively inhabit—that we can perform these essential reflections and moral inquiries.

John Gardner has argued that fiction is a laboratory in which we can explore in imagination the probable implications of people's character and choices. He describes what he calls "moral fiction" as a "philosophical method" in which art "controls the argument and gives it its rigor, forces the writer to intense yet dispassionate and unprejudiced watchfulness, drives him—in ways abstract logic cannot match—to unexpected discoveries and, frequently, a change of mind."[11] His point is that in a fictional setting we can explore the way a person with a certain character, placed within certain circumstances, might live his life. We can see how his self-knowledge, or lack of it, determines what he does and how that affects others. We can see how his care, or lack of it, determines the quality of his relationships and the morality of his actions.

The power of fictional narrative to develop our moral sensitivity, our ability to make subtle discriminations, and our empathy for others, is thus the result of the narrative structure of our lives. Even where moral laws do exist, we learn what they mean and how they apply only by seeing people, ourselves and others, try to live by them over extended periods.[12] To understand what certain virtues involve and how a person's character manifests itself, we need to see them realized in the narrative fabric of human lives. To see what the acceptance of certain values entails, we must trace out their implications over large periods of time, and in different contexts. *Narrative explorations of this sort are, in fact, what moral reasoning is all about.*

In short, we must recognize the narrative dimensions of our lives, both the narratives we inherit from our culture and the particular instantiations of those narratives that we are constructing in our own lives. Any adequate moral philosophy must give a central role to the narrative structure of experience and to the nature of the particular narratives that make up different moral traditions. Fictional narratives provide us rich, humanly realistic experimental settings in which we can make our own moral explorations. We make those explorations, not just in novels and plays, but also in the narrative construction of our lives. This, I take it, is what Richard Eldridge means when he says that "these texts, these readings, and the understanding of our moral personhood in the world that they develop will be true or successful not because a known method or criterion tells us so, but only insofar as we take them up, live them, make sense and assessments of our lives in their terms."[13]

What Difference Does Moral Imagination Make?

Let me summarize what I have been arguing concerning the difference that moral imagination ought to make in how we live our lives. A theory of morality should be a theory of moral understanding. Moral understanding is in large measure imaginatively structured. The primary forms of moral imagination are concepts with prototype structure, semantic frames, conceptual metaphors, and narratives. To be morally insightful and sensitive thus requires of us two things: (1) We must have knowledge of the imaginative nature of human conceptual systems and reasoning. This means that we must know what those imaginative structures are, how they work, and what they entail about the nature of our moral understanding. (2) We must cultivate moral imagination by sharpening our powers of discrimination, exercising our capacity for envisioning new possibilities, and imaginatively tracing out the implications of our metaphors, prototypes, and narratives.

The first requirement above, gaining knowledge of our moral understanding, entails that we will give up the illusions both of absolute moral values and of radical moral subjectivism. It requires us to give up the idea that moral reasoning is finding prearticulated rules and fitting them to situations. It demands that we study in detail the metaphoric structure of our morality, asking what it highlights and what it hides. Finally, it gives us a way to determine what might be changeable in our understanding and what such changes would entail for who we are and how we affect others.

The second requirement, that of developing our moral imagination, changes our conception of moral development. It sees our primary task as less a matter of learning how to apply moral laws and more a task of refining our perception of character and situations and of developing empathetic imagination to take up the part of others.

These, then, are some of the senses in which an experientialist view of moral theory can still give us some of the kinds of guidance we desire from a moral theory. It can't tell us what to do in given situations, but then neither could traditional Moral Law theories. Rather, it gives the kind of general guidance that comes from enhanced moral understanding and self-knowledge.

Empathetic Imagination

Traditional moral theories have almost entirely ignored one of our most important moral capacities—the capacity for empathy. Hume's treatment of what he called "sympathy" or "fellow-feeling"[14] touches on this issue, but it does not go to the heart of imaginative empathetic projection into the experience of other people.[15] As a limiting case, it requires the ability to imagine *ourselves* in different situations and conditions at past and future times. Unless we can put ourselves in the place of another, unless we can enlarge our own perspective through an imaginative encounter with the experience of others, unless we can let our own values and ideals be called into question from various points of view, we cannot be morally sensitive.

Hume was therefore at least partially correct in recognizing a general sympathy as the basis for morality: "Utility is only a tendency to a certain end; and were the end totally indifferent to us, we should feel the same indifference towards the means. It is requisite a *sentiment* should here display itself, in order to give a preference to the useful above the pernicious tendencies. This sentiment can be no other than a feeling for the happiness of mankind, and a resentment of their misery."[16]

What Hume misses is that, beyond a feeling for the well-being of others, we need also to imaginatively take up their experience. According to the traditional interpretation of Hume's moral theory, he misses this aspect because of his rigid separation of reason and feeling, which forces him to deny reason a central role in morality. But Annette Baier has argued that Hume is actually criticizing this strict separation of reason and feeling. She suggests that Hume's entire project gradually builds up a rich and subtle account of rational sentiment as underlying our ability to imaginatively take up the part of another person.[17] In any case, the most charitable way to construe Hume's sentiment for the welfare of others is as a blending of feeling, imagination, and reason.

This 'taking up the place of another' is an act of imaginative experience and dramatic rehearsal of the sort described by Nussbaum and Eldridge in their accounts of narrative moral explorations. It is perhaps the most important imaginative exploration we can perform. It is not sufficient merely to manipulate a cool, detached 'objective' reason toward the situation of others. We must, instead, go out toward people to inhabit their worlds, not just by rational calculations, but also in imagination, feeling, and expression.

Reflecting in this way involves an *imaginative rationality* through which we can participate empathetically in another's experience: their suffering, pain, humiliation, and frustrations, as well as their joy, fulfillment, plans, and hopes. Morally sensitive people are capable of living out, in and through such an experiential imagination, the reality of others with whom they are interacting, or whom their actions might affect.

I would describe this imaginative rationality as *passionate,* if that word were not so laden with subjectivist connotations. Roberto Unger describes as passionate "the whole range of interpersonal encounters in which people do not treat one another as means to one another's ends."[18] Passion is the basis of our noninstrumental relations to others, and it takes us beyond fixed character, social roles, and institutional arrangements.

Extending my earlier argument that Kant's categorical imperative requires imaginative (metaphoric) interpretation, we can now see that the Kantian imperative always to treat others (and oneself) as ends-in-themselves has no practical meaning independent of our imaginatively taking up the place of the other. Contrary to Kant's explicit claims, we cannot know what it means to treat someone as an end-in-himself, in any concrete way, unless we can imagine his experience, feelings, plans, goals, and hopes. We cannot know what respect for others demands of us, unless we participate imaginatively in their experience of the world.

We need this same reflective attitude toward, and imaginative knowledge of, ourselves, if we hope ever to rise above the level of creatures driven by immediate needs, desires, and whims. For we must be able to imagine how we might feel and think and act in various hypothetical situations.

It is extremely important to understand that the kind of empathetic imaginative understanding involved here is not merely personal or subjective. Such a romantic view of empathy, as a kind of flowing-into-the-other by giving oneself up to strong fellow-feeling, is an artifact of an erroneous traditional separation of reason, imagination, and feeling. However, even the romantic poets understood the shared, communal character of imagination and feeling. The poetry of both Wordsworth and Coleridge, for example, often involves meditations directed toward revivifying strong human feelings that bind us together in community. Both the *Lyrical Ballads* and the *Biographia Literaria* explore the communal and transformative character of an imagination that makes it possible for us to understand each other, to share a world, and to reach out to others in a caring way.

Now that we have seen the social, public, and constitutive dimensions of imagination (in conceptual structure, metaphor, image schemas, and narrative), we can dismiss subjectivist readings of imagination, as being cognitively and experientially false. We need not worry that empathetic imagination is a private, personal, or utterly subjective activity. Rather, it is the chief activity by which we are able to inhabit a more or less common world—a world of shared gestures, actions, perceptions, experiences, meanings, symbols, and narratives.

Moral imagination is public and shared.[19] It has the same public character as do our social relations, practices, and institutions, for all of these are defined by metaphors and other imaginative structures. Imagination, as I have described it, is the primary means by which social relations are constituted. Consider, for example, the imaginative dimensions of all sexual relations that have a truly social dimension. A sexual act can be meaningful only if it is more than a sequence of passive reactions to stimulation. Each person must imaginatively grasp the other's acts as responses to one's own intentions and acts. I must experience your touching of me as both expressing your desire and as directed toward me and my desire. I must take up and carry forward your desire in my active response to you. In happy cases the result is a reciprocal play between partners, a kind of erotic dialectic in which we share in each other's experience. Joseph Kupfer explains the nature of this reciprocity as

> sharing in each other's ends, each taking risks in respect to the same things and with regard to one another at the same time. . . . Sexual reciprocity is also responding to another's physical response: moving to the other's movement, stroking the caressing hand, embracing the embracer. It includes acting on the needs and desires which we perceive the other to have. At the same time, our partner is responding in like fashion to us. Furthermore, reciprocity includes responding both for our own sake and for the sake of the other, independent of our personal stake.[20]

Meaningful sexual relations are, in this way, social and deeply imaginative. As such, they are representative of human relations generally, which rest on the ability to take up the part of the other and to let one's ongoing interactions and relations be guided by one's imaginative grasp of the experience and intentions of other people. It is this kind of empathetic understanding that underlies the possibility of any morality that is more than mere rule-following.

The Imaginative Envisionment of Possibilities for Acting

Beyond knowledge of our own and others' cognitive and moral capacities and perspectives, beyond an abiding fellow-feeling, beyond the ability to inhabit imaginatively the world of another, something more is yet required. That 'something more' is an ability to imaginatively discern various possibilities for acting within a given situation and to envision the potential help and harm that are likely to result from a given action.

Care, concern, and good intentions are not enough. We are social creatures who live in communities, whose material and emotional well-being require social relationships and interactions, and whose individual and joint projects require actions directed toward goals, such as satisfying our material, interpersonal, and cultural needs. We need, not just to will purely, but rather to act in ways that promote the well-being of ourselves and others.

Kant is famous for denying that purposive activity is or ever could be definitive of the morality of our willing. He sought to remind us that a good will stands forth as morally praiseworthy in its own right, without regard to any ends it might or might not achieve: "Even if it should happen that, by a particularly unfortunate fate or by the niggardly provision of a step-motherly nature, this will should be wholly lacking in power to accomplish its purpose, and if even the greatest effort should not avail it to achieve anything of its end, and if there remained only the good will (not as a mere wish but as the summoning of all the means in our power), it would sparkle like a jewel in its own right, as something that had its full worth in itself" (*F,* 394).

Kant was right in observing that uncontrollable contingencies ought not to detract from the merit of good willing. However, moral action requires us to realize ends, both immediate (e.g., to assist an accident victim) and long-range (e.g., to educate the young), both narrow (e.g., to help someone find shelter) and comprehensive (e.g., to realize an overarching pattern of social relations). Good willing doesn't exist in itself, locked up in inner mental space and isolated from our actions. Will is not an entity separated from its directedness toward the realization of various ends, purposes, and plans, most of which require joint actions and projects. Our will is thus spread out in the activity of our ongoing lives, though it is not reducible to that activity.

The envisioning of possibilities for fruitful, meaningful, and constructive action requires moral imagination. Our ability to criticize a moral view depends on our capacity for imagining alternative viewpoints on, and solutions to, a particular moral problem. In order to adapt and grow, we must be able to see beyond our present vantage point and to grow beyond our present selves. We must be able to imagine new dimensions for our character, new directions for our relationships with others, and even new forms of social organization. Roberto Unger has articulated both the need and the conditions of possibility for imaginative transformation of this sort.

> So you know . . . that, though it is your fate to live within conditional worlds, you also have the power to break outside them. When you do that, however, you do not reach the unconditional: the thought beyond limiting method and language, the society beyond limiting practical and imaginative structure, the personality beyond limiting character. You can, nevertheless, work toward a situation that keeps alive the power to break the limits: to think thoughts that shatter the available canon of reason and discourse, to experiment with forms of collective life that the established practical and imaginative order of society locks out or puts down, to reach out toward the person beyond the character.[21]

It is precisely by recognizing the always partial nature of our metaphors, schemas, and narratives that we can keep ourselves alerted to the constant necessity of stretching ourselves beyond our present identity and context. No person can be moral in a suitably reflective way who cannot imagine alternative viewpoints as a means of understanding and transforming the limits of his own convictions and commitments. This is an activity of moral imagination.

Imaginative Moral Reasoning

The metaphors and other imaginative structures that make us aware of our conditioned state and the need to seek out alternative viewpoints turn out to give us the means we need to do this. The very character of metaphorical understanding that undermines absolutist pretensions—its relative indeterminacy and multiplicity of meanings—also supplies us with a range of possible meanings and directions that we might previously have overlooked. On the one hand, our imaginative understanding creates certain problems for us, since it introduces a multivalence and open-endedness into our understanding and reasoning. On the other hand, it does not leave us without resources for dealing with indeterminacies in our experience. It opens up a range of constrained alternatives that might help us solve our problem or accomplish our general goal.

As an example of the way this kind of imaginative transformation of our moral understanding operates in an open-ended, yet highly constrained, manner, I want to consider Steven Winter's analysis of the imaginative basis of a landmark case of legal reasoning.[22] The case examined by Winter is *legal,* but because his analysis focuses on imaginative structures present in conceptualization and reasoning generally, it can stand as an example of what typically goes on in the creative use of *moral* imagination, too.

The case, *NLRB v. Jones and Laughlin Steel Corp.,* concerns the issue of whether the federal government should have the power to regulate labor relations in manufacturing. The outcome established an important precedent for greater government regulation in this and many other areas as well. The steel company wanted to preserve its power to restrict union activities. Relying on well-established nineteenth-century precedent, the steel manufacturers argued that we must distinguish manufacturing from commerce. Manufacturing is *local* and thus subject only to the laws of the state in which the goods are made. Commerce, to the extent that it extends across state boundaries, would be subject to federal regulation. So construed, the federal government would have no jurisdiction over the steel company's handling of labor problems arising at the level of manufacturing.

The drafters of the National Labor Relations Act argued differently, building their argument on the metaphor of a STREAM OF COMMERCE. Taking that metaphor as fundamental, they reasoned that a corporation's interfering with labor's collective bargaining has "the necessary effect of burdening and *obstructing* commerce by (a) impairing the efficiency, safety, or operation of the instrumentalities of commerce; (b) *occurring in the current of commerce;* (c) materially affecting, *restricting, or controlling the flow* of raw materials or manufactured or processed goods from or *into the channels of commerce* . . . or (d) causing diminution of employment and wages in such *volume* as substantially to impair or disrupt the market for goods *flowing from or into the channels of commerce.*"[23]

What Justice Hughes discerned in this argument was not only the STREAM OF COMMERCE metaphor, but also the SOURCE-PATH-GOAL schema that underlies it. He used this schema as the basis for an alternative metaphorical understanding that would justify even greater governmental control over business. Arguing that the STREAM OF COMMERCE metaphor covers only a limited range of cases, Hughes then elaborates his alternative metaphoric frame: "The congressional authority to protect interstate commerce from burdens and obstructions is not limited to trans-actions which can be deemed to be an essential part of a 'flow' of interstate or foreign commerce. *Burdens and obstructions* may be due to *injurious action springing from other sources.* The fundamental principle is that the power to reg-ulate commerce is the power to enact 'all appropriate legislation' for its *'protection and advancement'* . . . and it is primarily for Congress to consider and decide the *fact of the danger* and to *meet it.*"[24]

Hughes is transforming the logic of the argument here from one of avoiding obstructions to the free flow of commerce (STREAM OF COMMERCE metaphor) to one of actively meeting potential dangers that might limit the *advancement* of commerce. A much more aggressive role for the government is being sanctioned. The basis for this expanded role is the emergence of a new metaphoric conception of COMMERCE AS JOURNEY. As Hughes says, what if we regard commerce as "*a great movement* of iron ore, coal and limestone *along well-defined paths.*"[25] Commerce, personified as a traveller, must then be supported and protected as it moves along its journey (following a SOURCE-PATH-GOAL schema). A much more active role of protector is justified for the federal government, in which antici-pated dangers or obstructions must be directly confronted. That would mean that the government could intervene at any point in the commerce journey, even at the 'start' of the journey in the manufacturing plants.

Winter summarizes Hughes's imaginative transformation of the underlying metaphors and their basic image schema:

> The older model was premised on a *stream* metaphor that entailed a quite limited congressional role: If commerce is a stream, then Con-gress's job is to *regulate* its flow and protect it from *obstructions.* Hughes' model, premised on the much richer *journey* metaphor, yields more wide ranging entailments. If commerce is a traveler on a journey, then the potential sources of interference are much more widespread. The focus now becomes not mere obstructions, but harms of many sorts such as *throttling, danger, injurious actions springing from other sources.* The correlative congressional power shifts from *regulation* to *protection and advancement.* Congress is now the interstate police pro-tecting the always vulnerable traveler and expediting her journey.[26]

Hughes goes on to explore the entailments of his new metaphor, including the key notion that "*stoppage* of those [manufacturing] operations by *industrial strife* would have a most serious effect on interstate commerce,"[27] so that the federal government may find it necessary to interfere with labor relations, insofar as they might pose a threat to the ability of commerce to make its journey.

The critical move, as we have seen, has already been accomplished—the shift of metaphors carried off by discerning their underlying shared SOURCE-PATH-GOAL schema. This is an important part of what I mean by the imaginative exploration of possibilities for action that lies at the heart of moral reasoning. What is crucial in such cases of reasoning is that we can employ metaphoric and other imaginative materials that are already operating in our present understanding of a situation to transform that situation by discovering novel alternatives for evaluation and action.

Justice Hughes's reasoning in *Jones and Laughlin* is imaginative in that it utilizes metaphoric resources available to all members of our culture, and it carries us, via an underlying image schema, from one systematic metaphor for commerce to a novel one that has very different entailments concerning the extent of government control in business. We have seen that Hughes's exercise of moral imagination is, although highly constrained by preexisting frames and values, nevertheless not altogether determined by them. He is able to reason creatively from one metaphorical conception to another by his imaginative elaboration of an image schema shared by both metaphorical mappings.

Hughes's reasoning in this legal case is exemplary of the nature of moral imagination generally. In our moral reasoning we use imaginative structures and contents given to us by our culture and articulated through our personal experience as a basis for imaginatively exploring new possibilities for meaning, relationships, social organizations, and forms of practice.

What is crucial is that our moral reasoning can be *constrained* by the metaphoric and other imaginative structures shared within our culture and moral tradition, yet it can also be *creative* in transforming our moral understanding, our identity, and the course of our lives. Without this kind of imaginative reasoning we would lead dreadfully impoverished lives. We would be reduced to repeating habitual actions, driven by forces and contingencies beyond our control. It is moral imagination that gives us the modest, but absolutely necessary, freedom we have to grow and develop morally and socially.

It is unsettling to some people to realize that there is a certain amount of ineliminable indeterminacy in our experience of situations, and that human moralities cannot escape this indeterminacy. But the fact that there are always multiple framings possible for any situation ought not to generate either despair or cynicism. Rather, we ought to celebrate the multivalence of situations that makes it possible for us to deal creatively and constructively with them, for this means that we are not locked into the same old fixed patterns of behavior and response. We can transform our experience, we can try out new ideas, and we can grow.

Moral Imagination and the Aesthetic Dimensions of Experience

I began this book with the observation that many people are likely to regard the term 'moral imagination' as an oxymoron, a juxtaposition of two contradictory concepts. Their reason for holding this mistaken view is that they accept the Moral Law conception of morality as a system of moral laws derived by pure reason alone, whereas they associate imagination with art, creativity, and our general capacity to *break* rules and transcend our present concepts.

As part of our Enlightenment heritage, we tend to regard imagination as an 'aesthetic' capacity whose primary function is creativity in art and science. Let us examine the false assumption that, because imagination is an aesthetic capacity, it can have no place in moral reasoning.

The rigid separation of the aesthetic from the moral is rooted in the following Enlightenment view of cognition that we have inherited: The Enlightenment folk theory of Faculty Psychology was used to support the view that our mental acts can be broken down into separate and distinct forms of judgment. One of the central tasks of epistemology was to explain the role of each of the cognitive faculties or powers in producing the types of judgments characteristic of science, morality, and art. Typically, 'theoretical' and 'scientific' judgments (judgments giving us determinate objective knowledge of the world) were analyzed as acts that unified sense perceptions under concepts and then conjoined those concepts into propositions that expressed our knowledge of the world. 'Moral' judgments, as we have seen, were supposed to involve the judging of particular cases as falling under a particular moral concept, and thereby being governed by a specific moral rule. In other words, moral reasoning (judgment) consisted in the application of moral laws to concrete cases, on the basis of shared moral concepts.

'Aesthetic' judgments, by contrast, were thought not to involve any concepts at all, and they were not products of reason. They were, instead, based on *feelings* and *imagination,* expressing our feeling response to certain perceptible forms of natural and artificial objects. It was regarded as crucial not to confuse moral with aesthetic judgments. Neither aesthetic judgments nor acts of artistic creation could be performed by following rules, since there were no concepts involved that could give rules (of the form 'If object X has properties A, B, C, then it is beautiful'). Moral judgments, in contrast, could supposedly derive determinate rules for action from determinate moral conepts.

As long as aesthetic and moral judgments are viewed as radically different in this way, the idea that imagination is central to moral judgment will be seen as utterly wrongheaded. If you take imagination to be an unconstrained, subjective play of images or representations, then placing imagination at the core of moral judgment would seem to undermine the possibility of definite moral laws.

Those folk theories that are based on Enlightenment Faculty Psychology, its distinction among types of judgment, and its correlative distinction among realms of experience (i.e., the theoretical, moral, and aesthetic) are, for the most part, shown to be wrong by cognitive science. I want to single out for criticism two views in particular that are based on this cluster of false assumptions: that aesthetic judgment pertains only to objects of beauty and works of art (and so is not part of morality), and that morality covers only that dimension of our lives where we guide our actions by rationally derived moral laws.

In sharp contrast, it has been an underlying assumption of this entire study that the 'aesthetic' permeates every aspect of our lives. I construe the 'aesthetic' broadly as including the imaginative structures, activities, orientations, and transformations by means of which we are able to have coherent experience that we can make some sense of. It was Dewey who saw most clearly that there are aesthetic dimensions to all our experience. Human beings tend to seek experience that builds to some level of fulfillment. The aesthetic is that which makes it possible for us to have relatively unified, coherent, and consummated experiences. Therefore, the 'aesthetic' is present and intermingles in what we think of as the 'scientific,' the 'theoretical,' and the 'moral.' We call a certain experience 'theoretical' to emphasize the importance of its descriptive, explanatory, and confirmation-oriented dimensions. We call an experience 'moral' to emphasize its practical, normative, and action-oriented dimensions. Dewey explains this enriched notion of the aesthetic:

> I have tried to show . . . that the esthetic is no intruder in experience from without, whether by way of idle luxury or transcendent ideality, but that it is the clarified and intensified development of traits that belong to every normally complete experience. . . .
> It is not possible to divide in a vital experience the practical, emo-

tional, and intellectual from one another and to set the properties of one over against the characteristics of the others. The emotional phase binds part together into a single whole; "intellectual" simply names the fact that the experience has meaning; "practical" indicates that the organism is interacting with events and objects which surround it. The most elaborate philosophic or scientific inquiry and the most ambitious industrial or political enterprise has, when its different ingredients constitute an integral experience, esthetic quality.[28]

We must stop making the mistake of thinking of the aesthetic as an escape from the practical or moral, that is, as a retreat from moral responsibilities into a realm of the cultivation of artistic taste. This requires us to acknowledge that the aesthetic dimensions of any experience are those that contribute to its possibilities for meaningful order, coherence, and consummation. In large measure, this is a matter of imaginative structuring. Seen in this light, morality is not the search for moral laws to guide our lives, but rather the ongoing imaginative exploration of possibilities for dealing with our problems, enhancing the quality of our communal relations, and forming significant personal attachments that grow.

Thus, it is neither scandalous nor threatening to regard morality as fundamentally a matter of moral imagination and as involving aesthetic development. The aesthetic dimensions of experience—including imagination, emotions, and concepts—are what make meaning and the enhancement of quality possible (or, correlatively, the disintegration and impoverishment of experience).

Imagination is no longer banished to the realm of allegedly subjective aesthetic experiences. Instead, it is precisely that capacity which allows us both to experience present situations as significant and to transform them in light of our quest for well-being. Imagination is the means for going beyond our selves as presently formed, moving transformatively toward imagined ideals of what we might become, how we might relate to others, and how we might address problematic situations.[29] Moral imagination is our capacity to see and to realize in some actual or contemplated experience possibilities for enhancing the quality of experience, both for ourselves and for the communities of which we are a part, both for the present and for future generations, both for our existing practices and institutions as well as for those we can imagine as potentially realizable.[30] And this holds true for whether we are experiencing and judging artworks or engaged in pressing moral deliberations that determine the course of our lives.

On the Metaphor of MORALITY AS ART

Saying that there are aesthetic dimensions woven into the fabric of our moral experience, understanding, and reasoning sounds a bit like saying that morality is art. While I do think that moral reasoning is a certain type of skillful imaginative activity, I am not proposing that we take the MORALITY AS ART metaphor as an unqualified truth. There are many aspects of prototypical artistic activity that are not part of moral reasoning, and vice versa.

What I *am* proposing is that we are likely to learn a great deal more about morality by examining how far it is like aesthetic discrimination and artistic creation than by studying traditional Moral Law accounts. Let me suggest how far I am willing to press the MORALITY AS ART metaphor as revelatory of the nature of moral reasoning. Consider the following characteristics of artistic activity as they bear on moral deliberation:

Discernment. Deciding how to act in a particular set of circumstances will depend on how we frame the situation. This is a matter of subtle discernment and discrimination of what is important in the situation. It is very much a matter of reading situations, character, and intentions. Without fine-textured perception of this sort, moral laws and rules are useless and empty. This is the basis of Martha Nussbaum's argument that "moral knowledge . . . is not simply intellectual grasp of propositions; it is not even simply intellectual grasp of particular facts; it is perception. It is seeing a complex, concrete reality in a highly lucid and richly responsive way; it is taking in what is there, with imagination and feeling."[31]

The work of morality is done, not in the grasping of moral laws or principles, but in discerning what is going on in the situations we face: who we are and what we desire, what others want and need, how we relate to them, what possible forms our action could take, and what is likely to result from various envisioned courses of action.

The capacity for subtle discrimination that is absolutely essential if we are to be morally sensitive is one of the things we prize most in artists. We value their ability to notice what we do not see, to imagine possibilities we have not imagined, and to feel in ways we might, but are not now, feeling. We value their ability to respond to situations and experiences in ways that we tend to overlook, thereby opening up to us new dimensions of our world.

Just as in our aesthetic perception, so also in our moral discernment, there are constraints on our imaginative vision of things. Nussbaum reminds us that, "if we think of the perception as a created work of art, we must at the same time remember that artists, as James sees it, are not free simply to create anything they like. Their obligation is to render reality, precisely and faithfully; in this task they are very much assisted by general principles and by the habits and attachments that are their internalization" (155).

Moral and artistic perception are alike in this way: they are acts of imagination and feeling for which there is no predetermined method (or algorithmic procedure), yet they are "assisted" by general principles and constrained by the nature of our bodily, interpersonal, and cultural interactions. Just as lack of aesthetic discrimination is an artistic fault, so lack of moral perception is a moral fault. Nussbaum concludes: "Obtuseness is a moral failing; its opposite can be cultivated. By themselves, trusted in and for themselves, the standing terms [general principles and rules] are a recipe for obtuseness. To respond 'at the right times, with reference to the right objects, towards the right people, with the right aim, and in the right way, is what is appropriate and best, and this is characteristic of excellence' (Aristotle, *EN* 1106b21–23)" (156).

Expression. At least since the romantic period, we have come to regard prototypical works of art as acts of expression by an artist. In *The Principles of Art* R. G. Collingwood argues that the work of art is actually identical with the act of expression by the artist.[32] In expressive activity the artist comes to give definition, individuality, and clarity to emotions, images, and desires. In this way art comes to be a form of self-disclosure and self-knowledge.

I am not claiming that *all* art is like this, nor that Collingwood's theory covers all forms of expression. But, just as in art, we do express our character and self-identity in our moral deliberations and actions. More importantly, we form and re-form ourselves in an ongoing fashion in and through our moral reasoning. We both find ourselves and transform ourselves through our thoughts and deeds.

We do not tend to think of morality as importantly concerned with self-expression, but it obviously is. Since we come to be who we are in and through our thoughts and actions, morality is one of our primary forms of self-expression and self-definition. It is the main arena in which we project ourselves and pursue our sense of what we hope to become.

Investigation. Art has always been valued as an investigation into the nature of things. Art as *mimesis* or creative imitation, and thus a form of knowledge, was the first theory to arise in the Western tradition. And, even though strictly imitative or naturalistic views of art are out of favor now, we continue to see art as an investigation of the possibilities of form, materials, language, institutions, relationships, and so forth.

Thinking of moral deliberation as a form of moral investigation is enlightening, therefore, because it highlights the exploratory aspects of morality. In order to act in the best way we can, we must try out various framings of situations, inquire into the motives and intentions of others, and explore possibilities for constructive interaction that are latent within situations. It is but a very small part of such investigations to find moral laws. Most of what we have to do is a form of engaged probing and experimentation with our understanding of situations, our relationships, and our grasp of the implications of various projected courses of action.

Creativity. In art we make things: physical objects, texts, tunes, events, or even conceptual entities. We mold, shape, give form to, compose, harmonize, balance, disrupt, organize, re-form, construct, delineate, portray, and use other forms of imaginative making.

In a very straightforward way, this is exactly what we do in morality. We *portray* situations, *delineate* character, *formulate* problems, and *mold* events. When we act we engage in various forms of creative making: we *compose* situations, *build* relationships, *harmonize* diverse interests, *balance* competing values and goods, *design* institutional practices, and *orchestrate* interpersonal relations. This is not merely an optional way of describing what we do, it is a precise account of what morally sensitive and perceptive people must do.

Everyone recognizes that imagination is the key to these artistic acts by which new things come into existence, old things are reshaped, and our ways of seeing, hearing, feeling, thinking, and so forth are transformed. And we have seen above that imagination, too, is the key to the moral acts by which old conceptions and values are reshaped, our ways of perceiving and responding to situations and people are transformed, and new realities come into existence.

The historical and evolutionary character of human experience entails that new kinds of problems and situations will arise over time, so that we must be constantly adjusting, adapting, and fine-tuning our lives. This requires continual experimentation with new possibilities for addressing these novel conditions that arise. Much of our experimental activity will prove inappropriate, misdirected, or even counterproductive, just as our artistic experiments often are. But, occasionally, we do come up with imaginative new forms of personal and institutional relationships, both at the modest level of our individual lives, and on the more grand scale of communities and whole cultures (such as the abolition of slavery and the institution of universal voting rights).

Certain people are particularly good at this sort of imaginative exploration and creation. They enlarge our understanding—our sense of the possibilities open to us for experiencing our world, understanding ourselves, and forming attachments with others. They appear to break the established rules of morality or law or propriety, going beyond canonical forms and practices to show us new ways of thinking, relating, and acting.

In the realm of art narrowly construed, for example, van Gogh's *Portrait of Patience Escalier* (1889) could violate accepted rules for the realistic use of color by painting eyes with red irises and beard and hair of a bluish green cast, yet what he gives us rings true to our experience, reshapes it, and reveals hitherto hidden dimensions not captured by our received aesthetic canons. In painting after painting he undermines any canonical presentation of color (e.g., the green faces of his self-portraits, the blue tree trunks in an olive grove), only to create an intensity of color that holds us captive and convinces us utterly of the rightness of what he has seen and done—not according to any set of rules for making art, but according to the flexible logic of our imaginative understanding of things.

We are not without parallels in morality. In his *Letter from a Birmingham Jail* Martin Luther King Jr. gave his eloquent response to his friends and supporters who were urging him to desist from civil disobedience and to let time work out the civil rights changes that would 'inevitably' come about. Nonviolent confrontation, they argued, would only alienate the very people who needed to be won over. Change must come gradually, as people adjust to new ideas and arrangements. Why submit people on both sides to pain, suffering, alienation, and even death, merely to speed up a process that should develop gradually?

King saw what so many people could not see. He saw that change would not happen by normal processes. He read the character and intentions and will of the people involved on both sides. He envisioned possibilities for human relationships that could inspire people to sacrificial action. He imagined ways to realize the ideal of human equality that others had missed. Today we see fairly clearly that he acted with justice, compassion, humility, courage, and insight. In the early 1960s none of this was clear at all. It required perception, imagination, and remarkable creativity to orchestrate the civil rights movement as he did. It is art to which we can all aspire.

Skill. There is thus a skillful dimension to morality, for morality requires skillful coping[33] with others and with the contingencies of life. I mean by 'skill' the Greek conception of *technē* as articulated by Martha Nussbaum: "*Technē*, then, is a deliberate application of human intelligence to some part of the world, yielding some control over *tuchē* (chance or contingency); it is concerned with the management of need and with prediction and control concerning future contingencies. The person who lives by *technē* does not come to each new experience without foresight or resource. He possesses some sort of systematic grasp, some way of ordering the subject matter, that will take him to the new situation well prepared, removed from blind dependence on what happens."[34]

There are artistic skills for which training is appropriate—they can be learned through practice. But skills must not be conceived merely as knowledge of effective means to some pregiven, definite end. The artist does not begin by framing an exact conception of what she wishes to produce and then applying skills to realize that end. The skill lies, rather, in a form of interaction with materials, forms, and ideas in which something determinate begins to take shape through the process of working with the materials of the art. One's conception evolves and grows by skillfully working the material, whether it is clay, fabric, paint, musical tones, or words. A *technē* of this sort, according to Nussbaum, "will be qualitative, plural in its ends, and in which the art activities themselves constitute the end."[35]

As in art, so also in morality, there is a dimension of skill. There are aspects of morality where practice and training are appropriate. Such practice is seldom a case of following verbal rules, though there is a place for this kind of teaching, especially for young children. The skillful coping that is required is the kind of understanding that allows some people to work their way creatively and constructively through situations that are developing as they confront them. This kind of skill, then, is never merely a fixed procedure that one applies mechanically to situations; instead, it is an elusive kind of knowledge of how to go on, in the midst of contingencies and unforeseen circumstances, to realize well-being. It is this form of creative making that I have in mind when I speak of 'orchestrating' relationships or 'composing' situations.

These, and other, parallels between art and morality are the basis for my taking seriously the MORALITY AS ART metaphor, as a way of opening up overlooked imaginative dimensions of our moral reasoning. *I am not, thereby, collapsing morality into art* (narrowly construed as the making of art objects). Rather, I have been arguing that the kind of imaginative judgment widely recognized as appropriate to the making, experiencing, and evaluating of artworks can serve as a model of moral judgment, insofar as it is pervasively imaginative in many of the same respects.

I am thus not sanctioning the 'aestheticization' of life and morality that has cropped up repeatedly during the last century as a cynical or despairing response to the disintegration of what was once regarded as *the* Western moral framework. As Kierkegaard showed us conclusively, the life of A (the aesthete) is both a flight from moral responsibility and a destruction of the possibility of meaningful human existence and action.[36] If we understand the aesthetic in the sense articulated above, then the idea of the aestheticizing of life becomes nothing more than a misuse of the term, predicated on an overly narrow and subjectivist definition of the aesthetic and on a false separation of the aesthetic from the moral.

What Is Moral Imagination Good For?

Everything I have said in this chapter constitutes my answer to this question. I have summarized many of the ways in which our moral concepts, our framing of situations, and our reasoning about what to do are typically based on various types of imaginative structure. I have argued that the imaginative character of moral understanding places certain obligations on us: (1) an obligation to know the implications for morality of the fact that human cognition is in large measure imaginative, and (2) an obligation to cultivate moral imagination in ourselves and others.

This will seem to some to be meager guidance for our lives. It is time to realize that this is all we have, and that it does not leave us helpless. A theory of morality, understood as a theory of moral understanding, does not give us moral laws, yet it does offer a certain kind of guidance for our lives. The guidance is provided by moral knowledge of ourselves and others. We will reflect and act differently, because we see the importance of moral perception and discernment, of imaginatively taking up the part of others, and of envisioning alternative possibilities for composing situations in ways that contribute to human flourishing.

People who fall back on rules and moral laws are people who are either afraid of the indeterminacy and contingency of life, or morally obtuse, or both. Rule-mongering is a sign of moral failure, and it cannot do what it promises, namely, to tell us how to act in every situation.

This brings me back to the story with which I began the chapter. Early in 1971 I had to make my decision. I did. I filed with my draft board for conscientious objector status. I broke my father's heart. I was called for my draft physical and was told that I would soon be called to report for induction into the army. My draft board had reportedly never issued a CO status to anyone. I was contemplating the ominous spector of imprisonment, having decided that it would be improper for me to flee the country.

Then something happened that is typical of the way in which unexpected, unpredictable contingencies that are utterly outside our control often change our lives. Instead of an induction notice, I received a letter disqualifying me from active service status on the basis of a joint deformity in my left knee—something left over from high-school basketball. I was classified 1-Y, which meant suitable for service in case of national emergency. So I did not go to Vietnam, I did not go to prison, and I did not perform alternative service.

The fact that an utter contingency changed my life does not alter the moral significance of the dilemma I posed above. The situation I faced was completely typical of all the difficult moral dilemmas we encounter in our lives. They are not solved by having moral laws. They are not solved by some preestablished method of moral reasoning. They are not matters of finding '*the* right thing to do.' Rather, they are matters that require discriminating, balancing, composing, envisioning, projecting, exploring—matters of imaginative perception, imaginative envisionment, and imaginative action.

Living without Absolutes: Objectivity

and the Conditions for Criticism

If our moral understanding is fundamentally imaginative in character, then what can moral objectivity possibly consist in? Is it a mere illusion, as extreme relativists claim? Or, if it is not an illusion, then what account of objectivity can we give that is consistent with the imaginative structure of our moral concepts and the reasoning we do with them? I propose to outline such an account.

What we need is a reasonable and empirically adequate conception of 'objectivity' and 'impartiality' based on imaginative rationality. The question is, Having given up the claim to an absolute standpoint for moral judgment, is there any realistic notion of objectivity that is not merely a matter of which person or group wields the power to set standards? We must find out whether there is any basis in structures of imagination that makes it possible for us to criticize and to transform some of our most basic beliefs and values.

As I have been arguing, especially in the previous chapter, the key to answering this crucial question is to focus on the public, social character of imagination. We have seen that image schemas and conceptual metaphors are typically grounded in our bodily experience. Imagination, therefore, is not merely a private, subjective, or idiosyncratic process. It can be the basis for concepts, frames, and points of view that transcend individual perspectives, although not in the sense claimed by absolutism.

Moreover, imagination is the means by which we are able to conceive of alternative perspectives and to explore their implications for action, relationships, and communal well-being. Thus, the very possibility of taking a critical stance toward a particular viewpoint depends on our imaginative ability to envision other viewpoints.

The crux of this view of moral criticism as fundamentally imaginative is that moral objectivity consists, not in having an absolute 'God's-eye point of view,' but rather in a specific kind of reflective, exploratory, and critical process of evaluation carried out through communal discourse and practice.

Notice also that, just as we must reconstruct our notion of objectivity, we must also reconstruct our sense of subjectivity and imagination. In earlier chapters I have argued that neither subjectivity (i.e., our identity as persons) nor imagination is merely individualistic and private. Both involve shared, communal, cultural, and even universal dimensions. Objectivity and subjectivity thus move closer to each other as correlative parts of an interactive process of experience. Objectivity is less transcendental and absolute than many people believe, while subjectivity is correspondingly less subjective and private than most people believe.

The Conception of Objectivity Underlying
Absolutism and Relativism

The standard of objectivity shared by both moral absolutism and, ironically, extreme moral relativism is the false one foisted upon us by the Moral Law folk theory. According to the absolutist version, objectivity can only be secured by the existence of universally binding moral laws. These absolute and objective moral laws must come from the essential structure of a Universal Reason that is supposedly shared by all moral agents. Moral objectivity consists in rising above your particular embodiment—your longings, interests, emotions, and specific attachments to others—to assume the point of view of a transcendent Universal Reason shared by all people. Our prejudices and biases are what supposedly set us apart from others and blind us to the light of Universal Reason. Our innate radical freedom permits us to overcome these prejudices, to rise above our bodily desires, and to take up a universally valid standpoint in our moral deliberations and evaluations.

The Moral Law account can acknowledge that the personality of each individual may change over time, but it must insist that what makes us moral agents— our Universal (practical) Reason—cannot change its essence. In moral absolutism, therefore, there is no room whatsoever for imaginative transformation or development, either in human rationality or in the concepts that ground morality.

Extreme relativism, which is regarded as the opposite of absolutism, turns out to share this same mistaken view of objectivity in moral judgment. The only difference between the two views in this: Absolutism thinks that we can meet this standard of objectivity, because it thinks people are exactly the way the Moral Law folk theory describes them (i.e., they possess an essential human reason that issues universal moral principles). The relativist agrees that objectivity, if it existed, would have to be secured by universal moral laws, but thinks that there is nothing universally shared across all cultures and times that could ground such a strong notion of objectivity. Consequently, relativists deny the existence of objectivity in the absolutist sense.

In sharp contrast with this static, nondevelopmental, and nonevolutionary absolutist view of our identity as moral agents, I have been emphasizing the temporal character of everything human. We are beings whose identities emerge and develop in an ongoing process of interactions within our physical, interpersonal, and cultural environments. To function successfully within these changing environments our reason must be expansive, exploratory, and flexible. The locus of our moral understanding is thus our imaginative rationality (a *human*, rather than *Universal*, Reason) that allows us to envision and to test out in imagination various possible solutions to morally problematic situations. By giving us alternative perspectives, it also thereby gives us a means for criticizing and evaluating those projected courses of action and the values they presuppose.

Those who regard objectivity as based solely on universally valid moral laws will typically see all forms of imagination as subjective and unconstrained, and therefore as undermining the very possibility of objectivity. When absolutists assume this false view of imagination, they are forced to conclude that it can have no important role in moral reasoning, since the moral laws are alleged to issue solely from an absolute, fixed, and essential reason.

Extreme relativism, in either of its two forms, assumes this same mistaken view of imagination. The first form agrees with the absolutist doctrine that morality is a set of rationally derived laws, but it argues that our concepts, rationality, and values are defined relative to particular cultural contexts. It thus denies both the universality of reason and also the role of imagination in applying moral laws to concrete cases.

The second form of relativism is distinguished by the fact that it acknowledges a role for imagination in our conceptualization and reasoning. However, since imagination is taken to be a nonrational process that is not governed by rules of any sort, relativists of this second variety can see no basis for any universal rationality or objectivity in morality. They see different moralities as different and incommensurable imaginative frames, having no grounding in human embodiment or experience. They describe change within systems of morality as one set of laws or values coming to be replaced by another set, but blindly, by virtue of contingent circumstances. They deny that there is any underlying rationality within which to assess differing moralities.[1]

When stacked up against such extreme forms of relativism and irrationalism, some form of moral absolutism has seemed to many people to be the only reasonable alternative to anarchy and chaos. But we have seen why this is a false and dangerously mistaken conclusion based on an incorrect understanding of conceptual structure, reason, moral personhood, and moral imagination that is shared by both absolutism and relativism alike. In order to understand more fully why this absolutist view of objectivity won't work, let us begin by asking why it is so natural for people to feel the need for moral absolutes.

What Motivates Moral Absolutism's View of Objectivity?

Moral absolutism received its clearest and most elegant expression in Enlightenment moral philosophy. It was a grand and important project that promised to set morality once and for all on absolutely firm rational foundations. Many of our most basic moral ideas found their classic articulation with this context—ideas such as autonomy, universal moral personality, respect, and universal laws of reason.

It would be a serious mistake to think that we could or ought to discard altogether these ideas on the grounds that they arose within a philosophical framework that is no longer defensible. To throw out these ideas wholesale would be to deny and reject our tradition, our history, our community, and thereby our very identity. *Yet we cannot keep these ideas unchanged,* for as they now stand, they are seriously at odds with our moral experience, our social needs, and our current understanding of cognition and knowledge. We must, instead, *transform* these crucial ideas in light of what we have learned about meaning, cognition, and reasoning, and in light of the demands of our present situation.

In order to see how these moral ideals might be revised, we need to understand why moral absolutism has the deep and broad appeal that it does within our culture. Its obsession with moral absolutes can be seen as a way of trying to deal with some of the more frightening and threatening aspects of human existence. We are born into a world full of need, conflict, hostility, and evil. Without denying the existence of kindness and love, it remains true that "the world is real and dense and dark,"[2] and that, as Hobbes observed, "the life of man, solitary, poore, nasty, brutish, and short."[3] We have needs (e.g., food, shelter, love, protection from harm) that must be satisfied if we are to survive and flourish in our environment. Yet the resources for satisfying these needs are quite limited and hard to come by, which gives rise to severe competition. Even worse, the conflicts that arise are not limited merely to understandable tensions over the distribution of scarce resources. For there is evil in the world that goes far beyond this—a seemingly ineradicable aggressive instinct that leads us to inflict suffering on others, as well as on ourselves, even when our basic needs are tolerably well met.[4] This unbridled aggression assaults us on every page of human history, in every period, and in every place we know of.

Hence, we cry out for constraints on the actions of others who affect us and also on our own actions, which can harm both others and ourselves. We need a certain measure of stability in our private lives, in our social interactions, and in our public institutions, and we perceive that specific restrictions must be observed in order to make such stable social arrangements possible. Consequently, we crave fixed standards of proper behavior that will both protect us from harm and ideally maximize our individual freedom in a way that is consistent with a like freedom of others to pursue their own ends. We furthermore realize that communally relative standards won't ultimately solve our problem, for various communities (understood via the SOCIETY IS A PERSON metaphor) are themselves in competition for scarce resources, and they experience conflict and disagreement about moral standards. It is no longer possible for different cultures and moral traditions to presume to stand apart in isolation from one another. We are forced to confront competing cultures with their competing practices of human flourishing.

In this way we are severely tempted to take the fatal step from the need for order, stability, and constraint to a demand for absolute moral constraints in the form of universal moral laws or principles. The unacceptable alternative to such absolutes is perceived to be a general erosion of moral constraints to the point where we fall back into uncontrolled competition among individuals and social groups. What is feared most is an extreme relativism that denies the possibility of justifying our moral principles and institutions outside of a particular, historically situated moral community.[5]

Recall that the absolutes required by absolutism to answer relativism were of two sorts: (1) the fundamental moral concepts and moral laws that are based on them, and (2) the essential structure of reason from which those moral principles are allegedly derived. Absolutism needs concepts that have a definite, fixed, univocal content, so that they can be applied directly to concrete situations on the basis of clearly perceived features of those situations. Without such concepts and principles, the argument goes, we would be left with a moral indeterminacy bordering on chaos—you understand a basic concept one way and I understand it quite differently, and there is no agreed-upon standard or procedure for determining who is right.

As an illustration of this perceived need for moral absolutes, consider the classic form of an argument prohibiting abortion:

1. Killing an innocent person is morally prohibited because it fails to respect his humanity (or his status as made in God's image, or as an end-in-himself).
2. A fetus is an innocent person.
3. Abortion is an intentional killing of a fetus.
4. Therefore, abortion is an intentional killing of an innocent person.
5. Abortion is morally impermissible (as failing to respect the humanity or personhood of the fetus).

Premises 1 and 2, of course, are the controversial ones, and the vast majority of moral debate centers on premise 2, which defines a fetus as a person. The question is, What view of the concept *person* is necessary in order to make this anti-abortion argument work? First, the concept *person* must be absolutely fixed and well-defined. Second, it must be either value-neutral or else itself based on an absolute value.

The concept *person* must be fixed, well-defined, and context-free, because otherwise each time we used the concept in a different context it could conceivably have a different meaning. But if each application of the concept determines its meaning, then either (1) we would need a *rule* for applying the concept in various cases (and this would be the same as saying that the meaning of 'person' is fixed), or (2) we would be left with the possibility that different people might apply the concept differently.

What about the requirement of value neutrality for the concept? This requirement is spawned by the fear that, if the way we apply the concept *person* depends on our values, then we might well vary in our judgments about what the concept applies to, and when it applies. We could try to avoid this variability in either of two ways. One way would be to insist that the concept *person* is value-neutral and that applying it in no way depends on any values we have. The other way would be to claim access to an absolute or ultimate value, binding on all people, that would make it possible for every one of us to apply the concept in the same way.

We have seen in previous chapters that some of our most basic concepts simply do not have either a fixed content or a classical category structure (specifying necessary and sufficient conditions). We also saw that some of our basic moral concepts are applicable only within contexts that presuppose certain values (e.g., the case of *lie*). But if contexts are not value-neutral, then we cannot avoid having to make value judgments in applying a concept, such as determining what counts as a person.

We are now in a position to address our question of the ultimate motivation for moral absolutism. Why is it thought to be so horrible that our moral concepts are neither fixed nor absolute? I have offered the following answer: Without such absolute fixed points (in the form of concepts and laws), we realize that we must depend on the judgments of *fallible, finite, and frail creatures living within evolving communities who are forced to make decisions by their best lights within what are typically highly ambiguous value-laden contexts.* The degree of fear that this prospect engenders in us is likely to depend on our faith in our fellow creatures. And there are certainly good reasons for skepticism and fear, since we are aware of just how often we ourselves make decisions with incomplete or faulty information, under stress, under the influence of our own perceived self-interest, or even out of mere aggression.

In sum, moral absolutism is motivated by a very widespread human longing for clarity, certainty, order, and constraint in a world that confronts us constantly with change, obscurity, doubt, contingency, and aggression. We become absolutist to the extent that we take this very normal longing and seek to satisfy it by projecting the *absolute* as a ground of meaning, truth, morality, and social structure, in order to give us an answer to our finitude. Driven by this strong desire to overcome our finitude, we search for absolute moral laws, as the ultimate constraints on human actions.

Moral absolutism offers itself as *the* definitive rebuttal to all forms of relativism, because it purports to identify absolute moral principles. *If* it could supply what it promises, in a manner consistent with what we are learning about human cognition, then perhaps it could satisfy our longing for clarity, certainty, and stability. But we have seen several ways in which *it does not work,* such as in its view of the self, action, conceptual structure, and reason. At the very heart of moral absolutism is an untenable view of objectivity. It is time to say what's wrong with that view and to determine what might replace it in a nonabsolutist account.

What Objectivity Isn't

To put it simply: objectivity cannot depend on a 'God's-eye point of view.' It cannot be the taking up of a perspective that encompasses all perspectives. It cannot be an ultimate context. It can be none of these things, for they are all illusory ideals impossible for finite, historically situated human beings.

We have seen that, for the most part, human concepts do not have such an absolute, noncontextual character. There is no single univocal concept, for instance, of *cause* or *rights* or *lie*. Where concepts have prototype structure, their appropriate application depends in large measure on idealized cognitive models and other contextual frames and values. Where concepts are metaphorically defined, those definitions are always partial, so that there is no single 'correct' understanding of the concept. Where concepts involve image-schematic structure, that structure can often be elaborated in various ways by metaphor.

To see exactly what is wrong with this view of objectivity, we need to examine the absolutist framework in which it is embedded. That framework is constituted in part by what Lakoff and I have called the UNDERSTANDING IS SEEING metaphor that structures a large portion of our concepts of knowledge and cognition.[6] As Sweetser has shown, most of our language about knowledge is structured by vision metaphors for various epistemic acts.[7] And Rorty has examined the extent to which philosophical treatments of knowledge have been dominated by the MIND'S EYE metaphor, with disastrous skeptical effects.[8] The metaphorical mapping from the source domain (vision) to the target domain (knowing) is as follows:

The UNDERSTANDING IS SEEING Metaphor

Visual Domain	*Understanding/Knowing*
Eye (organ of sight)	Mind's eye (organ of knowing)
Physical object seen	Ideas (mental objects)
Light	(Light of) reason
Visual field	Domain of knowledge
Visual acuity	Mental acuity

The UNDERSTANDING IS SEEING metaphor combines with two basic image schemas to form our absolutist folk model of objectivity. The first is the CONTAINER schema, which is basic to our bodily experience of ourselves both as containers and as objects contained within various bounded spaces and volumes (e.g., rooms). For example, we understand ourselves not merely as actual physical containers (as in "My liver is *in* me") but also as abstract metaphorical containers ("She was *filled* with emotion," "He's got a lot of courage *in* him"). Our minds are containers for ideas and thoughts ("Keep that idea *in* mind," "His mind is airtight—nothing gets *out* or *in*"). We also experience VISUAL FIELDS AS CONTAINERS, that is, as bounded spaces ("The ship came *into* view," "It has gone *out* of sight now").

If we take the UNDERSTANDING IS SEEING metaphor and comprehend the source domain (vision) via the VISUAL FIELD IS A CONTAINER metaphor, we get the conception of understanding or knowing as seeing idea-objects within a bounded space (the field or domain of knowledge). Thus, we think of intellectual disciplines as 'fields' that are divided into 'areas.' To gain knowledge we must take up the appropriate 'point of view' from which to 'see clearly' the properties of idea-objects and their relations to each other. The problem of objectivity is to find the proper point of view sharable by others that gives you a full view of idea-objects as they are in themselves. Anyone taking up an objective viewpoint would presumably see what anyone else would see from that perspective. Ideally, what is needed is a perspective that encompasses all possible points of view and thus gives the object as it really is. We call such an all-encompassing perspective the 'God's-eye point of view.'

Within this metaphorical conception of objectivity, a prejudice is a belief or idea that 'blocks' your ability to see clearly. It 'obscures' your intellectual vision. It may even make you 'blind' to what is the case. Prejudices are belief-objects that limit your perspective so that you cannot see things as they really are.

A prejudice constitutes an obstacle in either of two senses. First, it can block your intellectual vision. In this case, what one needs is to 'see through' or 'beyond' one's prejudices. Second, the prejudicial belief-object can block you from 'getting to' a belief, where BELIEFS ARE LOCATIONS (e.g., "I've *come to* the belief that love is pain," "Saul *returned to* a belief in God"). 'Overcoming' or 'getting beyond' one's prejudice is thus surmounting an obstacle and moving to a belief-location.

An objective viewpoint distances us from our prejudices so that we can see them for what they are in relation to other idea-objects. Getting the proper distance from one's prejudices can be achieved by elevating oneself above them. Here the second image schema—the VERTICALITY (or UP-DOWN) schema—comes into play. One must 'rise above' or 'transcend' one's prejudices to get the proper perspective on the object of one's knowledge.

Objective knowledge is the result of taking oneself 'out of' one's subjective stance and 'rising above' the limits imposed by your subjective preferences, needs, and interests. Strictly speaking, the only truly adequate transcendent perspective would be a God's-eye view—a view that could take in everything and every possible perspective at once! Anything less would be merely one more limited and partial perspective.

Practical-moral objectivity is modelled on theoretical objectivity. The problem of the moral point of view is to 'rise above' one's particular interests and prejudices to take up a universally valid perspective. For Moral Law theories the body is the source of one's particularity and difference. It is the locus of feelings, sensations, emotions, and desires that set us questing after personal self-interested satisfaction. Being moral requires transcending our embodiment and acting, as free rational wills, from the perspective of disinterested universal reason.

Objectivity, on this view, is a feature of our 'acts of judgment.' According to this ideal, morality is rational, reason has a universal essence, and so it is possible to make objective judgments based on universal moral principles. Armed with these principles and a pure practical reason for evaluating any moral judgment, there could be a 'rational method' for resolving disputes about morality. Objective judgments are those that *any* fully rational agent would make in similar circumstances. To be fully rational is to transcend one's subjectivity, which is regarded as peculiar to, and different for, each individual person. When our judgments are morally objective, we are realizing our purely rational natures as superior to our individual bodily sensations and desires. By getting beyond and above our subjective perspectives, values, interests, and ends, we achieve a transcendent viewpoint that can be shared with every other rational being who, like ourselves, has cast off its particularity and difference to become pure rational will.

What this gets wrong, of course, is that our embodiment is actually something we share in common. There are universal structures of bodily experience, even if they can be imaginatively elaborated in various ways. Our perceptual structures are universally shared, and so are our motor programs. The imaginative structures of our understanding are shared. Moreover, our feelings, sensations, and emotions have a public character. I cannot feel your feelings as you feel them, but there is as communicable dimension to our 'subjective' experience. I do not know your pain, but I do know pain. I do not experience your sadness, but I can share in it with you. Our embodiment, therefore, is far from being private—it is the ground for our shared experience of a world.

The absolutist view of objectivity assumes a pure, context-free rationality that simply does not exist. It assumes the existence of a God's-eye point of view, whereas human beings are always finite, perspectival creatures. There are numerous well-known arguments against the possibility of absolute foundations, pure reason, a priori methods, and ultimate contexts. These can be found in epistemology,[9] philosophy of science,[10] and moral theory.[11]

In the previous chapters I have argued against the possibility of a context-free, absolute reason, along the following lines: The meaning of some of our most basic moral concepts is determined, not in itself, but only in relation to a larger context that includes folk models, systematic metaphors, and complex values and interests that are culturally shared. But, if these meanings are context-dependent and value-laden, then our reasoning about them will implicate various values and ideals. If some of our most basic moral concepts are defined metaphorically, and often by multiple metaphorical frames, then we must always ask for any concept, *What metaphorical frame (or frames) is it defined relative to?*

Moreover, in addition to cognitive models and metaphors, our moral reasoning depends on various folk theories about the mind, the world, and society. The folk theory of Faculty Psychology, or something very much like it, is needed to define the metaphysical, epistemological, and psychological framework upon which the Moral Law folk theory is based. And I take it that virtually nobody familiar with our current scientific understanding of how cognition works could accept the Faculty Psychology folk theory at face value.

I argued in chapter 5 that our belief that our most basic moral principles must somehow constitute the essence of human reason is the result of elevating our most cherished cultural values to the level of moral absolutes. But we saw that there are very many competing values and competing goods, including various conceptions of rationality and of the self. We saw why it is a mistake to treat them as absolutes and why this makes it more difficult for us to act in morally sensitive and constructive ways.

Our very notion of rationality is evaluative through and through, since it is defined relative to particular values, interests, and purposes. MacIntyre argues that we cannot articulate a view of justice independent of its corresponding view of reason:

> each particular conception of justice requires as its counterpart some particular conception of practical rationality and vice versa. . . . conceptions of justice and of practical rationality generally and characteristically confront us as closely related aspects of some larger, more or less well-articulated, overall view of human life and of its place in nature. Such overall views, insofar as they make claims upon our rational allegiance, give expression to traditions of rational enquiry which are at one and the same time traditions embodied in particular types of social relationship. [12]

The interdependence of our conceptions of justice and rationality holds also for the intimate link between our conceptions of reason and moral well-being. Different standards of rational justification coevolve with different conceptions of human flourishing. [13] What counts as a 'good reason' in a moral argument will depend on a cluster of values that define our sense of what life is about and how it ought to be lived. A 'good reason' or 'good argument' within a utilitarian framework will be quite different from a 'good reason' with a Kantian framework. In fact, we saw that their very conceptions of reason are different. Utilitarian reason is economic (means-ends) rationality that has no motivating or practical force in itself. Kantian rationality is based on the idea that reason can move one to action, and thus it is never merely means-ends rationality. If such large differences exist *within* the Enlightenment tradition, we can expect radically different conceptions to occur in other cultures outside this narrow tradition. The false idea of a context-free rationality thus results from failing to understand fully the historical dimension of human meaning, knowledge, and reason. It is based on the illusion that we might somehow think ourselves *outside* or *above* time, tapping into the *eternal* and unchangeable.

But, as Gadamer has argued, even if it were possible to occupy an eternal standpoint (which it is not), this would utterly destroy the very conditions that make it possible for us to understand anything at all.[14] For it is precisely our tradition—through language, institutions, rituals, accumulated experience, symbols, and practices—that gives us the means to understand what we experience. To extract ourselves, per impossible, from our inhabiting of a tradition and a community would strip us of the resources for experiencing anything as meaningful.

The moral relativist is likely to step in at this point with the claim that, in the absence of absolute moral frameworks, concepts, and values, we are left only with tradition-bound moralities for which no external criticism is possible. They will see Gadamer's claim that we can never throw off all our prejudices as evidence of the cultural relativity of all values. Radical relativists claim that once absolutes fall, the entire notion of dialogue between, and criticism of, competing moral traditions falls, too.

In order to see why we are not left with radical relativism, we must consider more closely Gadamer's notion of prejudice, the nature of traditions, and the possibility of criticism within and across traditions.

Why the Absolutist Conception of Objectivity Is So Harmful

The absolutist view of moral objectivity we have been examining is not merely mistaken. Far worse, it poses a great obstacle to our attempts to lead moral lives. In its Enlightenment formulation, this view of objectivity leaves us with three extremely harmful ideas, the ideal of a *context-free rationality,* the dream of a single *method* of moral reasoning, and the illusion of a single ultimate perspective from which to discern the *one true set* of moral precepts. This cluster of bad ideas is harmful and morally irresponsible in three important ways.

1. It leads us to expect and demand what we cannot have, namely, absolute moral truths. It sets us in search of something that does not exist. It causes us to ask the wrong kinds of questions in trying to figure out how to live (questions such as "What rule applies here?" "What is *the* right thing to do here?" "How can I be certain that I am right?"). Instead of exploring a range of possibilities for resolving conflicts or problems, we end up being more concerned with finding the right rules, the definitive constraints, to which everyone is supposed to conform.

It is time to recognize, once and for all, that moral absolutism cannot give us the absolute moral laws it promises. We have seen that, even if such laws did exist, they wouldn't be the kind of laws that human beings like ourselves could use in our lives, since they presuppose a false view of concepts and reason.

When we give up the absolutist notion of objectivity, therefore, we are not losing something that is necessary for our lives. The fact is, we can't lose something that never existed and that cannot exist. Rather, we are releasing ourselves from the influence of an illusory ideal that was counterproductive to human well-being and community.

2. These false ideals tempt us into forms of self-deception and arrogance. We deceive ourselves into thinking that morality is just a matter of finding the right rules and obeying them. We deceive ourselves into thinking that concrete situations can fit neatly under fixed concepts and imperatives. And we are tempted to become arrogant through our belief that we are somehow plugging into absolute truth. Such arrogance is typically accompanied by an intolerance of alternative goods, values, and ideals.

Everywhere we look we find opposing figures or groups, each armed with the knowledge that they possess the one absolute set of moral values, and each utterly intolerant of the very existence of the other. The simple fact that each of us believes that *we alone* possess moral truth ought to be enough to wake us up to the existence of a plurality of conceptions of reason and human well-being. As I argued earlier, we need not even go outside our own moral tradition to discover quite different conceptions of rationality and different definitions of morality. Gilligan's two ethics—the ethics of rights, duties, and laws versus the ethics of care and responsibility for others—entail different conceptions of moral reasoning and circumscribe the domain of morality in two different ways.

3. The third harmful consequence of the absolutist view of objectivity is that it nourishes a faith in ultimate values. Such a faith blinds us to the plurality of possible values and alternative modes of living, some of which might make us better able to understand and live with each other, to know and criticize ourselves, and to find new possibilities for ordering our lives in more satisfactory ways. We need liberation from the fascist idea of *the one right method* for moral reasoning. Once we understand that there can be no God's-eye view, no ultimate context, no perspective that encompasses all perspectives, then we are freed to pursue a less ambitious and much more realistic ideal.

It ought to be clear now that the *worst thing* we could have in moral deliberation is someone who thinks he or she has a monopoly on truth. The history and philosophy of science have swept away the false idea of one method and of ultimate truth in the development of science, yet these phantoms persist in moral theory.

If there is no absolute, final truth, and if there can be no single method for getting truth, then what ought we to seek instead? The answer is that we want a number of competing methods, views, ideals, programs, and practices in continual dialogue. We want these rival views being tested through confrontation with each other and through the experience of various institutions, communities, and cultures.

What Thomas Kuhn says about science holds also for morality—we don't want uniformity in science; rather, we want an evolutionary ongoing exploration of many different programs and views.

> Given a group all the members of which are committed to choosing between alternative theories and also to considering such values as accuracy, simplicity, scope, and so on while making their choice, the concrete decisions of individual members in individual cases will nevertheless vary. . . . To many of my critics this variability seems a weakness of my position. When considering the problems of crisis and of theory-choice I shall want, however, to argue that it is instead a strength. If a decision must be made under circumstances in which even the most deliberate and considered judgment may be wrong, it may be vitally important that different individuals decide in different ways. How else could the group as a whole hedge its bets?[15]

The best program for morality will be a group strategy that prizes variation for the social group as a way of experimenting with possibilities for evolutionary survival and flourishing. It is important to see that what 'works best' is not some one fixed method or state or social arrangement as such. What seems to work at one time, in one place, within one set of historical conditions may not work under other conditions. Over and over and over again, history gives us examples of views that seem not to work. These views that fail are probably bad moral strategies. But this does not mean that our current view is somehow absolute, simply because we seem to be getting by with it for the present. We need, instead, to experiment with ways of meeting changing physical, economic, social, and political conditions.

Nor is the 'best program' simply that system which satisfies the desires of those who just happen, for the moment, to hold power. What is needed is rather a strategy that fosters ongoing criticism, self-reflection, and dialogue with competing views. If objectivity is anything, it is a *process* of continual reflection and criticism. The means for this criticism will, of course, arise from within various historical traditions. But that does not mean that we are condemned merely to assault one another with our received values, with no hope for change or growth. For we have seen how the workings of the moral imagination of a situated self can, in fact, lead to transformation and self-criticism. Let us examine this critical process more closely.

What Sense Can We Make of Objectivity?

The quest for eternal truths hides from us the fundamentally historical character of human existence. The important point here is not the obvious one that we are always historically, culturally, and communally situated in all that we think and do. That is true, but it does not capture the more important insight that our very possibilities for making sense of our experience and for transforming it to enhance our lives are grounded in the sedimented understanding and experience of our tradition. We must stop looking at our situatedness within a tradition as a problem and start to see it as the very means for our moral understanding and moral growth. We must cease to regard objectivity as the throwing off of all our prejudgments (our 'prejudices') or the casting aside of our tradition.

Here Gadamer's account of our 'prejudices' (*Vorurteilungen* = prejudgments) is relevant. Our prejudgments are conditions for our being able to make sense of things. Without them, we could understand nothing. If we somehow were able to give them all up, then our understanding of some situation would not be *our* understanding. Rather than overthrowing all our prejudgments, we need to open them up to possible transformation through our encounters with others, whose prejudgments may confront our own.

> It is not so much our judgments as it is our prejudices that constitute our being. This is a provocative formulation, for I am using it to restore to its rightful place a positive concept of prejudice that was driven out of our linguistic usage by the French and the English Enlightenment. . . . Prejudices are not necessarily unjustified and erroneous, so that they inevitably distort the truth. In fact, the historicity of our existence entails that prejudices, in the literal sense of the word, constitute the initial directedness of our whole ability to experience. Prejudices are biases of our openness to the world. They are simply conditions whereby we experience something—whereby what we encounter says something to us.[16]

The Enlightenment was animated by a vision of a universal community based on rational principles, rational communication, rational argument, and rational institutions. The ideal of a universal community of rational beings was noble and idealistic, even if the actual political and social realities of Enlightenment imperialism and domination were quite ugly. Our universally shared rationality was to be the basis for universal values and critical standards of evaluation. Whenever competing views came into conflict, there would exist an ultimate rational standpoint from which to assess the merits of each view. The idea of rising above one's subjective interests, inclinations, obsessions, and habits to take up an objective rational viewpoint seemed to many to be the only basis for any notion of criticism and objectivity.

But what if Gadamer is right that we can't rise above all our prejudices without losing ourselves and our capacity to understand and experience anything at all? If we must give up the Enlightenment ideal of objectivity, then how can we avoid merely wrapping ourselves in our culturally constituted prejudices?

In other words, if all conceptions of rationality turn out to be defined relative to particular historical traditions, then what can objectivity consist in? MacIntyre has argued that, although we are always tradition-bound, there are, nevertheless, resources within our traditions for transcendence and improvement: "What the Enlightenment made us for the most part blind to and what we now need to recover is . . . a conception of rational enquiry as embodied in a tradition, a conception according to which the standards of rational justification themselves emerge from and are part of a history in which they are vindicated by the way in which they transcend the limitations of and provide remedies for the defects of their predecessors within the history of that same tradition."[17]

But now we encounter a serious problem. MacIntyre argues for the possibility of a form of dialogue between competing moral traditions that can reveal the superiority of one set of rational standards for justification over another. If this process of criticism and rational evaluation of various views, values, and commitments is always situated within one or another particular moral tradition, how could there ever be progress in our debates with those who hold competing views of morality? How is it possible for us to do anything besides patting ourselves on our collective backs for the evident superiority of our *own* moral tradition? If the standards for rational justification and evaluation are context- and tradition-bound, then how can we avoid judging our progress by the very standards that are at issue between rival views?

MacIntyre responds to this perennial problem by arguing that, no matter what else a given moral philosophy does, it will always "articulate the morality of some particular social and cultural standpoint."[18] In the terms I have been using, this amounts to saying that any moral theory will be an attempt to refine, sharpen, and make consistent various folk theories of the culture within which that philosophical theory emerges.

Yet the confrontation between competing moral philosophies, as embedded in and expressive of moral traditions and folk theories, gives rise to a dialectical play that does occasionally show the superiority of one view over its present competitors. How can this be, especially since there are no context-free standards, and the very contexts or traditions themselves are at risk in the confrontation of competing moral philosophies? MacIntyre's answer is that one philosophy may actually reveal, explain, and overcome the limitations of another view: "As in the case of natural science there are no general timeless standards. It is in the ability of one particular moral-philosophy-articulating-the-claims-of-a-particular-morality to identify and to transcend the limitations of its rival or rivals, limitations which can be—although they may not in fact have been—identified by the rational standards to which the protagonists of the rival morality are committed by their allegiance to it, that the rational superiority of that particular moral philosophy and that particular morality emerges."[19]

But what can it mean for one philosophy to 'transcend' the limitations of its rivals, in a way that would be recognized and acknowledged by adherents to the rival view? MacIntyre answers by supplying three criteria for the notion of the superiority of a view.[20] (1) The new ('superior') theory or view must identify a crisis that has come to be recognized within the tradition that underlies the less adequate view, and it must then be able to furnish solutions to key problems that could not be solved within the earlier theory. (2) The superior view must be able to explain why the inferior view lacked the resources to solve these problems. (3) The superior theory must be in certain important respects continuous with the theory it supersedes. Otherwise, we could not see the new view as actually solving the problems of the old one. Without this continuity there would be only radical incommensurability of terms, concepts, laws, and arguments. If this were the case, we would experience the new theory as utterly foreign, since it would not seem to address *our* problems, that is, the problems that emerge and get their meaning within our moral tradition.

Contrary to extreme relativistic charges, moralities are not radically incommensurable forms of life. The fact of our embodiment guarantees this much. We all have bodies that have at least a core set of universal needs and desires. Beyond that small core there may be broad variation across cultures. Still, we all need love, shelter, food, and protection from harm. We all feel pain, joy, fear, and anger. There are certain basic-level experiences we all have—experiences of harm and help—based on our embodiment and the material and social conditions of human existence. That is why there are prototypes of *the bully, breach of promise, the good samaritan,* and *exclusion from the group* as basic human experiences, even though they may be variously elaborated in different traditions. Our common embodiment (and the role it plays in founding both our reason and our desire),[21] therefore, insures that there will always be at least a partial frame in common between competing moralities.

Contrary to certain absolutist views, therefore, there is not total commensurability between competing moral theories. Contrary to extreme relativist views, however, there is not total incommensurability. Instead, there is partial incommensurability that is always a matter of degree.

MacIntyre summarizes his account of moral progress as follows:

> Progress in rationality is achieved only from a point of view. And it is achieved when the adherents of that point of view succeed to some significant degree in elaborating ever more comprehensive and adequate statements of their positions through the dialectical procedure of advancing objections which identify incoherences, omissions, explanatory failures, and other types of flaw and limitation in earlier statements of them, of finding the strongest arguments available for supporting

those objections, and then of attempting to restate the position so that it is no longer vulnerable to those specific objections and arguments.[22]

The dialectical play of competing views and traditions described by MacIntyre captures important dimensions of the ongoing critical interaction of rival viewpoints or traditions that we actually encounter in history. Consider, for example, slavery. We appear to be on the tail end of a historical contest between views that sanction slavery and those that find it absolutely contrary to proper respect for human beings. Officially, if not completely in fact, slavery has been seen to be contrary to human autonomy and destructive of human dignity. We are now in a position to explain why proslavery views give rise to problems they cannot solve or to internal inconsistencies that erode their very credibility. We can supply a vision of life without slavery that captures the imagination of virtually everyone who encounters it. And we can explain the way in which our superior view preserves important values from the previous, less adequate morality. For example, slaveholders, such as some of the framers of our Constitution, held Enlightenment values concerning the dignity and autonomy of persons. Only they did not accord that status of personhood to slaves. Antislavery arguments were based, directly or indirectly, on the notion of the autonomy of persons and the argument that slaves possessed the essential features of human personhood.

Notice that it is the historical process itself—including war, struggle, suffering, economic change, and political conflict—rather than mere 'intellectual' debate, that is the locus or medium of this dialectical interchange of views. The dialectic, in other words, is worked out in the struggles of concrete economic, political, social, and religious traditions, and not in the debating hall.

Consider also the tearing down of the Berlin Wall. The Wall was, by almost everyone's standards, a very bad idea that embodied an inadequate view of morality and political organization. In the twenty-eight years that it stood, it and its moral framework were subjected to a kind of experiential (social, political, moral) testing. A dialectic was playing itself out. Through this historical process, the Wall came to be seen as a bad experiment in human living.[23] This does not mean that it will not go back up, that it will not be tried again, or that it might not turn up again as part of a larger moral scheme that gains ascendancy in years to come, perhaps because of economic, political, or natural (e.g., drought, flood, environmental deterioration) contingencies. Yet we can see the crumbling of the

Wall as the outcome of a test within a dialectical interaction of different moral philosophies.

What I find most valuable in MacIntyre's account is his description of the way in which a historically situated dialectical process can sometimes reveal *how* and *why* one moral tradition (with its attendant moral philosophy) is superior to another. Yet we must always remember that this superiority is relative to our purposes, interests, and concrete historical conditions. The merits of rival moral theories, or the traditions they represent, are not identified by theoretical comparisons from a God's-eye perspective, according to abstract external criteria. They are determined, rather, within the context of economic, political, social, and religious interactions among differing organizations, institutions, and traditions. There can be no once-and-for-all validation of any moral viewpoint, because, to repeat, we do not and cannot stand outside of time, or above all particular contexts.

Martha Nussbaum has applauded MacIntyre's analysis of the way in which standards of rational justification are defined relative to moral traditions, but she is rightly critical of his suggestion that the only way to stabilize criteria of reason is via a shared commitment to authority.[24] MacIntyre is led to this overly strong view because he sees it as the only answer to the problem of how it is possible to unite conviction and rational justification when there exists no ultimate theoretical or practical context. MacIntyre's mistake, according to Nussbaum, is to think that there is only one possible way to secure widely shared rational standards: "Why is a view justified only if its backers can beat dissenters into line? The answer seems to be: because of the fact of original sin. Political authority, MacIntyre tells us on Augustine's behalf, is 'the necessary, and in the Christian conception the divine, remedy for sin.' And 'the central human experience of morality' is that 'of our inability to live by it.' MacIntyre concludes that the way in which Augustine shows Aristotle's view to be 'radically defective' is by pointing to a 'radical defectiveness in the natural human order'" (40). In other words, MacIntyre, taking the 'fact' of original sin as a given, claims that natural human reason is intrinsically defective and can be redeemed only by a superior (divine) authority.

This begs a host of important questions, including whether original sin is a fact, whether there is a divine basis for authority, and whether there might be other ways of securing agreement on standards. Nussbaum defends Aristotle's view of shared human characteristics as making possible rational inquiries that could be both intelligible and compelling to nearly everyone: "Aristotle gives a general account of what it is to live as a human being with both limitations and abilities. The story he tells should, he thinks, be intelligible to any human being who hears it, despite differences of language and culture. 'One can see in one's travels to distant countries,' he writes, 'the experiences of recognition and affiliation that link every human being to every other human being.' And it is on this basis that he holds out hope for a persuasive inquiry into the good that is not exclusively tied to one culture or another" (41).

There is no argument here, nor could there be, for the existence of a universal essence that would guarantee agreement among all fully rational creatures. But there is the closest thing to this that we can get, once we have given up essences and absolutes. The argument runs as follows: Human beings share a basic biological makeup, they share the same general cognitive mechanisms, and they share certain general physical, interpersonal, and cultural needs that are the basis for universally shared purposes, interests, and projects that show themselves in every culture we have encountered, even though they may take different forms in each culture. Given the nature of our bodies, our brains, and our physical and social interactions, we would expect that certain *basic-level experiences* (e.g., of harm, of help, of well-being) would be common across cultures. Shared purposes and experiences of this sort are the basis for Aristotle's "experiences of recognition and affiliation that link every human being to every other human being." That is why, when we encounter other cultures, or envision previous societies, the people we encounter are never utterly alien to us. Rather, we meet something of ourselves and our experience in them. And that is the common basis for a possible dialogue.

The existence of such universal constraints and basic-level experiences will not, to be sure, select any one position as either all-encompassing or final, yet they will limit us to a range of reasonable alternatives. Furthermore, they indicate relevant considerations for constructing productive dialogue among competing views. They give us a way of discussing the relative merits of competing theories, practices, and traditions. The extreme relativist view that competing moralities may be radically incommensurable just seems to be false, in light of considerations such as these.[25]

Someone might object that these alleged constraints are too general, too loose, and too few to really give us a robust sense of objectivity. But that is simply not true, once we have given up our craving for absolute laws, univocal terms, and value-neutral concepts that were the hallmark of the false absolutist conception of a God's-eye objectivity. We're not going to have *that* kind of objectivity, since

it is an impossible ideal. However, a different view of objectivity is now possible
—one that is based on the following aspects of human experience:

Biological purposes. There are certain purposes that, as a matter of empirical
fact, all human beings do seem to share. These include bodily nourishment, sexual satisfaction, procreation, shelter, safety from bodily harm, and various forms
of social interaction. [26] Virtually every society known to us has, each in its own
way, made provisions for the satisfaction of these needs and desires. There are
rare cases of individuals or groups who have tried to ignore or reject these purposes in their conceptions of human flourishing, but at a price. The Shakers, for
instance, prohibited sexual intercourse on the grounds of the imminence of the
Second Coming of Christ. Only a handful of these people are left. Likewise,
various forms of sexual repression have been tried throughout history. But the
fact of repression testifies to the power and pervasiveness of sexual urges. Freud
may have been right that the possibility of civilization depends on widespread
repression of our sexual and aggressive urges, but no morality can work over an
extended period of time if it does not recognize these drives and find appropriate
means for satisfying them to some degree.

Biological purposes such as these establish general limits on possible so-
cial/economic/political interactions. I mean 'limits' in the sense that a so-
ciomoral system must provide meaningful opportunities for the fulfillment of
such purposes. This doesn't entail that celibacy, for instance, should be banned.
Of course not. It means only that there would be something defective about a morality that required universal celibacy, simply because it would eventually lead to
the extinction of that society. It is in this sense that such biological purposes
would allow us to judge the relative superiority of one view over another, by virtue of how well the competing views permit us to *realize and harmonize* our basic
purposes.

Cognitive structure. There is much that we are learning about the nature of the
human conceptual system, cognition, and knowledge, such as the nature of
category structure, how people make inferences, how perception works, and the
conditions for communication. In previous chapters I have used some of this research to explore the role of various kinds of imaginative structure in our moral
concepts and our reasoning based on them. Theories of morality that are inconsistent with our best (though in principle revisable) empirical understanding of
cognition must be highly suspect, since they would not be compatible with the

way people actually understand things and reason about them. This is the upshot of Owen Flanagan's sustained argument that any adequate moral theory must satisfy a "PRINCIPLE OF MINIMAL PSYCHOLOGICAL REALISM: Make sure when constructing a moral theory or projecting a moral ideal that the character, decision processing, and behavior prescribed are possible, or are perceived to be possible, for creatures like us."[27]

Thus, we have seen that any theory relying on univocal, fixed, essentialist concepts and rules simply cannot be adequate to the requirements of actual human understanding. We just do not think and reason, for the most part, with such concepts. Any account that tries to exclude or minimize the imaginative character of our moral reasoning is bound to prove bankrupt, lacking the resources necessary to explain moral deliberation. Any view that treats goals and purposes as pre-established, fixed, determinate givens that we then deliberate about and pursue, could never be adequate to the way we ordinarily acquire a more and more definite understanding of our goals only in, and by means of, our exploratory moral activity. Any view that treats metaphor and other imaginative structures as marginal, dispensable, and undesirable could never have a chance of making sense of our moral experience. So, these cognitive constraints really do rule out a great many candidate moral theories, while at the same time recommending directions for constructing more realistic and adequate ones.

Social relations. There are certain types of social relations and organizations that appear to undermine their own legitimacy and that make it difficult for us to pursue our shared goals. Societies founded on domination, raw power, intimidation, and repression have existed for limited periods of time and do still exist today. But no one has ever made any case for their desirability under the conditions we typically encounter in our world in any but the most extreme circumstances. Totalitarian states may provide a certain degree of stability and order, but it is a stability based on the prohibition of certain basic human forms of expression and social interaction that make it possible for societies to grow and adapt. Again, this is not a knockdown argument against totalitarianism, but rather one of several considerations that reveal its repressive and stultifying character.

Consider, next, lying. Any social system founded on lying would do itself in. As Kant, the great denouncer of lying in any form, saw, lying is pernicious chiefly because it destroys the trust necessary for successful social relations that make it possible for us to achieve our joint purposes. A moral system that sanctions lying to foreigners or people who are outside of one's social framework is quite conceivable. But a morality that allowed for lying within a society would undermine the possibility of trust, communication, and cooperative action.

As another example, there have certainly been, and are now, hermits who shun social interaction. Yet those individuals are themselves products of social interactions, including sexual union of their parents, complex forms of nurturing necessary for their growth and survival, and extensive educational practices without which they would be only marginally human.

Ecological concerns. Any theory that ignores our ecological situation threatens the subversion of all our other goals and practices. Any view that regards our natural environment merely as a tool or resource—as nothing but a commodity to be used up—is evidently inferior to one that recognizes the complex way in which organism and environment are coevolving and constituted by their mutual interaction. The most obvious cases are those cultures that die out because they completely exhaust their natural resources and make their environment uninhabitable. More typical cases, such as our own current situation, are those where we are gradually and irreversibly degrading the overall quality of our environment, and thereby diminishing our possibilities for flourishing and enhancing the quality of our existence.

Systems of morality are thus dependent on ecological considerations at least to the extent that certain ends, purposes, and goods defined within a morality may not be attainable unless certain ecological requirements are met first. Those goods, such as sufficient food and protection from the elements for all people, might become impossible as a result of our ecological irresponsibility. In this way, our material conditions place restrictions on the forms our moralities can take.

Objectivity as Transperspectivity

These four basic dimensions of human life—physical, cognitive, social, and ecological—give us a very substantial basis for reflecting on the merits of competing moral philosophies. They do not—could not—single out one 'right' theory, but they give us many considerations for ruling out many views altogether, and for deciding the relative merits of the remaining alternatives, although always within a given historical situation and relative to purposes that are themselves open to criticism and to change.

We are now in a position to make some general claims about the nature of a reasonable and realistic *human objectivity,* as opposed to an impossible God's-eye-view objectivity. Human objectivity is what characterizes a reflective process by means of which we are able to take up multiple perspectives as a way both of criticizing and transforming our own views and those of others.

Steven Winter has characterized such a human objectivity as a form of *transperspectivity*, which is the ability of a physically, historically, socially, and culturally situated self to reflect critically on its own construction of a world, and to imagine other possible worlds that might be constructed.

> Once we give up the notion of the transcendent position (for God, consciousness, or anything else), then, "objectivity" becomes a question of *transperspectivity*. "Impartiality," in turn, is no longer a matter of an aperspectival position, but rather an exercise of the empathetic ability to imagine what a question looks like from more than one side. "Situated self-consciousness," in this view, is a two-part process. First, it involves the capacity to unravel or trace back the strands by which our constructions weave our world together. Although we may be situated in a web of belief, there is nothing that prevents us from making those beliefs *translucent* and, thus, amenable to reflection. Nothing, that is, except lack of imagination.
>
> Second, situated self-consciousness involves the ability to imagine how the world might be constructed differently. . . . In either event, situated self-consciousness depends upon an act of the imagination that transports one "beyond" his or her previous conceptions. . . . it is a process of first rendering our constructions translucent and then seeing *past* them to different, perhaps more productive constructions.[28]

Here is a vision of a realistic human objectivity. It involves understanding, and being able to criticize, the way in which you and others have constructed their worlds, and it involves the imaginative capacity to conceive and carry out modest transformations of those constructed worlds. In other words, it involves a limited freedom to imagine other values and points of view and to change one's world in light of possibilities revealed by those alternative viewpoints.[29]

Transperspectivity involves acts of imagination. To some it will seem strange and even inappropriate to combine 'objectivity' and 'imagination.' But forms of imaginative rationality are, in fact, what make human objectivity possible. They are what permit us to take up various perspectives as a way of criticizing any given position, our own or others'. We do this, as we have seen, by means of different kinds of imaginative acts: by envisioning different framings and metaphorical structurings of situations, by empathetically taking up the part of others in order to understand what they experience and how various possible actions might affect them, and by exploring the range of possibilities for action open to us.

Imaginative activity of this sort is our sole means for assuming different perspectives and tracing out what they would mean for how we develop our identity, how we affect others, and how we compose our relationships. Such acts of imagination are what allow us to see *that* and *how* things might be different, and better.

I have argued that there is no single correct method for figuring out what to do in a situation. There are general principles and imaginative ideals, but they do not determine one true method. It is important to see, however, that the absence of any absolute method does not mean that there are *no* methods (as some relativists think). There are several imaginative methods. Trying out different imaginative framings of a situation is one of them. Examining hitherto unnoticed implications of a shared metaphorical concept is another. Empathetically exploring the experience and feelings of other people is another. And envisioning how various continuations of our individual and cultural narratives are possible, and what they would entail for oneself and others, is yet another.

We ought to use as many of these imaginative methods as we can. Transperspectivity requires it, for that is the only way we can criticize our present moral understanding, take up the part of others, and expand our sense of the possibilities for constructive action.

As I have argued before, this dialogue of different perspectives—this dialectic of transperspectivity—is not merely an intellectual endeavor carried out through conscious reflection and argument. It is, rather, a process of individual and group experience. It is *worked out through the experience of a people over long periods of time*.[30] It is a form of cultural and transcultural experimentation, which ultimately tests a culture's imaginative resources.

Objectivity, then, does not consist in approximating the impossible ideal of a God's-eye perspective. In fact, we can now see that such an absolute standpoint would be counterproductive for creatures like ourselves who confront an *evolving* world and who evolve along with it. What we need is an adaptive capacity and a flexibility that allows us to confront and deal constructively with new problems (even new *kinds* of problems) that emerge in our changing experience. This requires taking up different critical perspectives on our present moral understanding and figuring out how we can extend or change aspects of it in light of our present situation. There are no absolutes for dealing with an experience that has this kind of evolving character. What is required, instead, is imagination in the various forms discussed above.

Objectivity-as-transperspectivity is precisely what creatures of our sort need if we are going to deal intelligently and constructively with the problems we encounter. Objectivity for us consists in our ongoing individual and communal attempts to bring multiple perspectives to bear on our deepest folk theories, values, and conceptions of reason—to see what they entail for our lives, to see when and how they should be changed, and to envision new possibilities for how things might be carried forth in constructive ways. This is the imaginative basis of a realistic human objectivity. Living without absolutes, therefore, means replacing the impossible ideal of moral knowledge as a system of absolute moral laws with the humanly realistic notion of moral knowledge as imaginative moral understanding.

TEN

Preserving Our Best Enlightenment Moral Ideals

I have framed and motivated my account of imaginative moral understanding by contrasting it with aspects of our Moral Law folk theory. A large part of my critical argument has been directed against absolutistic Enlightenment versions of this folk theory that have exercised a profound influence on both our common-sense views about morality and the philosophical theories that emerge from them. I have also criticized the relativism that grew out of these same basic philosophical assumptions. For each of these Enlightenment legacies (e.g., views of the self, reason, moral law, objectivity) I have tried to answer three questions: (1) From a philosophical and psychological perspective, how are these views motivated? (2) How are they based on image schemas, conceptual metaphors, idealized cognitive models, and other imaginative devices? (3) Given what we have learned about the imaginative character of human conceptualization and reasoning, in what specific ways are these views either false or misleading as a basis for a theory of morality?

In light of these criticisms, it may seem as though I am claiming that there is nothing good about our Enlightenment moral tradition. To interpret my analyses as nothing more than Enlightenment bashing is to miss the whole point of my argument. The point is not to throw out our most important Enlightenment moral ideals, but rather to reframe them in a way that is consistent with what we know about the self, reason, concepts, and so forth. We cannot simply deny our moral heritage, for it in large measure defines our moral sensibility. Moreover, since our identity as a person is embedded within our moral tradition, we cannot utterly reject our tradition without losing ourselves. What we must do, instead, is to transform aspects of our tradition to make them consistent with our knowledge of the way human beings make sense of things, reason about them, and are motivated to act. Only in this way can we determine what our inherited moral ideals might mean and how they might be useful for us in our present situation.

In order to say what is *good* about our Enlightenment heritage, it is useful to summarize, one last time, its most problematic assumptions. By looking at its excesses and overstatements, we can better understand what animated the entire project and what sort of vision it expresses. We can then determine what is psychologically realistic, morally noble, and worth redeeming within this vision.

Problematic Assumptions of Enlightenment Morality

The following is a short list of the key Enlightenment assumptions I have been criticizing, which also lie at the heart of the Moral Law folk theory:

1. *The split self.* The Enlightenment preserved the Judeo-Christian conception of humans as metaphysically bifurcated creatures. This creates insurmountable problems concerning how our bodily side (as the seat of our perceptions, desires, feelings, emotions, and actions) could ever interact with our mental side (the seat of our understanding, reason, and will). If we really are split in this way, then how could desire ever affect reason and how could reason ever guide desire? Given only the resources of the folk theory of Faculty Psychology, this is an insoluble problem.

2. *Faculty Psychology.* Enlightenment philosophy adopted and refined the folk theory of Faculty Psychology, with its rigid distinctions among discrete mental capacities. Perception passively receives sensations. Imagination forms them into images. Feeling arises from those sensations. Understanding conceptualizes. Reason calculates and formulates principles. Will chooses. We have seen that separating the faculties in this rigorous manner leaves no room for an imaginative rationality. Neither does it leave any place for the emotional dimensions of our moral concepts and reasoning. Moral judgments end up being 'pure' rational applications of concepts and laws to concrete situations. On this account, the imaginative capacity that is so crucial to our moral understanding and reasoning is simply excluded as irrelevant.

3. *Universal, essential, disembodied reason.* Universal Reason is what supposedly distinguishes people from brute animals. It is the essential capacity that we all share, and so it is what defines our identity as moral agents. We saw how this view of a pure, Universal Reason ignores the crucial role in our moral understanding that is played by our bodily experience, our emotions, our imagination, and our interpersonal and cultural relations.

4. *Radical freedom.* The Moral Law folk theory presupposes a radical freedom of the will to act on rational principles independent of any influence from our bodily nature, or from any other 'external' source (e.g., habit, social custom, or the authority of another person). Such a freedom requires a separate metaphysical realm, distinct from our bodily being, which is not determined by any bodily need, desire, or habit. As Kant saw, there is no way to prove the existence of such

an absolute freedom, nor even to explain how it is metaphysically possible. Conceiving of human beings as free in this way only reinforced the picture of a radically split self whose rational essence resided in a mysterious noumenal realm of which we could have no direct experience and about which we could know nothing.

5. *Absolute moral laws.* Moral objectivity was founded on the notion of universal moral laws, derived from Universal Reason, and capable of guiding our action in any conceivable situation that might arise. I argued that the classical account of concepts and of Universal Reason required by this view are both challenged by what we have recently learned about conceptualization and reasoning.

6. *The scope of morality.* If you put the previous assumptions together, what results is an extremely narrow definition of what counts as morality. Morality is a set of restrictive rules that are supposed to tell you which acts you may and may not perform, which you have an obligation to perform, and when you can be blamed for what you have done. It is not fundamentally about how to live a good life, or how to live well. Instead, it is only a matter of 'doing the right thing'—*the* one right thing required of you in a given situation. This drastic narrowing of the scope of morality has monumental consequences. Treating moral reasoning as if it consists only in discovering and applying moral laws ignores the imaginative structure of our moral concepts and reasoning, and thus excludes from consideration all of the evidence that would support the central role of imagination.

There are two basic strategies within this narrow conception of morality for denying the role of moral imagination and for excluding from morality all questions about living well. I want to examine both of these strategies and to argue for the broad view of morality suggested by the central role of moral imagination in our moral knowledge.

What's Wrong with the 'Institution of Morality'?

The Enlightenment ideal of a pure reason that transcends all contexts, values, and interests has turned out to be a dangerous illusion, dangerous because it leads us into believing that we might actually grasp some absolute value, principle, or perspective. Once we deceive ourselves into believing that there could be such a transcendent viewpoint, we can easily fool ourselves into believing that our own tradition, in terms of which we make sense of our moral experience, might somehow be the highest expression of the essence of a universal and absolute reason.

We have seen in detail how the narrow description of moral reasoning as limited to operations of an allegedly Universal Reason ends up excluding all imaginative structures of cognition from morality. The kinds of argument for the importance of imagination that I have been giving are typically dismissed by calling upon two basic distinctions that have traditionally been used to define the scope of morality and moral theory.

1. *Morality v. prudence.* According to Moral Law theories *moral reasoning* concerns the practical use of reason to derive the appropriate moral laws that dictate correct action in a particular situation. *Prudential reasoning,* on the other hand, involves the practical use of reason to determine the most efficient means to attaining the comprehensive human end of happiness or well-being. Thus, as we saw earlier, Donagan distinguishes rigidly between 'living morally' (morality) and 'living well' (prudence). He asserts that one cannot live well without living morally, but that one can live morally without living well. Moral theory is then defined by Donagan as concerned only with living morally in this highly restricted sense.

Armed with this distinction, a Moral Law theorist can dismiss as 'mere' prudential reasoning all of my discussion of imaginative reasoning concerning how to compose situations, build relationships, create and enhance harmony, and explore possibilities for action. This is a particularly difficult strategy to counteract, for it effectively excludes from consideration many of the phenomena and much of the evidence that might challenge the Moral Law theory. It amounts to the claim that most of what goes on in our deliberations about how we ought to act and feel and think is irrelevant to the morality of our actions.

2. *Moral theory v. moral psychology.* Another related dichotomy that is similarly used to exclude possible counterevidence is the infamous distinction between moral philosophy and moral psychology. Moral philosophy is supposed to consider only how we *ought to* reason and act, and how we might justify the laws or principles upon which we act. Moral psychology, on the other hand, is supposed to be concerned only with the motivations, patterns of moral development, psychological influences, and modes of understanding that describe how people do, in fact, reason and make decisions in actual practice. This distinction is used to relegate any description of the imaginative structure of moral understanding to the domain of 'mere' moral psychology. Moral theory is supposed to be concerned, not with how we understand things, but with determining the fundamental moral laws and showing how they can be applied to concrete cases.

Although these two sets of distinctions are not identical and are thus the basis for two different arguments for dismissing imaginative rationality, the general form of both arguments is the same. Each excludes from consideration any descriptions or explanations of various phenomena of imaginative cognition as not properly falling under morality and moral theory. The upshot of this is to dismiss any potentially problematic data that might call the dominant Moral Law paradigm of morality into question.

What's wrong with these two strategies for marginalizing moral imagination is that they drastically narrow the scope of morality to what Bernard Williams has called "morality, the peculiar institution."[1] The 'institution of morality' reduces all moral considerations to a single univocal notion, that of *moral obligation:* "In the morality system, moral obligation is expressed in one especially important kind of deliberative conclusion—a conclusion that is directed toward what to do, governed by moral reasons, and concerned with a particular situation" (174–75).

Understood in this narrow sense, morality has three central features: it concerns inescapable obligations to perform, or refrain from, certain actions; it denies the possibility of an ultimate conflict among our obligations; and its characteristic reactions are blame, guilt, and self-reproach. The 'institution of morality' thus tries to force every significant moral consideration into a highly specific kind of 'moral' obligation. It sees morality as solely a matter of constraining laws. Consequently, within this system, one can only justify an action by citing some obligation to perform it. Faced with two conflicting principles of action, it becomes necessary to establish one of them as supplying an overriding obligation. This gives rise to the fundamental criterion that "*only an obligation can beat an obligation*" (180).

Richard Shusterman has observed that this conception of morality requires a vast hierarchy of obligations that would exclude a large part of what is actually important in our moral deliberations: "Thus, if the performance of a noble unobliged act of kindness prevents me from meeting a trivial obligation, say arriving to work on time, a vague general obligation relating to kindness must be posited to justify my act's obvious worth. The idea that certain things can be good regardless of obligation and can even outweigh obligation in ethical deliberation is utterly foreign and intolerable to the system of morality."[2]

It is time to call the absolutists' bluff, by turning their charge of irrelevance against them. It is time to recognize moral absolutism and its 'institution of morality' for what they are, namely, the privileging of a very narrow and limited set of values as definitive of morality. The overly restrictive scope of morality as it is conceived by the Moral Law folk theory is, to be sure, part of morality. But it is crucial to keep in mind that it is *only a part,* only one subset of a number of relevant values, considerations, and principles.

As we saw in chapter 5, the Moral Law folk theory is fundamentally a reductionistic strategy that tries to ignore, or marginalize as less relevant, what Taylor calls the great "diversity of goods" that make up the content of our moral experience and that present us with real moral dilemmas that cannot be resolved by absolute principles. Williams makes the same point by asking rhetorically, "If there is such a thing as the truth about the subject matter of ethics—the truth, we might say, about the ethical—why is there any expectation that it should be simple? In particular, why should it be conceptually simple, using only one or two ethical concepts, such as *duty* or *good state of affairs,* rather than many? Perhaps we need as many concepts to describe it as we find we need, and no fewer" (17).

Given the variety of human interests and purposes, given the various levels at which human needs arise (e.g., bodily, interpersonal, social, political), and given the range of possible ways to imaginatively satisfy our multilevel desires, there is no reason to think that there should exist a single standard of human good that presents itself as nothing more than a system of obligations. In fact, the idea that there might be a single overarching value or conception of human flourishing seems highly improbable in light of the diversity of our needs, desires, and practices. Moreover, since many of our most fundamental moral concepts are defined by multiple partial metaphorical structurings, our concepts are typically not going to be univocal and our values are typically not going to reduce to a single standard of valuation.

I have been arguing that moral absolutism excludes as irrelevant those imaginative dimensions of our understanding, experience, and reflection that lie at the heart of our sense of morality. It gives us an account of what we should pay attention to, what we should do, and how we should evaluate what we do that tends to close off those very considerations and modes of reasoning that may be the key to our acting nobly, responsibly, and with foresight in the face of problems that make up the fabric of our moral lives.

Another way to put my objection is to say that absolutist morality overlooks the background conditions, models, values, and practices that make possible those few occasions when there do seem to be absolute principles, namely, the unproblematic prototypical cases. As Williams points out, the "system of blame" that is part of the institution of morality presupposes a massive background of assumptions. It can presume to focus exclusively on very specific aspects of particular acts (as meriting praise or blame) only because it assumes a highly determinate defining context for those actions. The system of blame is surrounded by other practices of encouragement and discouragement, acceptance and rejection, which work on desire and character to shape them into the requirements and possibilities of ethical life.

Morality neglects this surrounding and sees only that focused, particularized judgment. There is a pressure within it to require a voluntariness that will be total and will cut through character and psychological or social determination, and allocate blame and responsibility on the ultimately fair basis of the agent's own contribution, no more and no less. It is an illusion to suppose that this demand can be met. (194)

The Moral Law theory, with its institution of morality, can only seem to work, in short, because it is based on a background of physical and social conditions, moral practices, and a large set of assumptions about reason, character, freedom, self-identity, will, and so forth. In order to understand the crucial role played by this 'background' it is necessary to pay attention to many sorts of considerations that Moral Law theories dismiss as moral psychology. The problem, as we have seen, is that you can't make sense of applying moral laws to situations without bringing in these background assumptions. You cannot separate moral theory from moral psychology. You cannot separate moral reasoning from (imaginative) moral understanding.

The crux of an adequate response to the morality/prudence and moral theory/moral psychology gambits is thus simply to point out that both dichotomies rest on a wholly untenable narrowing of morality to a reductive set of values, situations, and principles. The key concepts of absolutist morality could only have meaning relative to a background of values and cognitive models, which they then try to exclude from consideration.

I have argued that moral absolutism (and Moral Law theory in general) depends on a view of moral personality, concepts, rules, and reason that is largely at odds with our best empirical understanding of how the mind works. Consequently neither can it be an adequate account of our moral understanding and cognition, nor can it supply moral principles that could actually be used by real human beings. We have seen, for example, that some of our basic moral concepts are not of the classical objectivist sort. Instead, they have prototype structure, are often radial categories with metaphorical principles of extension, are dependent for their meaning on idealized cognitive models, and are value-laden. Our categorization, and our reasoning based upon those categories, is thus typically non-absolutist.

For these reasons, we cannot make morally effective use of absolutist moral theory. *That* type of theory was founded too much on allegedly a priori reasoning that is supposed to be in no way dependent on empirical considerations. But it is wrong to think of morality as an activity of pure reason. Since before Quine,[3] the pure/empirical split has been demolished as too problematic to be used for any serious metaphysical, epistemological, or logical work.

Therefore, since the pretended separation of 'moral theory' from 'moral psychology' is but an artifact of that ill-advised and unsupported pure/empirical dichotomy, it must be given up. While we may grant that some statements are less empirical than others, and that some methods are more like what were traditionally regarded as a priori, this gives us at best only a continuum ranging from an ideal a priori pole over to its opposite empirical pole. Quite obviously, this undermines the possibility of distinguishing a pure moral philosophy from an empirical moral psychology.

To sum up, the ideals of a pure method of practical reasoning and of a univocal standard of value in terms of which any action could be morally evaluated are as false as they are seductive. They tempt us unmercifully with the lure of univocal concepts, strict moral laws, and the security of absolute values. Unfortunately, as we have seen, these ideals have very little to do with the realities of human understanding and experience. Williams has summarized the kinds of allurements, and the corresponding errors, of an absolutist 'institution of morality.'

> Many philosophical mistakes are woven into morality. It misunderstands obligations, not seeing how they form just one type of ethical consideration. It misunderstands practical necessity, thinking it peculiar to the ethical. It misunderstands ethical practical necessity, thinking it peculiar to obligations. Beyond all this, morality makes people think that, without its very special obligation, there is only inclination; without its utter voluntariness, there is only force; without its ultimately pure justice, there is no justice. Its philosophical errors are only the most abstract expressions of a deeply rooted and still powerful misconception of life. (196)

The Broad Scope of Morality

If morality is not definable narrowly by the 'institution of morality,' then how is it to be defined? There is no simple answer to this crucial question. But let us start with the minimal claim that morality concerns the kind of lives we ought to lead, given the fact that our actions can help or harm people. However we define 'help' and 'harm,' we notice at once that most of what we do in our lives affects the well-being of both other people and ourselves. Acts that were before thought of as merely 'technical,' 'aesthetic,' or 'theoretical' turn out to have moral dimensions as well. Acts that were previously thought of as strictly 'moral' in character turn out to have theoretical, technical, and aesthetic dimensions, too.

For example, is it strictly an aesthetic issue whether or not I choose to have a beautiful lawn? The very question is misleading, for it is predicated on the rigid distinctions between 'aesthetic,' 'theoretical,' and 'moral' judgments that I am challenging. What if I need to water my lawn to keep it green? Then I am using a precious natural resource. Isn't that a moral issue? What if I decide to fertilize it? Won't some of that fertilizer find its way into the ground water? The same holds for pesticides. There is nothing morally neutral about any of this, for it affects our entire ecosystem, and thus the lives of other people, including future generations.

What if I should decide to paint my house Day-Glo orange? On the received view, that is a matter of aesthetic taste. But can there be any doubt that it affects the well-being of others? The reply might be made that it affects only their aesthetic well-being, not their moral well-being. But how can we possibly make such a distinction, when the 'aesthetic' dimensions are woven into the fabric of all our experience, as I argued above? Distinguishing so-called 'aesthetic' from 'moral' well-being merely begs the question. What principled way could there be to make such a distinction?

I am not urging moral fanaticism. Moral fanaticism turns every little action into a moral problem. By making every deed a moral choice, it makes the living of an ordinary life a massive moral burden, as though in each act we were deciding the fate of humankind. Rather, issues of help, harm, and well-being do not enter into every aspect of life equally. Brushing your teeth is not, for the most part, a moral issue. To treat it as such would be moral fanaticism. Nevertheless, brushing your teeth is part of a conception of hygiene that bears on your personal well-being. As such, it is a tiny part of what you might do to keep yourself as healthy as possible. To think of brushing your teeth as a moral *duty,* however, would be ridiculous. This only shows that there is something wrong with the idea that 'duty' and 'obligation' are the only criteria for motivating and evaluating actions.

What I am urging is the recognition that morality reaches, in varying degrees, into most aspects of our lives. Restricting morality to the 'institution of morality' therefore misses much of what is crucial if we are to live good lives. As an example, consider business education. It is typical for courses in business schools to be oriented around a number of modules that each student is expected to master— finance, accounting, marketing, personnel management, and so forth. In each of these modules there are standard kinds of problems encountered, and the student is supposed to learn the relevant procedures and techniques for solving those problems. It then occurs to some people that there ought to be a 'business ethics' component, too. It will be construed in terms of the same model as the other modules. Ethics, then, will be regarded as just another matter of problem solving— there are typical (ethical) problems, and the student is supposed to learn theories and techniques for solving them.

Unfortunately, this whole way of proceeding is mistaken. It makes ethics just one more module. It makes it seem as though ethical concerns are separate from finance, accounting, and marketing, which are supposed to have their own distinct principles. But the fact is that ethics pervades *every aspect of business,* from accounting, to hiring, to management, to marketing, to deciding what products one will manufacture and what resources one will use. It is just this conception of a compartmentalized education (based on a compartmentalized view of human cognition and experience) that makes it seem to many people perfectly appropriate to perform cost-benefit analyses concerning moral issues, such as in the case of the Pinto gas tank.

Another problem with this conception of morality is that it presents ethical problems as if they were like technical problems, where one calculates the most efficient means to some preestablished end. But moral problems are often about the ends themselves, about what we ought to choose and pursue. They are seldom merely matters of technical means-ends reasoning alone. It is a short step from regarding all moral reasoning as means-ends reasoning to the reduction of morality to cost-benefit analyses of the sort performed in the Pinto case.

In sum, the scope of morality is far broader than the 'institution of morality' allows. It reaches into virtually every aspect of our lives. This need not turn our mundane decisions into grand existential dilemmas, as though in every minute act we were choosing for all humankind. Rather, it should simply make us far more aware of the potential of our actions for affecting human welfare. It confronts us with the task of always trying to see as broadly as possible the implications of our attitudes, judgments, and way of life. It simply tries to make us more finely attuned to our interconnectedness with other people, animals, and organic processes as a whole.

So far, I have remained within an anthropocentric orientation, tying value to *human* well-being. Many of the most pressing moral debates, however, concern whether we should extend the scope of morality beyond our anthropocentric world to embrace other forms of life and even the ecosystem as a whole. It is one thing to say that we ought to be kind to animals whenever we can, and it is quite another to say that they have as much right as we do to immunity from harm. It is one thing to say that we should be good stewards of our natural resources because we cannot survive without them, while it is quite another to say that the locus of value lies outside humans in nature as an ongoing process. However understandable it is that we humans are likely to see ourselves as the locus of moral value, there seems to be little reason to give ourselves a special status when we view our tiny niche in the natural process as a whole. It may be psychologically unrealistic to think that we will ever see ourselves as perhaps dispensable for the well-being of a larger natural system, but this issue is certainly one that must be addressed by a suitably broadened conception of morality.

The overly neat and rigid distinctions of traditional Moral Law theory serve various purposes by restricting our focus concerning what counts as a moral issue and how it ought to be dealt with. However, the price for this relative simplicity is too high, for it has led us to overlook a great deal of what is relevant to our moral deliberations. It has impoverished our conception of morality. It has supported false and unattainable ideals, some of which are actually harmful. It has encouraged us to blame ourselves and others in unjustified ways, and it has also permitted us *not* to blame ourselves for certain things that we really are responsible for.

The question of the scope of morality is, therefore, itself a moral issue. It is a deep moral issue concerning what a person will count as morally relevant in deciding how to act. Contrary to the Moral Law theory, we do not usually have preestablished criteria at hand to decide this for every case. Some issues, such as surrogate motherhood and in vitro fertilization, were not moral issues thirty years ago, but they are important issues today. Our conception of morality must change along with our evolving experience. Though I have not done the necessary analysis to demonstrate this, I suspect that the concept 'morality' is an essentially contestable radial category,[4] where certain kinds of cases are prototypically recognized as moral, while noncentral cases are the subject of ongoing heated debate. The scope of morality, then, is an open question that ought to be kept open, if our moral deliberations are to be sensitive to our changing experience.

Saving Our Noblest Enlightenment Ideals

Having summarized the harm done by our Enlightenment conception of morality, what's left? Quite a lot, but the good ideals that are left need to be reinterpreted in light of a more empirically adequate view of concepts and reasoning of the sort we have been exploring. What follows is a suggestion as to how some of our most noble moral ideals might be interpreted in a suitably revised, empirically responsible form.

Universal moral personality. The principle of universal moral personality requires us to count each person and to count each person as equal to every other. The Enlightenment view ascribed moral personality (and, hence, equality) to any creature who possessed an essential Universal Reason. If we deny the existence of Universal Reason (i.e., a transcendent, pure reason with an essential logical structure), we can still attribute moral personhood to all creatures who have human reason, which is embodied, imaginative, and tied to our historically situated self-consciousness. There will be an overriding presumption of equal treatment, unless the most compelling argument can be supplied that identifies relevant differences among people. However, we must remember that there is nothing fixed or absolute about our present way of determining who falls under the category *person*. Whereas the Enlightenment attributed moral personality only to rational beings like ourselves, we might conceivably come up with good reasons (such as empirical studies of animals) for extending this status to nonhuman creatures. There is no a priori way to decide this issue. As our knowledge of what makes us what we are and of how we are similar to and different from other creatures grows, we may find it necessary to redraw our lines of equality.

Respect. As rational and equal, people are entitled to a respect that recognizes their right to the conditions of full moral agency, such as freedom from slavery, bodily harm, and psychological coercion. We may not, that is, use other people merely as means (objects or utensils) to ends that they would not or should not make their own.[5] This respect extends not only to others but also to ourselves, so that we should not use ourselves in ways that would deny or degrade our moral capacities.

In the Enlightenment context, with its Judeo-Christian roots, respect was a *duty* owed to others by virtue of their essential rationality. Abstracted from essentialism, respect for ourselves and others becomes an ideal for treating people (and perhaps animals and the environment?) in a way that makes it possible for us to live together with some measure of harmony. We know, psychologically, that without proper self-respect we come to despise and abuse ourselves and other people, and we lack the ego strength to relate constructively with others. We know that when we fail to respect other people we come to distrust them, we fail to understand and communicate with them, and we are more prone to resort to violence and other destructive behaviors toward them. Respect is not an absolute duty stemming from pure reason; rather, it is a requirement for living together in some modest degree of harmony and for pursuing almost every conception of human flourishing we know of.

Moral principles. Yes, there are moral principles, and they are important. But they are not the absolute, univocal principles of Moral Law theories. We have seen that, where 'moral laws' exist, they are best understood as capsule summaries of the collective wisdom we derive from our shared moral experience as a community. They are reminders of important considerations that should be figured into our moral deliberations. They are not technical rules telling us precisely how to act in a given case. At best, they will apply unproblematically only to the unproblematic central or prototypical cases within a moral category that provided the experiential basis from which the rules were derived in the first place.

The crucial thing is not to be fooled into thinking that, just because there are a few moral laws, all moral reasoning must be discovering and applying such laws. On the contrary, I have tried to show that much of what matters is hidden by Moral Law theories. We need a different model of moral reasoning that encompasses the imaginative dimensions of conceptualization and thought.

Autonomy. Perhaps our greatest Enlightenment legacy is the idea of autonomy, the idea that morality depends on our ability to act on principles that we have given freely to ourselves, without being subject to laws imposed upon us by another (heteronomy). Morality thus preserves our autonomy, for it is the rational exercise of our freedom to guide ourselves in ways that guarantee the mutual freedom and autonomy of everyone.

The Enlightenment conception of autonomy assumed an essential Universal Reason as the basis for our radical freedom (our freedom not to be determined by anything beyond our own reason). But without such a defining essence, what can autonomy become? The answer is Rawls's answer[6]—that autonomy is not a given metaphysical fact, but rather an ideal to be pursued. It is the ideal of not being determined in your actions by forces or authority to which you do not rationally and freely consent. It is the ideal of each person charting his or her own life in a way that is consistent with the maximal freedom of others to do the same.

This ideal of autonomy rests, not on the false idea of radical freedom, but instead on the situated freedom of human beings. Our freedom is embodied and socially situated. We are not free to act on *any* principle we might happen to choose, nor are we free to become anything we desire. But we do have the imaginative capacity to make modest transformations in our experience, and in our self-identity, by using our imaginative resources (such as image schemas, metaphors, idealized cognitive models, and frames). Autonomy is self-determination in this limited, situated sense.

Rational criticism. The Enlightenment aspired to universal rational standards of evaluation and criticism in all areas of human experience, such as science, morals, politics, and art. If morality stemmed from an essential Universal Reason and consisted of absolute moral laws, then there would be a universally valid standpoint from which to evaluate any moral claims. Moreover, if people were radically free, then they could be held solely responsible for their acts, and it would always be appropriate to praise or blame them for what they have done.

But if you strip away all of these absolutistic metaphysical and epistemological supports, then what is left of moral criticism? Our answer is that we are left with the basis for criticism that we had all along, namely, transperspectivity. We can be critical through an ongoing dialectical process in which we bring different perspectives to bear on our present moral understanding to see what it entails for our lives, how it affects others, what it misses that might be significant, and how it might be changed. Criticism becomes a social practice in which individuals and entire groups subject their values, principles, and fundamental frames to continual scrutiny. Criticism of this sort is not carried on from an absolute or totalizing perspective, for there isn't any such thing for human beings. Human reason gives us a human objectivity (as transperspectivity), and, as Putnam reminds us, "If our 'objectivity' is objectivity humanly speaking, it is still objectivity enough."[7]

Morality beyond the Rules

What we are left with from the Enlightenment is a small cluster of important moral ideals that have been severed from their origins in the essentialist, universalist, and absolutist metaphysics and epistemology of that period. Instead of regarding these ideals as ultimate moral facts grounded on our essence as rational beings, we should regard them as imaginative ideals we seek to realize and to harmonize in the way we live our lives and treat others.

Some people will find this view disgustingly relativistic, since it recognizes the possibility of a broad range of realistic visions of human flourishing. It recognizes that there is almost never only one single way to be moral. We have seen, in fact, that the idea of discovering '*the* single right thing to do' must be rejected because it is incompatible with what we know about the imaginative character of human conceptualization and reasoning. Moreover, it is the very thing we don't want if we are trying to act morally, because it tends to close us off to morally significant aspects of situations.

The absolutist will accuse us of having no way to convince others who have different values from ours that they are wrong. We all know of cultures who live by at least some values that we (not just ourselves personally, but our entire culture) find morally reprehensible. How are we supposed to regard such cultures?

The answer is this: To start with, we must recognize that there is no way to bludgeon those who disagree with us into submission by claiming privileged access to the essence of reason. It is time to give up the Moral Law conception of REASON AS FORCE. Morality isn't about *forcing* people to draw certain 'rational' conclusions and then acting on them. Instead, moral 'argument' (which is a bad word for the kind of open dialogue we should be engaging in) ought to be about holding up ideals for living that capture people's imagination, because they really do inspire them with a vision of human flourishing that is realizable in their lives.

Everybody knows that moral education and moral growth do not consist primarily in the learning of moral rules. We learn from experience and example. We develop our moral sense because of how people have treated us, what we have experienced, and the moral ideals and frames our culture supplies us. Our moral understanding is built up around the moral prototypes we have encountered and the meaning they have for us. We are inspired by the lives, either actual or fictional, of people who seem to us to be caring, sensitive, intelligent, courageous, and wise. We get a sense of what we might become and how we might live by observing how they live and by trying to act as they would in a given situation.

When we confront persons who disagree with us about a moral issue, it is not as though *we* are being rational and they are not. Reason is just not that narrow and restrictive. Rather, there are usually plenty of 'good reasons' for both of the competing views. There are several things we might say to them in discussing our differences. Perhaps we can identify an inconsistency in their position. Or maybe we can show them implications of their view that they have not noticed—implications that either make them question their view, or else that show them a new way to think about things. We can also present persons who have a different view with an account of how things might be for all of us if certain values were lived out, certain types of relationships were formed, and certain social practices were realized. We can hold up for their consideration a vision of what is possible, and we can explain how various values, principles, and ideals hang together according to our idea of human flourishing. But we cannot accuse them of being irrational simply because they do not happen to see things our way.

In the course of our explanation and dialogue, we will perhaps discern limitations in our own view, or some prejudice that blinds us to certain constructive possibilities in a situation. We may see that some model we are working with is not rich enough to encompass all that is morally relevant in a particular case. If we are fortunate, we will escape the trap of merely trying to convince others that we are right and they are wrong. Perhaps we will actually understand that neither of us has the truth, whole and absolute.[8]

So, how much relativism are we saddled with? The answer is that what we know about human experience, conceptualization, and reasoning leaves us with a fairly robust relativism, but not a total relativism. There are universal human experiences of pain, pleasure, suffering, joy, and fulfillment. There are universal human needs, such as shelter, food, love, and protection from harm. There are widely, if not universally, shared moral prototypes (e.g., *the bully, fair distribution, undeserved kindness*). All of these universals, if they really are universals,[9] place general constraints on what moralities must be like. Furthermore, the facts of human psychology—how we conceptualize, what motivates us, how our identity is formed, and how we develop—place restrictions on the form of any humanly realistic morality.

As we have seen, however, the fact that human conceptualization and reasoning are largely imaginative entails that there will exist a large variety of ways for imaginatively interpreting and elaborating these apparently universal bases. There are many different ways to understand the meaning of basic-level experiences of pain, pleasure, sadness, and joy. And there are a variety of ways to satisfy basic human needs. Thus, for example, something as universal as pain may be experienced in different ways—as an awful suffering, as an unremarkable fact of life, or even as an ennobling experience. A need as basic and universal as love can be given widely divergent meanings across cultures, and can be satisfied in a wide variety of human relationships. A prototype as common as *undeserved kindness* will mean one thing within a Kantian-style rational ethics and something very different within a Judeo-Christian ethics of love.

This brings up a final, crucial point. We examined the way in which the Moral Law folk theory, especially when articulated within the framework of Enlightenment psychology, metaphysics, and epistemology, gives us an extremely narrow, restrictive, and unimaginative conception of morality. By getting rid of Enlightenment absolutism, morality is opened up to certain virtues and moral ideals that were previously hidden, but which now come to seem central to moral understanding and moral wisdom. I have in mind such virtues and feelings as tenderness, mercy, forgiveness, love, and humility.[10] I have in mind the recognition that absurdity, inescapable tragedy, and luck play a central part in all human existence.[11] I have not done the necessary analysis to give an empirically responsible account of the way in which these virtues, ideals, and facts of human moral experience can be woven together into a coherent morality. It would be a morality that goes beyond restrictive laws and the ethics of obligation and duty. It would be morality that goes beyond our instrumental relations to others and to our environment. It would explore forms of relationship that go beyond those given by our culture. And it would be based on our ability to take up the part of others through imagination and feeling.

It looks as though we had better learn to live, therefore, not only with multiple moral systems, but also with the multiplicity of values and goods that we experience in our own lives. That there exists an irreducible and sometimes conflicting diversity of goods, values, and ideals, and that there is no single criterion against which to rank order them, will seem obvious once we have managed to free ourselves from the spell of a totalizing moral absolutism. It takes no great insight to recognize that our moral understanding is complex, multidimensional, messy, anything but transparent, and utterly resistant to absolutes and reductive strategies. This is not to say that we shouldn't seek as much clarity, determinateness, and stability as we can realistically manage, but only that we must never be fooled into thinking that our formalizations can stand for our embodied, ongoing, historically situated, and imaginative moral experience. We negotiate our way through this tangled maze of moral deliberation, one step at a time, never sure where we will end, guided only by our ideals of what we, and others, and our shared world might become. In this journey through sometimes uncharted territory, we must rely on what illumination we can get from our flickering moral imagination.

INTRODUCTION

1. For an account of the 'classical theory of categories' and its fundamental shortcomings, see George Lakoff, *Women, Fire, and Dangerous Things: What Categories Reveal about the Mind* (Chicago: University of Chicago Press, 1987).

2. The most influential body of research on prototype effects in categorization has been done by Eleanor Rosch and her colleagues, for example, Eleanor Rosch, "Natural Categories," *Cognitive Psychology* 4 (1973):328–50; Eleanor Rosch, "Human Categorization," in *Studies in Cross-cultural Psychology,* ed. Neil Warren (London: Academic Press, 1977), 1:1–49; Eleanor Rosch and B. B. Lloyd, eds., *Cognition and Categorization* (Hillsdale, N.J.: Lawrence Erlbaum, 1978).

3. This characteristic of concepts has been studied in cases of legal reasoning by Steven Winter, in "The Metaphor of Standing and the Problem of Self-governance," *Stanford Law Review* 40, no. 6 (1988):1371–1516, and in "Transcendental Nonsense, Metaphoric Reasoning, and the Cognitive Stakes for Law," *University of Pennsylvania Law Review* 137, no. 4 (1989):1105–1237.

4. See, for example, Charles Fillmore, "Frame Semantics," in *Linguistics in the Morning Calm*, ed. Linguistic Society of Korea (Seoul: Hanshin, 1982), 111–38; Charles Fillmore, "Frames and the Semantics of Understanding," *Quaderni di Semantica* 6, no. 2 (1985):222–53.

5. The nature of systems of conceptual metaphor is explored in George Lakoff and Mark Johnson, *Metaphors We Live By* (Chicago: University of Chicago Press, 1980). For an update on more recent work on this subject, see George Lakoff, "The Contemporary Theory of Metaphor," in *Metaphor and Thought,* 2d edition, ed. Andrew Ortony (Cambridge: Cambridge University Press, 1993). An example of ways to test for the existence of conceptual metaphors is presented in Raymond Gibbs, Jr., "Psycholinguistic Studies on the Conceptual Basis of Idiomaticity," *Cognitive Linguistics* 1, no. 4 (1990):417–51.

6. For the parallel situation in legal reasoning see Winter, "Transcendental Nonsense"; Steven Winter, "Indeterminacy and Incommensurability in Constitutional Law," *California Law Review* 78, no. 6 (1990):1443–1541.

7. Following the work of Eleanor Rosch, George Lakoff has examined the phenomenon of basic-level categorization in *Women, Fire, and Dangerous Things*.

8. Alasdair MacIntyre, *After Virtue*, 2d edition (Notre Dame, Ind.: University of Notre Dame Press, 1984); Paul Ricoeur, *Time and Narrative*, translated by K. McLaughlin and D. Pellauer (Chicago: University of Chicago Press, 1984).

9. Richard Eldridge, *On Moral Personhood: Philosophy, Literature, Criticism, and Self-understanding* (Chicago: University of Chicago Press, 1989).

10. Owen Flanagan has examined many of the changes and qualifications that are required in contemporary moral theory if we are to have a "psychologically realistic" ethics (*Varieties of Moral Personality: Ethics and Psychological Realism* [Cambridge: Harvard University Press, 1991]).

CHAPTER ONE

1. For an extended analysis of the fundamental metaphorical systems defining the passions and emotions, See Zoltan Kovecses, *Metaphors of Anger, Pride, and Love: A Lexical Approach to the Structure of Concepts* (Philadelphia: Benjamins, 1986); Zoltan Kovecses, *The Language of Love: The Semantics of Passion in Conversational English* (Lewisburg, Pa.: Bucknell University Press, 1988); Zoltan Kovecses, *Emotion Concepts* (New York: Springer-Verlag, 1990).

2. Alan Donagan, *The Theory of Morality* (Chicago: University of Chicago Press, 1977), 7.

3. "And God said, Let us make man in our image, after our likeness . . . . So God created man in his own image, in the image of God created he him; male and female created he them" (Genesis 1:26–27).

I leave aside questions concerning the existence of immaterial rational creatures (e.g., angels) as well as questions concerning whether they would be subject to moral obligations.

4. "What is man, that thou art mindful of him? . . . For thou hast made him a little lower than the angels, and hast crowned him with glory and honour. Thou madest him to have dominion over the works of thy hands; thou hast put all things under his feet" (Psalms 8:4–6).

5. "Thou has avouched the Lord this day to be thy God, and to walk in his ways, and to keep his statutes, and his commandments, and his judgments, and to hearken unto his voice" (Deuteronomy 26:17).

6. "And God blessed them, and God said unto them, Be fruitful, and multiply, and replenish the earth, and subdue it: and have dominion over the fish of the sea, and over the fowl of the air, and over every living thing that moveth upon the earth" (Genesis 1:28).

7. For example, various actions are required or prohibited as befitting beings created in God's image: "Whoso sheddeth man's blood, by man shall his blood be shed: for in the image of God made he man" (Genesis 9:6); "He that oppresseth the poor reproacheth his Maker: but he that honoureth him hath mercy on the poor" (Proverbs 14:31).

8. As in St. Paul's admonition, "Owe no man any thing, but to love one another: for he that loveth another hath fulfilled the law" (Romans 13:8).

9. Jesus is reported as saying, "Think not that I am come to destroy the law, or the prophets: I am not come to destroy, but to fulfil" (Matthew 5:17). I am also very much aware of alternative traditions within Judaism and Christianity, such as mystical forms of life and what might be called an 'ethics of love.' Mysticism has never constituted a dominant or mainstream tradition in Western morality. And while an ethics of love would, indeed, go beyond a mere morality of rules, St. Paul, for one, argues that all of the moral

commandments are comprehended in the requirement "Thou shalt love thy neighbor as thyself. Love worketh no ill to his neighbour: therefore love *is* the fulfilling of the law" (Romans 13:9–10).

10. Donagan, *The Theory Morality,* chap. 1.

11. In the *Euthyphro* Plato raises the fundamental question of whether piety is pious because it is loved by the gods (i.e., it is piety because they arbitrarily say it is so), or whether the gods love piety because it is pious (i.e., there is a reason why they love it).

12. The following description of Kant's project is taken from my essay "Imagination in Moral Judgment," *Philosophy and Phenomenological Research* 46, no. 2 (1985):265–80.

13. Immanuel Kant, *Critique of Practical Reason,* translated by Lewis White Beck (Indianapolis: Bobbs-Merrill, 1956), 8n. Hereafter, all references to Kant's works will be cited by referring to the Akadamie edition page numbering.

14. Immanuel Kant, *Foundations of the Metaphysics of Morals,* translated by Lewis White Beck (New York: Bobbs-Merrill, 1959), preface, 392, hereafter referred to by *F* followed by the page number (Akademie edition pagination).

15. Kant recognizes the hypothetical character of his argument several times in the *Foundations,* as, for example, when he sums up what he has accomplished in the first two sections: "We showed only through the development of the universally received concept of morals that autonomy of the will is unavoidably connected with it, or rather that it is its foundation. Whoever, therefore, holds morality to be something real and not a chimerical idea without truth must also concede its principle which has been adduced here" (*F,* 445). Kant, of course, believed that traditional morality is not chimerical, but he was aware that there could never be any proof of this.

16. Kant repeats, on several occasions, the impossibility of proving such claims, given the nature of the concept of freedom as a 'rational idea' to which no sensible intuition could ever be adequate (see, especially, *F,* sec. 3).

17. In *The Absent Body* (Chicago: University of Chicago, 1990) Drew Leder has examined the experiential basis that exists for this Cartesian dualism, by showing how our embodiment tends to disappear and recede from our awareness in various cognitive activities. And he explains how the body comes to be regarded (mistakenly) as the locus of epistemic and moral error.

18. Kant makes it quite clear that morality stands as a constraint only for beings who, like us, are imperfectly rational by virtue of having bodies. Thus, Kant describes an objective principle of morality as "that which would serve all rational beings also subjectively as a practical principle if reason had full power over the faculty of desire" (*F,* 401n). It is precisely because we have bodies with desires and inclinations that reason does not have "full power." Because of this, the commands of reason are, for us, *imperatives:* "All imperatives are expressed by an 'ought' and thereby indicate the relation of an objective law of reason to a will which is not in its subjective constitution necessarily determined by this law. This relation is that of constraint" (*F,* 413).

19. See, for example, John Silber's account (in his introduction to his edition of Kant's *Religion within the Bounds of Reason Alone* [Chicago: University of Chicago, 1960]) of

Kant's change of view from the *Foundations* to the *Critique of Practical Reason* as he attempted to reconcile apparently conflicting intuitions about the nature of freedom, morality, and responsibility.

20. Silber (ibid.) traces Kant's problems with a conception of a will that is disembodied, for it then becomes impossible to say anything about how will can be affected by, and can affect, our bodily desires and inclinations. Kant is forced to posit a will split into two parts, *Wille* (= practical reason, which gives us the moral law) and *Willkür* (= the capacity for free choice, which is connected with desire). But this only restates, at a different level, the fundamental problem of uniting the two radically separated metaphysical realms.

21. R. M. Hare, *Freedom and Reason* (Oxford: Oxford University Press, 1963); Alan Gewirth, *Reason and Morality* (Chicago: University of Chicago Press, 1978); John Rawls, *A Theory of Justice* (Cambridge: Harvard University Press, 1971); Robert Nozick, *Anarchy, State, and Utopia* (New York: Basic Books, 1974); Donagan, *The Theory of Morality*.

22. Rawls, *A Theory of Justice,* 47.

23. Donagan, *The Theory of Morality,* chap. 1. Hereafter page numbers will be in the text.

24. Nozick, *Anarchy, State, and Utopia.*

25. Thomas Aquinas, *Summa Theologica,* question 90, art. 1.

CHAPTER TWO

1. "Three Cheers in Dearborn," *Time,* March 24, 1980, 24.

2. I have spelled out these traditional prejudices against metaphor in my introduction to *Philosophical Perspectives on Metaphor,* ed. Mark Johnson (Minneapolis: University of Minnesota Press, 1981).

3. This research group includes faculty and students at the University of California, Berkeley, with a core group consisting of George Lakoff, Eve Sweetser, Jane Espenson, Sharon Fischler, Adele Goldberg, Karin Myhre, and Alan Schwarz. They are producing a metaphor survey that includes mappings, representative expressions for each mapping, and relations of various metaphors.

4. Part of this analysis of the EVENT STRUCTURE metaphor is taken from Lakoff, "Contemporary Theory of Metaphor."

5. The PURPOSES ARE DESTINATIONS metaphor is analyzed in detail in my *Body in the Mind* (Chicago: University of Chicago Press, 1987), chap. 5.

6. See Lakoff, "Contemporary Theory of Metaphor," for a fuller analysis of the extent to which the LOCATION metaphor structures our conceptual system.

7. The SOCIETY IS A PERSON metaphor is discussed in George Lakoff, "Metaphor and War: The Metaphor System Used to Justify War in the Gulf," *Journal of Urban and Cultural Studies* 2, no. 2 (1991).

8. The hostility and aggression toward deviance that is generated in many people surely requires further (psychological) explanation, including our deepest anxieties about our

identity, our fear of that which is other, and our inability to deal with ambiguity and change. I do not pretend to understand the deepest origins of our intolerance for deviance.

9. The following account of the metaphoric mapping is based on the analysis done by Chris Klingebiel, "The Bottom Line in Moral Accounting" (Department of Linguistics, University of California, Berkeley, 1989, manuscript).

10. Once again, many of the following examples are taken from, or are variations on, those given in ibid.

11. Sarah Taub, "An Account of Accounting" (Department of Linguistics, University of California, Berkeley, 1989, manuscript).

12. I am giving a significantly different formulation of this schema than the one provided by Taub.

13. Taub, "Account of Accounting," 8.

14. Kovecses, *Language of Love,* analyzes the structure of these and related metaphorical concepts.

15. See, for example, Zoltan Kovecses, "Happiness: A Definitional Effort," *Metaphor and Symbolic Activity* 6, no. 1 (1991):29–46.

16. Naomi Quinn, "Marriage as a Do-It-Yourself Project: The Organization of Marital Goals," in *Proceedings of the Third Annual Conference of the Cognitive Science Society* (Berkeley: University of California Press, 1981), 31–40. The analysis I will be giving of selected parts of Quinn's data was worked out in collaboration with Nancy Tuana and George McClure.

17. See, for example, Naomi Quinn, "Convergent Evidence for a Cultural Model of American Marriage," in *Cultural Models in Language and Thought,* ed. D. Holland and N. Quinn (Cambridge: Cambridge University Press, 1987), 173–92.

18. My formulation of these metaphors does not always conform to the specific names Quinn gives them, though I believe that I have captured the basic mappings underlying each metaphor.

19. Quinn, "Marriage as a Do-It-Yourself Project," 31. All quotations from 'Alex' are taken from this source.

20. David Hume, *A Treatise of Human Nature,* ed. L. A. Selby-Bigge (1777; Oxford: Clarendon Press, 1888), bk. 3, secs. 1, 2; David Hume, *An Enquiry concerning the Principles of Morals,* ed. L. A. Selby-Bigge (1777; Oxford: Oxford University Press, 1902).

21. Kant, who is perhaps the most famous purveyor of the morality/prudence dichotomy, did, in fact, recognize this point. He saw that, if there is no connection between our being moral and our being happy, then morality must appear to us to be utterly mysterious—a command of reason imposed as if from on high, without any relation to our happiness. Even Kant found this distressing! And so, he devoted considerable effort in his *Critique of Practical Reason* to the argument that morality and virtue would be rewarded with happiness in a life beyond this world, just as reason requires.

22. Much of the relevant evidence, with reference to the appropriate studies, can be found in Lakoff, *Women, Fire, and Dangerous Things.*

23. Cognitive semantics is a program of empirical research in linguistics, psychology,

philosophy, and the other cognitive sciences that stresses the embodied and imaginative character of human cognition. Various versions of it are set out in the first issue of *Cognitive Linguistics* (1990). I have articulated the basic assumptions of my particular version of it in *The Body in the Mind*.

24. For instance, there are what I call 'image schemas' (e.g., CONTAINMENT, UP-DOWN, INSIDE-OUTSIDE, BALANCE, and SOURCE-PATH-GOAL) of which we have non-metaphorical concepts. However, as we will see, these image schemas often provide the basis of various metaphorical projections.

CHAPTER THREE

1. In chapter 5, I give an explanation of why and how moral theories typically come to regard themselves as giving absolute and definitive analyses of moral issues. The key idea is that they presuppose a mistaken conception of reason as having direct reflective insight into its own essence.

2. MacIntyre, *After Virtue,* 268.

3. Hilary Putnam, *The Many Faces of Realism* (La Salle, Ill.: Open Court, 1987), 51.

4. "The Kantian moral image does include the claim that thinking for oneself about how to live *(für sich selbst denken!)* is a virtue, to be sure, but it contains other ideas as well. It contains the idea that this virtue is not just a virtue, but that our capacity for exercising this virtue is the most significant moral capacity we have; it includes the claim that a human being who has chosen not to think for himself about how to live, or has been coerced or 'conditioned' into being unable to think for himself about how to live, has failed to live a fully human life. It contains also the vision of a community of individuals who respect one another for that capacity" (ibid., 61–62).

5. One might cite here any of a number of works by contemporary defenders of Kant, such as Marcia Baron, Alan Donagan, Richard Eldridge, Barbara Herman, Thomas Hill, Christine Korsgaard, Robert Louden, Onora O'Neill, Rick McCarty, and a host of others.

6. Barbara Herman, "On the Value of Acting from the Motive of Duty," *Philosophical Review* 90, no. 3 (1981):359–82; Marcia Baron, "The Alleged Moral Repugnance of Acting from Duty," *Journal of Philosophy* 81, no. 4 (1984):197–220.

7. Andrews Reath, "Kant's Theory of Moral Sensibility," *Kant-Studien* 80, no. 3 (1989):284–302; Rick McCarty, "Kantian Moral Motivation and the Feeling of Respect," *Journal of the History of Philosophy* (forthcoming).

8. Robert Louden, "Kant's Virtue Ethics," *Philosophy* 61, no. 238 (1986):473–89; Onora O'Neill, "Kant after Virtue," *Inquiry* 26 (1984):397.

9. Henning Jensen, "Kant and Moral Integrity," *Philosophical Studies* 57, no. 2 (1989):193–205.

10. Eldridge, *On Moral Personhood.*

11. The following analysis is a revision of selected parts on my essay "Imagination in Moral Judgment."

12. Kant provides what he calls a "transcendental deduction" of moral law. The form of the argument is as follows: Moral laws can have the character we attribute to them (i.e.,

necessity and universality) only if reason has a certain nature. Transcendental arguments are not proofs in the sense of deductions from axioms.

13. Immanuel Kant, *Critique of Pure Reason*, translated by Norman Kemp Smith (1781; New York: St. Martin's, 1968).

14. A maxim "contains the practical rule which reason determines according to the conditions of the subject (often its ignorance or inclinations) and is thus the principle according to which the subject acts" (*F*, 421n).

15. This way of formulating complete maxims is given by Michael Green, "Using Nature to Typify Freedom: Application of the Categorical Imperative," *International Studies in Philosophy* 14 (1982):17–26.

16. Kant, of course, cites more than one version of the categorical imperative, but he insists that this 'universal law' version is *the* basic formula. I will discuss the several formulas and their relations below. H. J. Paton, *The Categorical Imperative* (London: Hutchinson, 1947), still remains one of the best treatments of the different formulas and their interrelations and significance. Bruce Aune, *Kant's Theory of Morals* (Princeton: Princeton University Press, 1979), is also quite useful in briefly contrasting the versions of the supreme principle.

17. John Dewey, *Experience and Nature*, rev. edition (1929; New York: Dover, 1958).

18. Kant, *Critique of Practical Reason*, 8n.

19. Immanuel Kant, *Critique of Judgment*, translated by J. H. Bernard (New York: Hafner, 1968), introduction, iv. Hereafter abbreviated *CJ* followed by the section number.

20. Kant, *Critique of Pure Reason*, A132/B175.

21. Kant, *Critique of Practical Reason*, 69.

22. Paul Dietrichson, "Kant's Criteria of Universalizability," in *Kant: Foundations of the Metaphysics of Morals*, text and critical essays ed. Robert Paul Wolff (Indianapolis: Bobbs-Merrill, 1969), 176–77.

23. Hence, we get Kant's 'typified' form of the categorical imperative, "Act as though the maxim of your action were by your will to become a universal law of nature" (*F*, 421), which Kant uses to assess a large number of maxims he discusses.

24. Kant, *Critique of Practical Reason*, 69–70.

25. The problem of determining when a contradiction exists is notoriously difficult, and I cannot address it here. I recommend Dietrichson's thorough and insightful account of this evaluation procedure ("Kant's Criteria of Universalizability").

26. Mark Johnson, "Imagination in Moral Judgment," 265–80.

27. Donagan, *The Theory of Morality*, 232.

28. This weaker interpretation would be consistent with Eldridge's attempt to show how we can develop a socialized, historically situated Kantianism by focusing on narratives that manifest fundamental Kantian moral notions (*On Moral Personhood*).

CHAPTER FOUR

1. Different aspects of this new view of category structure were first explored by Ludwig Wittgenstein, *Philosophical Investigations* (translated by G. E. M. Anscombe

[New York: Macmillan, 1953]), and John Austin, *Philosophical Papers* (2d edition, ed. J. O. Urmson and G. J. Warnock [Oxford: Oxford University Press, 1970]). The major body of research that has defined categorization studies today was done by Eleanor Rosch and her colleagues: Rosch, "Natural Categories," 328–50; Eleanor Rosch, "Cognitive Reference Points," *Cognitive Psychology* 7 (1975):532–47; Eleanor Rosch, "Cognitive Representations of Semantic Categories," *Journal of Experimental Psychology* 104 (1975):192–233; Rosch and Lloyd, *Cognition and Categorization*.

2. Rosch, "Natural Categories," 328–50; Rosch, "Human Categorization," 1–49; Eleanor Rosch, "Principles of Categorization," in *Cognition and Categorization,* ed. Eleanor Rosch and B. B. Lloyd (Hillsdale, N.J.: Lawrence Erlbaum, 1978), 27–48.

3. Wittgenstein, *Philosophical Investigations*.

4. The fact that absolutism and some forms of relativism are *both* versions of the Moral Law folk theory was pointed out to me by Steven Winter, who identified the real culprit as not just absolutism or relativism, but rather the idea that morality is rule-following.

5. Donagan, *The Theory of Morality,* 7.

6. Thus, Hare focuses primarily on what he takes to be the supreme logical principle governing the nature of more specific rules of conduct, namely, a universalizability principle (*Freedom and Reason,* especially chap. 3). Alan Gewirth also sees the supreme principles as a general constraint on morally permissible actions: "every agent, by the fact of engaging in action, is logically committed to the acceptance of certain evaluative and deontic judgments and ultimately of a supreme moral principle, the Principle of Generic Consistency, which requires that he respect his recipients' necessary conditions of action" (*Reason and Morality,* x). Robert Nozick conceives of the rules as "side constraints" that prohibit certain sorts of actions against persons (*Anarchy, State, and Utopia,* 11). And in a more obvious Kantian fashion, Donagan identifies a substantive fundamental principle ("Act always so that you respect every human being, yourself or another, as being a rational creature") from which he tries to derive more specific precepts concerning the basic kinds of morally permissible, impermissible, and obligatory actions (*The Theory of Morality,* 65).

7. Donagan, *The Theory of Morality,* 66. Hereafter page numbers will be in the text.

8. The following schemas and specificatory premises are cited directly from ibid., 67–68.

9. Hare's treatment of this case occurs in "Abortion and the Golden Rule," *Philosophy and Public Affairs* 4 (1975):201–22. The example is taken from H. L. A. Hart, "Positivism and the Separation of Law and Morals," *Harvard Law Review* 71 (1958):593–629, and his debate with Lon Fuller, "Positivism and Fidelity to Law—A Reply to Professor Hart," *Harvard Law Review* 71 (1958):630–72.

10. Hart, "Positivism," 593.

11. Hare reasons, "If a normative or evaluative principle is framed in terms of a predicate which has fuzzy edges (as nearly all predicates in practice have), then we are not going to be able to use the principle to decide cases on the borderline without doing some more normation or evaluation" ("Abortion and the Golden Rule," 204).

12. Winter, "Transcendental Nonsense."

13. I am using 'objectivist' here to refer to what Lakoff (*Women, Fire, and Dangerous Things*) calls the 'objectivist' or 'classical' theory of categorization. The crux of this theory is that the meaning of a given concept is specified by a defining list of properties a thing must have if it is to fall under that concept. In this sense, a concept or category is defined by a set of necessary and sufficient conditions for membership within that category. As such, those categories get their meaning by their objective relation to objects and properties that exist independently in the world.

14. Linda Coleman and Paul Kay, "Prototype Semantics: The English Verb *Lie*," *Language* 57, no. 1 (1981):26–44.

15. Ibid., 43.

16. For an account of radial category structure see Lakoff, *Women, Fire, and Dangerous Things,* especially chap. 5: "A radial structure is one where there is a central case and conventionalized variations on it which cannot be predicted by general rules" (84).

17. Eve Sweetser, "The Definition of Lie: An examination of the Folk Models Underlying a Semantic Prototype," in *Cultural Models in Language and Thought,* ed. D. Holland and N. Quinn (Cambridge: Cambridge University Press, 1989):43–66.

18. Lakoff, *Women, Fire, and Dangerous Things.* The concept of an idealized cognitive model is discussed and illustrated throughout the entire book, especially in the lengthy case studies of part 3.

19. Robert McCauley, "The Role of Theories in a Theory of Concepts," in *Concepts and Conceptual Development,* ed. Ulric Neisser (Cambridge: Cambridge University Press, 1988):288–309.

20. Sweetser does not employ the term 'idealized cognitive model' but speaks instead of "folk theories." My names for, and formulations of, these models are taken from similar analyses by Lakoff (*Women, Fire, and Dangerous Things*) and Winter ("Transcendental Nonsense").

21. This maxim of helpfulness is a version of Paul Grice's principle of cooperation as articulated in "Logic and Conversation," *Syntax and Semantics,* vol. 3, *Speech Acts,* ed. P. Cole and J. Morgan (New York: Academic Press, 1975):41–58.

22. The extent to which females are regarded as prototypical persons varies from culture to culture and from one historical period to another. But it is clear that in American and European culture women have not yet attained prototypical status, insofar as they have not been accorded rights and privileges on an equal basis with men. Moreover, as feminist philosophers have shown in detail, there exists a profound gender bias in our very conceptions of reason, knowledge, morality, and politics.

23. Remember Donagan's claim that "the concept of respecting every human being as a rational creature is in large measure understood in itself" (71). The qualification "in large measure" is irrelevant to the argument I am giving, since I am claiming that no part of the concept is "understood in itself" in the sense that Donagan gives that phrase. What he takes as "understood in itself," I am arguing, is always understood only relative to background cognitive models and to the purposes and interests of those for whom the concepts play a significant role.

24. Steven Winter, "An Upside/Down View of the Countermajoritarian Difficulty," *Texas Law Review* 69, no. 7 (1991):1881–1927, gives a brief account of our changing conception of the purpose of public parks, and how such culturally contingent normative views have affected legal reasoning.

25. Richard Rorty, "The Contingency of Language," in *Contingency, Irony, and Solidarity* (Cambridge: Cambridge University Press, 1989):3–22.

26. Winter, "Transcendental Nonsense," 1194 ff. Hereafter page numbers will be in the text.

27. In later chapters I attempt to flesh out this view of the imaginative character of human cognition, with an emphasis on nonpropositional dimensions of understanding and reasoning.

28. This is a point that even Kant, with all of his objectivist leanings, saw with great clarity. He argued that one can never be certain of having acted morally, for two basic reasons: (1) *Psychological:* one can never know for sure what one's deepest motives are: "It is in fact absolutely impossible by experience to discern with complete certainty a single case in which the maxim of an action . . . rested solely on moral grounds. . . . For we like to flatter ourselves with a pretended nobler motive, while in fact even the strictest examination can never lead us entirely behind the secret incentives" (*F,* 407), (2) *Ontological:* to act morally requires acting freely, but we can never prove that we are free (see *F,* sec. 3).

29. John Dewey, *Theory of the Moral Life* (New York: Holt, Rinehart, and Winston, 1960), 141. This book is part 2 of Dewey's and Tufts's 1932 edition of their *Ethics.*

30. In her discussion of Aristotle's view of moral deliberation, Martha Nussbaum has made the same point about the proper way to regard general rules: "Principles are perspicuous descriptive summaries of good judgments, valid only to the extent to which they correctly describe such judgments. They are normative only insofar as they transmit in economical form the normative force of the good concrete decisions of the wise person and because we wish for various reasons to be guided by that person's choices" (*The Fragility of Goodness: Luck and Ethics in Greek Tragedy and Philosophy* [Cambridge: Cambridge University Press, 1986], 299).

31. Dewey, *Theory of the Moral Life,* 141.

32. On this basis (of the constant evolution of human experience) Dewey argues that "the need for constant revision and expansion of moral knowledge is one great reason why there is no gulf dividing non-moral knowledge from that which is truly moral. At any moment conceptions which once seemed to belong exclusively to the biological or physical realm may assume moral import" (ibid., 144).

CHAPTER FIVE

1. Owen Flanagan, *Varieties of Moral Personality,* mounts a sustained and comprehensive argument that shows why moral theory must conform to moral psychology. The key point is that any acceptable moral theory must be compatible with what we know generally about the nature of persons, human motivation, moral development, and so forth.

Flanagan argues that, although the restrictions imposed by such knowledge on the form and content of a moral theory are very general, nevertheless they do exclude certain kinds of views as being psychologically unrealistic.

2. It would be an interesting and eye-opening exercise to try to find even one instance of the expression 'moral imagination' in any of the standard works of moral theory. One is far more likely to find the term either ignored or disparaged. In any case, the idea of moral imagination as central to our reasoning is foreign to our mainstream tradition.

3. Charles Taylor, "The Diversity of Goods," in *Utilitarianism and Beyond*, ed. Bernard Williams and Amartya Sen (Cambridge: Cambridge University Press, 1982), 129–44. Hereafter page numbers will be in the text.

4. The attribution of universal moral personality is most clearly evident in the following three formulas of the categorical imperative: (1) *Universalizability:* "Act only according to that maxim by which you can, at the same time, will that it should become a universal law" (*F*, 421). (Everyone stands equally under universally valid moral laws.) (2) *Humanity as an end:* "Act so that you treat humanity, whether in your own person or that of another, always as an end and never as a means only" (*F*, 429). (Each person is treated equally as an end-in-itself.) (3) *Autonomy:* "The concept of each rational being as a being that must regard itself as giving universal law through all the maxims of its will" (*F*, 433). (We are equal in respect of standing under the requirement to give ourselves universally valid laws.)

5. That is, it is because we possess practical reason that we have this status of moral personality, and it is practical reason that informs us of our obligation to recognize this status in every other rational creature.

6. Kant argues that the nature of moral law (its origin in pure practical reason) requires that it be in no way dependent on any empirical content, end, or feeling. But this leaves only the *form* of law as such, which is universality. The supreme pure principle of morality can be nothing other than a universalizability criterion for evaluating particular maxims of actions. So, it appears that this universalizability constraint is nothing but the essence of pure practical reason itself (*F*, secs. 1, 2).

7. I am thinking here, minimally, of the denial of equal moral status to slaves in Greek society, and of the relativizing of duties, rights, and obligations to one's place in the caste system in modern India. One can, of course, insist that these conceptions are simply wrong or immoral, but such an argument rests on the presumption of a hierarchical ranking of values along with the assumption of a correlative notion of practical reason.

8. Richard Shweder and Edmund Bourne, "Does the Concept of the Person Vary Cross-culturally?" in R. Shweder, *Thinking through Cultures: Expeditions in Cultural Psychology* (Cambridge: Harvard University Press, 1991), 113.

9. Rawls, *A Theory of Justice*, 11–22, 251–57. This constructivist view of moral theory is articulated also in Rawls's "Kantian Constructivism in Moral Theory," *Journal of Philosophy* 77, no. 9 (1980):515–72, especially 554–72.

10. In *Whose Justice? Which Rationality?* (Notre Dame, Ind.: University of Notre Dame Press, 1988), Alasdair MacIntyre has argued at great length, on the basis of three

extensively elaborated cases from different historical periods, the parallel point that the notions of 'justice' and 'practical reason' are correlative, so that neither can be defined independently of the other.

11. In *Reason, Truth, and History* (Cambridge: Cambridge University Press, 1981), Hilary Putnam has argued that any conception of reason or rational acceptability will depend on some conception of cognitive flourishing or, more generally, of human flourishing. Hence, every conception of reason is value-laden (see, especially, "Fact and Value," 147–49).

12. Carol Gilligan, *In a Different Voice: Psychological Theory and Women's Development* (Cambridge: Harvard University Press, 1982). Hereafter page numbers will be in the text.

13. Lawrence Kohlberg, *Essays on Moral Development*, vol. 1, *The Philosophy of Moral Development*, and vol. 2, *The Psychology of Moral Development* (New York: Harper and Row, 1981, 1984).

14. Many of the relevant arguments formulated within Anglo-American analytic philosophy against essentialist views of reason (and the analytic/synthetic dichotomy) are summarized in Richard Rorty, *Philosophy and the Mirror of Nature* (Princeton: Princeton University Press, 1979). Nelson Goodman's *Ways of Worldmaking* (Indianapolis: Hackett Publishing Co., 1978) is also a useful summary of the arguments he has offered over the years in a number of his works.

15. Jeremy Bentham, *An Introduction to the Principles of Morals and Legislation* (Oxford, 1789), selection from *Ethics: Selections from Classical and Contemporary Writers*, 5th edition, ed. Oliver A. Johnson (New York: Holt, Rinehart, and Winston, 1984), 212.

16. Ibid., 218

17. Donagan, *The Theory of Morality,* 194 ff.

18. Owen Flanagan observes that act utilitarianism "requires an impossible amount of attention to one's action options" (*Varieties of Moral Personality,* 34).

19. A summary of the most telling criticisms appears in the introduction by Amartya Sen and Bernard Williams to their anthology, *Utilitarianism and Beyond* (Cambridge: Cambridge University Press, 1982).

20. As an example of the dominance of these models of rationality in contemporary psychological, social, and political theory, see MacIntyre, *After Virtue,* especially chaps. 7, 8. In economic theory, see Julie A. Nelson, "Gender, Metaphor, and the Definition of Economics" (Working Paper Series no. 350, Department of Economics, University of California, San Diego, January 1990).

21. Nussbaum, *Fragility of Goodness.*

CHAPTER SIX

1. Donagan, *The Theory of Morality,* 53.

2. Ibid.

3. Moral objectivism thus presupposes what George Lakoff (in *Women, Fire, and Dangerous Things*) has named the 'classical' view of categories, according to which a category is defined precisely by a set of necessary and sufficient conditions which must be

satisfied by anything that can truly be said to fall under that category. The objectivist theory of categorization leads quite naturally to the mistaken view that any given situation, by virtue of its definite properties, must either fall or not fall under some given concepts. And this leads, in turn, to the view that we can determine how we ought to act by discovering whether or not a given situation falls under a specific moral principle.

4. Roberto Unger, *Knowledge and Politics* (New York: Free Press, 1976). Hereafter page numbers will be in the text.

5. The second principle Unger names "the Arbitrariness of Desire," by which he means that what we want, as well as our justification of our wants, cannot be a matter of reason or understanding. It is merely a matter of arbitrary desire, either finding itself directed toward an object or choosing to pursue some end (42).

6. One thinks immediately of Thomas Hobbes's contract theory, in which a justification is needed for an individual to pass from a state of nature to the condition of a commonwealth (*Leviathan;* [1651]; Oxford: Clarendon Press, 1909), or of Locke's contract theory in his *Two Treatises of Government* (1690; rev. edition, ed. Peter Laslett [Cambridge: Cambridge University Press, 1960]). However, the basic problem that gives rise to contract theories, the atomic individualistic self, lies at the heart of much modern political theory, as in, for example, Rawls, *A Theory of Justice,* and Nozick, *Anarchy, State, and Utopia.*

7. Kant argues that the only thing good without qualification is a good will (*F,* 393) and that "an action performed from duty does not have its moral worth in the purpose which is to be achieved through it but in the maxim by which it is determined. Its moral value, therefore, does not depend on the realizations of the object of the action but merely on the principle of volition by which the action is done without any regard to the objects of the faculty of desire" (*F,* 399–400).

8. Bernard Williams, *Ethics and the Limits of Philosophy* (Cambridge: Harvard University Press, 1985), 64.

9. Flanagan, *Varieties of Moral Personality,* 142.

10. Dewey, *Theory of the Moral Life,* 150–51.

11. MacIntyre, *After Virtue,* 12.

12. Hume, *Treatise of Human Nature,* bk. 3, pt. 1, sec. 1, 457. Hereafter cited in the text in the form 3.1.1.457.

13. Annette C. Baier, *A Progress of Sentiments: Reflections on Hume's* Treatise (Cambridge: Harvard University Press, 1991), chap. 12. I am grateful to Owen Flanagan for correcting my presentation of Hume by directing me to Baier's work.

14. Ibid., 288.

15. A. J. Ayer, *Language, Truth, and Logic,* 2d edition (1946: New York: Dover, 1952), 107.

16. The only rational critique could come from the point of view of 'economic rationality,' that is, a criticism of a course of action as not being the most efficient means to some end. No rational criticism of values or ends is possible on this view.

17. G. E. Moore, *Principia Ethica* (Cambridge: Cambridge University Press, 1903), viii. Hereafter page numbers will be in the text.

18. Whether there *is* a naturalistic fallacy and, if so, what it consists in has been a subject of much debate. Most supporters and critics of Moore alike seem to agree at least that Moore held that any attempt to define 'good' was an instance of the fallacy. For a discussion of the debate on this question, see William Frankena, "The Naturalistic Fallacy," in *Theories of Ethics,* ed. Philippa Foot (Oxford: Oxford University Press, 1967), 50–63; Mary Warnock, *Ethics since 1900,* 2d edition (Oxford: Oxford University Press, 1966), 11–38. A more cynical and critical view of Moore, which I endorse, has been articulated by Bernard Williams, *Ethics and the Limits of Philosophy,* 121–22.

19. J. M. Keynes, "My Early Beliefs," in *Two Memoirs* (New York: Augustus Kelley, 1949), 83.

20. Keynes, "My Early Beliefs," 84–85.

21. G. J. Warnock, *Contemporary Moral Philosophy* (Oxford: Oxford University Press, 1967), 16.

22. MacIntyre, *After Virtue,* chap. 3.

23. In criticizing the bifurcation of the self, I do not intend to deny the relevance of Faculty Psychology. It may turn out that there is no adequate substitution for a robust Faculty Psychology (see Robert McCauley, "The Role of Cognitive Explanations in Psychology," *Behaviorism* 15, no. 1 [1987]:27–40). Rather, what I am criticizing is any psychology that presupposes a radical split into distinct metaphysical categories as underlying various faculties.

24. I include among Kantian approaches views as diverse as those of Rawls, Nozick, Gewirth, Donagan, and Hare, all of whom express a considerable debt to Kantian themes, concepts, and conceptions of moral philosophy.

25. Kant repeats, again and again, that it is impossible to show either how the categorical imperative is possible, how freedom is possible, or that morality is not chimerical. Virtually all of section 2 of the *Foundations* is concerned with this problem, but see especially pages 460–62.

26. Silber, introduction, lxxxv.

27. Thus, Donagan acknowledges that the Judeo-Christian moral tradition presupposes a distinction between event-causation and agent-causation, and he asserts that, "in my opinion, both this conception of action and the presupposition about causation on which it rests are philosophically defensible" (*The Theory of Morality,* 46–47). Furthermore, he supports the possibility of agent-causation by claiming that "neither the determinist nor the purely physicalist interpretations of human action are results of modern science: rather, they are anticipations of what its results will be, which are disputed within the relevant sciences" (233).

28. Rawls's strongest anti-essentialist and antimetaphysical arguments come out in "Kantian Constructivism in Moral Theory," 515–72, and in "Justice as Fairness: Political Not Metaphysical," *Philosophy and Public Affairs* 14, no. 3 (1985):223–51.

29. John Rawls, "A Well-Ordered Society," in *Philosophy, Politics, and Society,* 5th series, ed. P. Laslett and J. Fishkin (Oxford: Oxford University Press, 1979), 18.

30. Rawls, "Kantian Constructivism in Moral Theory," 519.

31. Rawls, *A Theory of Justice,* 21.

32. Michael Sandel, *Liberalism and the Limits of Justice* (Cambridge: Cambridge University Press, 1982), 15–16.

33. Rawls, *A Theory of Justice*, 3.

34. See Thomas Hill, Jr., "Humanity as an End in Itself," *Ethics* 91, no. 1 (1980):84–99, for a detailed exposition of Kant's argument.

35. Rawls, *A Theory of Justice*, 560.

36. Sandel, *Liberalism and the Limits of Justice*, 58–59.

37. Rawls, "Justice as Fairness," 238.

38. Flanagan, *Varieties of Moral Personality*, 105–32.

39. Rawls, "Justice as Fairness," 240, n. 22.

40. Sandel, *Liberalism and the Limits of Justice*, 59.

41. Rawls says of Sandel's charges, "I cannot discuss these criticisms in any detail" ("Justice as Fairness," 239, n. 21).

42. Ibid., 160–61.

43. Ibid., 172.

44. Dewey, *Theory of the Moral Life*, 149.

CHAPTER SEVEN

1. MacIntyre, *After Virtue*, 213.

2. This basis for criticism, moral development, and social change is taken up in chapter 8.

3. It is important to keep in mind how utterly different this account of agency and selfhood as embedded in narrative histories is from the objectivist view, which treats moral deliberation as the bringing of particular cases under universal moral rules.

4. MacIntyre, *After Virtue*, 216.

5. Flanagan, *Varieties of Moral Personality*.

6. Studs Terkel, *Working* (New York: Avon, 1972), 93.

7. Narratives are "of considerable value as vehicles for self-reflection on our personhood and its moral dimensions, for in narratives of action, descriptions of deliberation, motivation, and action vary (within some limits set by facts) at the author's discretion, so that ranges of narrative test and establish the limits of the possible in human deliberation and action" (Eldridge, *On Moral Personhood*, 33).

8. Thomas Merton, *Love and Living* (New York: Farrar, Straus, and Giroux, 1965). Merton speaks of the "package concept of love," but this is the same as what I am calling the LOVE IS A MARKET TRANSACTION metaphor.

9. Steven Winter, "*Bull Durham* and the Uses of Theory" (*Stanford Law Review* 42 [1990]:639–93), develops this duality of self formation (i.e., as both 'constituted' and 'constituting') in terms of M. Merleau-Ponty's notions of 'advent' and 'adversity.'

10. Dewey, *Theory of the Moral Life*, 150–51.

11. As Steven Winter has reminded me, it is quite possible that worrying about meaningful life stories is primarily a Western preoccupation, dependent in large measure on relative wealth and the leisure it provides. I am in no position to supply the massive supporting evidence that would be required to support the universal claim that all people pur-

sue narrative unities. My view is that no sooner do people secure the most meager existence than they begin to worry about meaning, value, and purpose in their lives. As soon as our lives are not immediately threatened, we emerge once again as questers after significant narrative unity in our lives, however differently such significance and unity might be defined from culture to culture.

12. Flanagan, *Varieties of Moral Personality,* 148–58.

13. Steven Winter, "The Cognitive Dimension of the *Agon* between Legal Power and Narrative Meaning," *Michigan Law Review* 87, no. 8 (1989):2225–79. My brief analysis of narrative structure is essentially a modified summary of Winter's treatment.

14. Ricoeur, *Time and Narrative,* 1:65.

15. The concept of an 'image schema' is elaborated in my *Body in the Mind* and in Lakoff, *Women, Fire, and Dangerous Things.* Both works treat the SOURCE-PATH-GOAL schema and other imaginative patterns of our experience that are the basis for metaphorical and metonymic extensions in our understanding of abstract domains.

16. See Lakoff and Johnson, *Metaphors We Live By,* for a discussion of metaphors for time.

17. Ricoeur, *Time and Narrative,* 1:66.

18. The nature of inheritance hierarchies for metaphor systems is explained in Lakoff, "Contemporary Theory of Metaphor."

19. As an example of how our overarching narratives can change through history, consider the difference between, for example, an Enlightenment history of the Fall of Rome and any form of contemporary history. The Enlightenment history will look for 'progress' in the story it tells, judging the events of Roman history by Enlightenment standards of progress. Most contemporary histories would consider 'progress' to be an illusory notion, having no place in historical explanation, which would more appropriately focus on, say, material economic conditions, class struggle, or even climatic changes that altered economies. The *meaning* and *moral import* of events change relative to these different narrative orientations.

20. Ricoeur, *Time and Narrative,* vol. 1, chap. 3.

21. Some would say that, precisely because it *is* the unconscious, it can never be brought to consciousness directly. But we do get glimpses of it indirectly by reflecting on our dreams, language, feelings, and actions.

22. The term 'basic action' was coined by Arthur Danto in "What We Can Do," *Journal of Philosophy* 55 (1963):435–45, and in "Basic Actions," *American Philosophical Quarterly* 2 (1965):141–48. In the latter article Danto defines a basic action as follows: A is a basic action if and only if (1) A is an action, and (2) whenever S performs A, there is no other action A′ performed by S such that A is caused by A′. The idea here was to find some *physical* movement that could be the grounding basis for other *intentional* actions performed in doing that basic action.

23. As Ricoeur says, "There is no action that does not give rise to approbation or reprobation, to however small a degree, as a function of a hierarchy of values for which goodness and wickedness are the poles" (*Time and Narrative,* 1:59).

24. Ibid., 52.

25. MacIntyre, *After Virtue,* 206–7.

26. Ibid., 208.

27. I owe the formulation of this principle objection to Steven Winter.

28. This is why certain speech act accounts of meaning and many institutional accounts of meaning, art, and morality turn out to be so unsatisfactory. Their mistake is to treat an institution, for example, as though it were a static thing definable by a set of rules, conditions, or constraints. What this misses is the temporal dimension that tends to undercut any attempt to fix the character of an institution, practice, or ritual.

29. MacIntyre, *After Virtue,* 212.

30. We see this even in someone as clear-sightedly and honestly absurdist as Camus, who creates, with obvious approval, characters like the doctor in *The Plague,* who understands without self-deception that there is no escaping his (our) fate yet throws himself into acts of charity *as if it really did matter after all.*

31. Thomas Nagel, "The Absurd," in *The Meaning of Life,* ed. Steven Saunders and David Cheney (Englewood Cliffs, N.J.: Prentice Hall, 1980), 155–65.

32. Perhaps a figure like Camus's Meursault in *The Stranger* presents an authentic challenge to my claim, for he seems to live as if there were no stories to be told, either of his own making or those sanctioned by his culture. Yet even Meursault begins to remember his past, to recount it to himself, during his trial and afterwards. He remembers what he liked, what tied his days together, and what mattered to him enough to move him (such as the warmth of the sun, Marie's soft skin, and Celeste's attempt to defend him in court). Even in this stark psychological landscape a minimal narrative structure emerges.

33. For an account of the nature of 'life stories' and their structure and role in our self-understanding, see Charlotte Linde, "Explanatory Systems in Oral Life Stories," in *Cultural Models in Language and Thought,* ed. D. Holland and N. Quinn (Cambridge: Cambridge University Press, 1987), 343–56.

34. John Dewey, *Human Nature and Conduct* (1922), in *The Middle Works of John Dewey, 1899–1924,* ed. Jo Ann Boydston (Carbondale: Southern Illinois University Press, 1988), 194.

35. Ibid., 195–96.

CHAPTER EIGHT

1. Of course, one did not need to rely on fiction and poetry to imagine the realities of war. They came graphically into our homes every night on the evening news—images so horrible that one was afraid even to imagine the experiences of those who both carried out and suffered these deeds.

2. Paul Churchland, *A Neurocomputational Perspective: The Nature of the Mind and the Structure of Science* (Cambridge: MIT Press, 1989), 299.

3. Thomasz Krzeszowski, "The Axiological Parameter in Preconceptional Image Schemata" (in *Conceptualization and Mental Processing in Language,* ed. R. Geiger and B. Rudrka-Ostyn [Berlin and New York: Mouton de Gruyter, 1991], 315–38), shows that there is an affective and evaluative dimension to even our most basic image schemas, and therefore to all of the concepts that use those schemas.

4. The assertion that *most* of our moral reasoning is based on metaphors does not mean that *all* of it is metaphorical. My claim is, rather, that no account of moral reasoning can get very far without running into metaphor and other imaginative devices. Consequently, the pretension of giving a nonfigurative account of moral reasoning is merely a bluff waiting to be called.

5. Our standard way of determining what the basic conceptual metaphors are is via linguistic analysis. However, Raymond Gibbs has begun a series of psychological studies that confirm the existence, and determine the nature, of certain deep conceptual metaphors, using nonlinguistic evidence. See Gibbs, "Psycholinguistic Studies," 417–62.

6. I am using the sense of 'generative entrenchment' spelled out by Mark Turner, *Reading Minds: The Study of English in the Age of Cognitive Science* (Princeton: Princeton University Press, 1991), 138–42.

7. Rorty, *Contingency, Irony, and Solidarity.*

8. Nussbaum, *Fragility of Goodness;* Martha Nussbaum, *Love's Knowledge: Essays on Philosophy and Literature* (Oxford: Oxford University Press, 1990).

9. Nussbaum, *Fragility of Goodness,* 14.

10. Martha Nussbaum, "Perceptive Equilibrium: Literary Theory and Ethical Theory," in *Love's Knowledge: Essays on Philosophy and Literature* (Oxford: Oxford University Press, 1990), 184.

11. John Gardner, "Moral Fiction," in *Moral Fiction* (New York: Basic Books, 1978), 108.

12. See Eldridge, *On Moral Personhood,* for several excellent examples of how we come to understand the meaning and force of our key moral concepts and principles by seeing them enacted in fictional narratives.

13. Ibid., 14.

14. Hume, *Principles of Morals,* sec. 5, pt. 2, 181–83, 221–22.

15. I have in mind what Hans Georg Gadamer describes in *Truth and Method* (New York: Crossroad Publishing, 1975) as "horizon fusion," the merging through a dialectical interaction with others, of the horizon of one's own world with that of another, in such a way as to lay one's own prejudgments open to criticism and possible transformation.

16. Hume, *Principles of Morals,* appendix 1.

17. I want to repeat my earlier qualification that the Hume presented in Annette Baier's *Progress of Sentiments* does seem to recognize the form of empathetic imagination I am describing.

18. Roberto Unger, *Passion: An Essay on Personality* (New York: Free Press, 1984), 105–6.

19. For examples of the role of imagination in the constitution of our shared reality, see my *Body in the Mind.*

20. Joseph Kupfer, *Experience as Art: Aesthetics in Everyday Life* (Albany: State University of New York Press, 1983), 103–4.

21. Unger, *Passion,* 262–63.

22. Winter, "Transcendental Nonsense."

23. *United States Code* 29 (1982):151 (congressional findings in sec. 1 of the act). Emphasis added by Winter ("Transcendental Nonsense," 1200).

24. *NLRB v. Jones and Laughlin Steel Corp.*, in *United States Reports* 301:36–37 (quoting *The Daniel Ball, United States Report* 77 [1870]:557, 564, and *Stafford v. Wallace, United States Reports* 258 [1922]:495, 521), as quoted in Winter, "Transcendental Nonsense" 1202, emphasis added.

25. *Jones and Laughlin,* 42 (emphasis added by Winter).

26. Winter, "Transcendental Nonsense," 1204.

27. *Jones and Laughlin,* 41 (emphasis added by Winter).

28. John Dewey, *Art as Experience* (1934; New York: G. P. Putnam's Sons, 1958), 46, 55.

29. "Imagination is not an abstract schematic power much less a faculty of fancy, of imaging. It is an activity which weaves the flux of experience into a meaningful continuity by constantly organizing and reconstructing the situational event so that it develops a horizon and focus which reveal its temporal possibilities for consummatory integration. Imagination grasps experience as *growth of meaning through action*" (Thomas Alexander, *John Dewey's Theory of Art, Experience, and Nature* [Albany: State University of New York Press, 1987], 261).

30. Thus, Alexander describes imagination as "the ability to grasp the meaning of the present in terms of a possible situation which may be realized *because* its ideal possibility has been grasped and used to mediate the situation and direct action" (ibid., 262).

31. Martha Nussbaum, "Finely Aware and Richly Responsible: Literature and the Moral Imagination," in *Love's Knowledge: Essays on Philosophy and Literature* (Oxford: Oxford University Press, 1990), 152. Hereafter page numbers will be in the text.

32. R. G. Collingwood, *The Principles of Art* (Oxford: Oxford University Press, 1935).

33. I adopt the term 'skillful coping' from Hubert Dreyfus's use of the term to describe Heidegger's understanding of that dimension of our being-in-the-world that is prior to conscious reflection and theoretical analysis.

34. Nussbaum, *Fragility of Goodness,* 94.

35. Nussbaum, *Fragility of Goodness,* 99.

36. Søren Kierkegaard in *Either-Or* and *Fear and Trembling.*

CHAPTER NINE

1. This view of moral imagination is presented most clearly in Richard Rorty, "Freud and Moral Reflection" (in *Essays on Heidegger and Others* [Cambridge: Cambridge University Press, 1991], 143–63).

2. Unger, *Passion,* 95.

3. Thomas Hobbes, *Leviathan* (1651; Oxford: Clarendon Press, 1909), pt. 1, chap. 13, 96.

4. Sigmund Freud, *Civilization and Its Discontents,* translated by James Strachey (New York: W. W. Norton, 1961).

5. An extended treatment of this problem can be found in MacIntyre, *Whose Justice? Which Rationality?*

6. Lakoff and Johnson, *Metaphors We Live By.*

7. Eve Sweetser, *From Etymology to Pragmatics: The Mind-as-Body Metaphor in Semantic Structure and Semantic Change* (Cambridge: Cambridge University Press, 1990).

8. Rorty, *Philosophy and the Mirror of Nature.*

9. Ibid.; Putnam, *Reason, Truth and History.*

10. Paul Churchland, *Scientific Realism and the Plasticity of Mind* (Cambridge: Cambridge University Press, 1979); Thomas Kuhn, *The Structure of Scientific Revolutions* (Chicago: University of Chicago Press, 1962); Paul Feyerabend, *Against Method,* 2d edition (1975; London: Verso, 1978).

11. MacIntyre, *Whose Justice? Which Rationality?;* Bernard Williams, *Ethics and the Limits of Philosophy.*

12. MacIntyre, *Whose Justice? Which Rationality?* 389.

13. Hilary Putnam, "Fact and Value," in *Reason, Truth, and History* (Cambridge: Cambridge University Press, 1981), 127–49.

14. Gadamer, *Truth and Method.*

15. Thomas Kuhn, "Reflections on My Critics," in *Criticism and the Growth of Knowledge,* ed. Imre Lakatos and Alan Musgrave (Cambridge: Cambridge University Press, 1970), 241.

16. Hans Georg Gadamer, "The Universality of the Hermeneutical Problem," in *Philosophical Hermeneutics,* translated by David Linge (Berkeley: University of California Press, 1976), 9.

17. MacIntyre, *Whose Justice? Which Rationality?* 7.

18. MacIntyre, *After Virtue,* 268.

19. Ibid., 268–69.

20. MacIntyre, *Whose Justice? Which Rationality?* 362.

21. The way in which our embodiment founds our reason and desire is examined in Lakoff, *Women, Fire, and Dangerous Things;* Mark Johnson, *The Body in the Mind;* Eleanor Rosch, F. Varela, and E. Thompson, *Embodied Mind* (Cambridge: MIT Press, 1991).

22. MacIntyre, *Whose Justice? Which Rationality?* 144.

23. This Marxist conception of a historically situated dialectical process that is material, social, and cultural (rather than merely intellectual) is set out by Merleau-Ponty in *Phenomenology of Perception,* translated by Colin Smith (London: Routledge and Kegan Paul, 1976).

24. Martha Nussbaum, "Recoiling from Reason," *New York Review of Books,* December 7, 1989, 36–41. Hereafter page numbers will be in the text.

25. The incoherence of the radical incommensurability thesis is set forth in Donald Davidson, "On the Very Idea of a Conceptual Scheme," *Proceedings and Addresses of the American Philosophical Association* 47 (1973):5–20.

26. The role of several of these factors in defining a person's identity and in his or her moral development is discussed in Flanagan, *Varieties of Moral Personality.*

27. Ibid., 32.

28. Winter, "*Bull Durham* and the Uses of Theory," 685–86.

29. On this view, "freedom consists not in an unrestricted capacity to define meaning, but in an ability to modulate meanings by transforming elements of the sedimented field of perception. Our freedom comes from our ability to focus our attention on those background decisions, to bring them to the foreground, and to see previously unperceived possibilities for change" (Kerry H. Whiteside, *Merleau-Ponty and the Foundation of an Existential Politics,* (Princeton: Princeton University Press, 1988); 68–69).

30. Donald Rutherford, "Whither Theory in Ethics: The Case of Williams' *Ethics and the Limits of Philosophy*" (Department of Philosophy, Emory University, 1989, manuscript).

CHAPTER TEN

1. Williams, *Ethics and the Limits of Philosophy,* chap. 10. Hereafter page numbers will be in the text.

2. Richard Shusterman, "Postmodern Aestheticism: A New Moral Philosophy?" in *Theory, Culture, and Society* (London: Sage, 1988), 344.

3. I refer to W. V. O. Quine's argument that there is no noncircular way to ground the analytic/synthetic distinction (see "Two Dogmas of Empiricism," in *From a Logical Point of View* [Cambridge: Harvard University Press, 1953], and later *Word and Object* [Cambridge: MIT Press, 1960]). This and other foundational methodological dichotomies of philosophy had already been challenged by Dewey, Blanshard, and others. Subsequent to Quine's formulation of the argument, the untenability of the analytic/synthetic and other attendant distinctions has been repeatedly demonstrated in one discipline and context after another. Still, as Rorty has documented (in *Philosophy and the Mirror of Nature* and *Consequences of Pragmatism* [Minneapolis: University of Minnesota, 1983]), such distinctions die hard, especially in philosophies whose pretense of a superior critical status rests entirely on claiming to be an activity of pure reason.

4. For an account of radial category structure see Lakoff, *Women, Fire, and Dangerous Things*.

5. This, I take it, is the force of Kant's second formulation of the categorical imperative, the end-in-itself formula: "Act always so as to treat humanity, whether in your own person or that of another, always as an end, and never as a means only" (*F,* 47).

6. Rawls, "Kantian Constructivism in Moral Theory," 515–72.

7. Putnam, *Reason, Truth, and History,* 168.

8. Some people will accuse us of holding the view that the Nazis were right in their own way, and the Allies were right in their way. They will want to know what you are supposed to say, then, to the Nazi who is beating down your door to haul someone off to the death camps. Does the fellow in jackboots simply have *different* values from you, values that must be given equal respect? The answer, I believe, is that you don't *say* anything to the Nazi, because there is nothing to say. You think his values are horribly wrong because they lead to a certain awful world of human suffering, degradation, and social disintegration. In other circumstances, you might try to point these things out to him, in order to show why

his view is harmful to human well-being. But in your present situation, rational discourse has utterly broken down, there is no communication, and you are confronted with the horror of brute violence. Reasoning is just not an issue. You either run, or fight, or die.

9. My claim that these are universal aspects of human experience is merely an armchair observation. I have not done any of the cross-cultural and historical research that would be necessary to confirm this account. What I have identified as universal seems to me to be relatively unproblematic, but certainly not unquestionable or immune to revision in light of empirical evidence.

10. Unger, *Passion,* explores some dimensions of a morality centered on such virtues.

11. Nussbaum, *Fragility of Goodness.*

INDEX